SEARCHING FOR GOD

SEARCHING FOR GOD

CATHOLIC THEOLOGY PAST AND PRESENT

Gregory C. Higgins

Paulist Press
New York / Mahwah, NJ

Library of Congress Cataloging-in-Publication Data

Higgins, Gregory C., 1960-
    Searching for God : Catholic theology past and present / Gregory C. Higgins.
    pages cm
    ISBN 978-0-8091-4894-3 (alk. paper) — ISBN 978-1-58768-417-3
    1. God (Christianity)—History of doctrines. 2. Catholic Church—Doctrines—History. 3. Theology, Doctrinal. I. Title.
    BT98.H54 2014
    230`.2—dc23

                                                                    2014006428

ISBN 978-0-8091-4894-3 (paperback)
ISBN 978-1-58768-417-3 (e-book)

Published by Paulist Press
997 Macarthur Boulevard
Mahwah, New Jersey 07430

www.paulistpress.com

Printed and bound in the
United States of America

For James and Emily

CONTENTS

CONTENTS

II. THE CRITICAL CLUE

III. THE SEARCH INTENSIFIES

PREFACE

I would like to thank a number of people who kindly assisted me in the composition of this text. First, the students and faculty at Christian Brothers Academy in Lincroft, New Jersey, have been my primary conversation partners on all things theological for the past thirty years. Many of the ideas presented in the pages that follow rightfully belong to them. Second, Christopher Bellitto, my editor at Paulist Press, has been a sure and steady guide through the writing process. Third, my special thanks to Bexley and Calli King as well as Ryan, Colin, and Brandon Schneider. Thanks, too, to Joe Incandela, Kevin Coyne, and J. Nolan Higgins, Mayor of Freehold Borough, New Jersey. Lastly, for things too numerous to count, thanks always to my wife, Eileen, and our two children, James and Emily, to whom I lovingly dedicate this work.

INTRODUCTION

Who is God? How can we come to a greater knowledge and love of God? How do our beliefs about God alter our understanding of our self, others, and the world? These are the questions that are at the heart of Christian theology. Like all academic endeavors, theology often seems focused on issues that are peripheral to these central concerns. However, in its best moments, theological discussion—whether it occurs in a lecture hall or in conversations around the dinner table—can shed much needed light on the deepest questions of human existence. We might say, then, that theology is the disciplined search for God. More broadly conceived, it is the systematic investigation of the various issues relevant to the question, "Who is God?" and the collection and organization of our findings into a coherent account of who God is and how God acts in our world.

MANY PATHS TO GOD

Because of the complexity of the human personality and the mystery of the divine presence, no two persons' search for God takes exactly the same form.

For example, in his memoirs, the theologian Stanley Hauerwas makes an interesting comment about his own sense of God's presence. Hauerwas observes:

God is just not "there" for me. God is "there" for some. God is there for Paula, my wife.... But God is not there for me in the same way. Prayer never comes easy for me. I am not complaining. I assume this to be God's gift to help me think hard about what it means to worship God in a world where God is no longer simply "there."[1]

God is "there" for certain people, while for others this is simply not the case. For those for whom God's presence is not obvious, there are intimations of the divine, but no theophanies.[2] These intimations can appear in any moment in one's life: in the playful smile of a child, in the sage advice offered by an elder, or in a stranger's act of kindness. These moments are the pearls of great value that we wisely treasure.

The theologian John Dunne adds another element into the mix: Two people can understand their relationship with God in fundamentally different ways. In an interview, Dunne noted, "What comes to mind here is what a friend of mine, a Dutch Calvinist theologian, once said to me: 'You,' he said, 'see life as a journey with God; I see it as wrestling with God.'"[3] Dunne best captured his own view of his relationship with God when he wrote in his journal, "My life is a journey in time, and God is my companion on the way."[4] In *Time and Myth*, Dunne offers this description of his own journey:

The question for me is not "Is there a God?" so much as "What is God?" The question "Is there a God?" supposes that one already understands what God would be if there were a God. It supposes that no voyage of discovery is necessary. The question "What is God?" on the contrary, calls for a voyage of discovery, for a whole lifetime of discovery. As I explore the height and depth and the breadth of life, each discovery I make about life is a discovery about God, each step is a step with God, a step toward God.[5]

For some people, their relationship with God is best captured in the image of Jacob struggling with an angel; while for others, it is Job questioning God or Abraham journeying to an unknown land.

A third example of the different paths open to those searching for God in the Christian tradition appears in an observation by the spiritual writer Evelyn Underhill, "You see I come to Christ through God, whereas quite obviously lots of people come to God through Christ. But I can't show them how to do that. All I know is the reverse route."[6] Christians can either arrive at God by thinking about Christ or arrive at Christ by thinking about God. The two different routes reach the same destination.

THE APPROACH IN THIS TEXT

A search involves careful preparation (part 1), examination of the critical clue in the search, and the development of an ongoing means of assessing new findings (part 2). The search then branches out into some of the areas that are most impacted by our initial findings (part 3). In each of these steps, we call upon the wisdom of the past as well as the present, so in each chapter there is a pairing of a classic work in Christian theology with a widely discussed contemporary work. The aim is to include a wide range of perspectives in our search for God.

In theological matters, preparation involves first tackling the problems inherent in speaking about a God who, by Christians' own admission, surpasses all our understanding (chapter 1). For Christians, speaking about God requires that we immerse ourselves in the biblical narrative. Its plot, its characters, and its tensions are the essential elements that comprise Christian discourse about God (chapter 2). Without a critical testing of our intellectual positions, our thinking can become shoddy and ill-informed. The field of philosophical theology brings an analytical rigor to bear on some of the thorniest questions about God (chapter 3). This exercise of human reason allows us to acknowledge the dilemmas that arise in our thinking about God and, when possible, help us move to some resolution. Last, but certainly not least in our preparation, is a critical reflection on the human person, on both the innate human receptivity to God and the resistances that we put in place in a futile effort to keep God confined to our own preconceived notions of who God is (chapter 4).

The central clue in the Christian search for God is, of course, Jesus Christ. As both a figure in human history (chapter 5) and the basis of the Christian faith (chapter 6), we can apply modern historical standards to the Gospels in an attempt to discover "the Jesus of history," or we can follow the theological debates that led to the church's credal statements regarding the union of the human and divine natures in the personhood of Christ. Theologically, the life, death, and resurrection of Christ constitute the framework in which our claims about God, including those that we have held since our childhood and those that we have most recently considered, are evaluated.

This centrality of Christ has been expressed in different ways in the Christian tradition: Biblical theologians speak of Christ as being the center of history; various church mosaics depict Christ as the Pantocrator, the ruler and sustainer of all creation, and certain schools of spirituality emphasize that Christ lives in our heart, the center of our being. For example, the founder of the Christian Brothers, John Baptist de La Salle, wrote in his work on prayer that when we place ourselves in God's presence by considering Christ, we begin to see "that all our actions refer to Jesus Christ and tend toward him as their center."[7] Luke Salm, one of the leading authorities on La Salle writes, "In Chapter 27 of the primitive Rule, it is prescribed that the Brother appointed should ring the rising bell at 4:30 AM and then say in a loud voice 'Live Jesus in our hearts!' to which the Brothers would respond 'Forever!'"[8] The custom soon moved into the classrooms and continues to this present day in schools run by the Christian Brothers. A custom such as this reminds us that Christ is at the center of who we are and what we do.

Taking Christ as their critical clue, Catholics intensify their search for God through their participation in the sacramental life of the church (chapter 7), in their moral lives (chapter 8), in their dialogues with neighbors of other faiths (chapter 9), and finally, in their hope for the day when they will see God face to face (chapter 10).

The search for God radiates outward in all directions like the ripple effect of a stone tossed into a pond. All that surrounds it is caught up in its wake. In the same way, in the intellectual, spiritual, and moral dimensions of our lives there is a continuous movement toward the mystery of God. Spiritual reading of the Bible gradually becomes a means of metaphorically hearing God. Critical intellectual study becomes disciplined thinking about God. Reflections on the human person become a consideration of how we desire God, and so on. Our lives become, as Dunne put it, "voyages of discovery," so that as we "explore the height and depth and the breadth of life, each discovery [we] make about life is a discovery about God, each step is a step with God, a step toward God."[9]

PART ONE

Preparing for the Search

1

INTRODUCTION: SPEAKING ABOUT GOD

Thomas Aquinas and Elizabeth Johnson

Norman Rockwell's (1894–1978) romantic depictions of scenes drawn from American life are among some of the most widely recognized works of twentieth-century art. His paintings captured the idealism of the American spirit, and were rarely overtly political in nature. However, one of his most popular works is the exception to the rule. At the center of "The Problem We All Live With" (1964) stands a young African American school girl carrying her books and supplies with federal marshals both in front and behind her. On the wall of the building that she passes is scrawled a racial epithet and the spattered remains of a recently thrown tomato trickle to the sidewalk. The inspiration for Rockwell's simple, but powerful artistic statement was the six-year-old Ruby Nell Bridges, who on November 14, 1960, became the first African American child to enroll in the William Frantz Elementary School in New Orleans. In a photo accompanying the news accounts of the desegregation of the News Orleans schools, one of the protesters carries a sign that reads, "God demands segregation."[1]

The story of the desegregation of the New Orleans schools serves as a cautionary tale for us as we begin our search for God.

History is littered with examples of people claiming God's endorsement of all sorts of causes. Because the aims of these causes were often contradictory, it is safe to assume that not everyone had correctly identified God's will. We need to remain open to possibility, then, that our own most cherished beliefs about God may be wrong. Equally important, however, is our relentless pursuit of a life lived in conformity with God's will. Unfortunately for us, this pursuit is carried out in the midst of the messiness and uncertainties of life. As we strive to do God's will, we do so with the awareness—the often frustrating awareness—that while certainty is unattainable, decision-making is unavoidable.[2]

To assist us in negotiating our thoroughly modern predicament, we turn first to the work of the medieval theologian, Thomas Aquinas. In Book One of his *Summa Contra Gentiles*, which he completed around 1260, Aquinas addresses the very concerns that we have raised regarding human knowledge of God and the adequacy or inadequacy of the language we use to describe God. Because his theology is so logical and systematic, Aquinas provides a very helpful guide to the thought process in dealing with questions related to God, including the potential pitfalls we need to avoid when searching for God and the avenues that offer the best chances for collecting a few hard-earned insights about God. We then turn our attention to Elizabeth Johnson, a contemporary Catholic theologian who incorporates several elements of Aquinas's theology into her own feminist reappraisal of our traditional images of God.

SEARCHING FOR GOD: AQUINAS'S GROUND RULES

At the outset we need to ask whether the entire project of searching for God is misguided. Does the quest for knowledge of God distract us from experiencing the love of God? Does the endeavor simply yield insights *about* God rather than bringing us into contact *with* God? The anonymous author of the fourteenth-century spiritual classic *The Cloud of Unknowing* cautioned, "[God] can be loved, but not thought. By love, God can be embraced and held, but not by thinking."[3] Thomas Aquinas, by contrast, believed that far from being a distraction, thinking about God is built into our very nature as human beings. God has implanted in us a "natural appetite for knowledge."[4] In the spirit of Aquinas, the late Dominican scholar Herbert McCabe once observed, "Theology is a difficult and very rewarding occupation but for the most part it is not concerned with trying to say what God is but in trying to stop us talking nonsense, trying to stop people making God in their own images, to stop us from mistaking our concepts and images for the mystery towards which they point."[5] Aquinas invites us to consider the fundamental questions that we will tackle throughout our investigation. How do we guard against speaking nonsense about God? How do avoid making God in our own image? To what extent can we know the mysterious reality that is God?

For starters, Aquinas was quite clear about the limits of human reason when considering questions about God. "Some truths about God exceed all the ability of the human reason," Aquinas declares in an early chapter of the *Summa Contra Gentiles*.[6] Truths in this category, for example, that God is triune, are accepted on the basis of faith, not reason. However, Aquinas also insists that reason plays a positive role in the search for God. He confidently asserts that "natural reason" is able to arrive at certain truths about God. "Such are that God exists, that He is one, and the like. In fact, such truths about God have been proved demonstratively by the philosophers, guided by the light of the natural reason."[7] While many thinkers today would not share Aquinas's conviction that God's existence has been "proved demonstratively," his balanced integration of both faith and reason in the search for God is compelling.

Aquinas's understanding of the relationship between faith and reason also reveals a great deal about his view of God.

According to Aquinas, through the use of human reason we can know that God exists, but we can't know God's essence for the simple reason that God is not an "object" that our minds can grasp. As Thomas explains in his *Commentary on John's Gospel*, "The reason why no created species can represent the divine essence is plain: for nothing finite can represent the infinite as it is....Therefore, the knowledge by which God is seen through his creatures is not a knowledge of his essence, but a knowledge that is dark and mirrored, and from afar."[8] While our knowledge of God is always "dark and mirrored, and from afar," it is nevertheless knowledge. More specifically, it is a knowledge about the "effects" of God. Aquinas states that "because we are not able to see [God's] essence, we arrive at the knowledge of His being, not through God Himself, but through His effects."[9] Chief among these "effects" are the very existence of the material world and the design and order of nature. Aquinas strikes a balance here: Our knowledge of God is reliable, but it is always indirect.

Within the parameters that he has established, Aquinas proposes an initial strategy for thinking about God that he calls "the method of remotion." The way of remotion—also known as the negative way—proceeds to a clearer understanding of God by saying what God *isn't* rather than what God *is*. For example, while we may not fully understand what we mean when we say that God is a purely spiritual reality, we can grasp that God is not a material substance like a tree, a book, or any of the millions of things we can name. By eliminating certain concepts about God, Aquinas suggests, we slowly narrow the range of possible meanings that we can attach to the word *God*. If Aquinas is correct, the way of remotion helps minimize the chances that we are creating an idol rather than discovering the living and true God.

While the negative way remains a constant refrain in Aquinas's discussion of God, it is not the final word. He believed that not only can we say what God is not, we can also make affirmative statements about the nature of God. Because humans are created in the image and likeness of God, we share in some imperfect way in the qualities of God. We can have some sense of the goodness of God, for example, by seeing its reflection in God's creatures. "Since it is possible to find in God every perfection of creatures, but in another and more eminent way, whatever names unqualifiedly designate a perfection without defect are predicated of God and of other things: for example, goodness, wisdom, being, and the like."[10] Again, Aquinas's sense of balance plays a critical role in his theology. We can know something about God's goodness or wisdom, but because we can't grasp God's nature, we also need to realize that God possesses these qualities "in another and more eminent way" than humans do. We get an inkling of God's love when we experience the love of another human being, for example, but the fullness of God's love surpasses all understanding (1 Cor 2:9; Phil 4:7).

Just as for Aquinas, our knowledge of God is reliable, though incomplete, so too is our language about God. Take the ordinary statement that God is good. If God's nature is radically dissimilar to our own, then this statement would have no real meaning. There would be no point of reference between our concept of goodness and God's nature. This would reduce us to silence about God. If we take the opposite approach and claim that God's nature is exactly the same as our own and that therefore God's goodness corresponds exactly to our own concept of goodness, then there is no longer any mystery to God. We have limited God to the categories of our own thought and language. Aquinas steers a middle course between these two options. For Aquinas, when we speak of God, we recognize that we are speaking by way of analogy, that is, we have confidence that our understanding of goodness rightly applies to God, but we readily admit that the full meaning of that statement eludes our understanding.[11]

THREE INSIGHTS INTO THE SEARCH FOR GOD OFFERED BY AQUINAS

In the midst of Aquinas's carefully constructed philosophical and theological arguments are several helpful reminders that will serve us well in our search for God. In keeping with Aquinas's deep respect for "the negative way" of approaching God, we will phrase his insights in terms of what God is not, rather than what God is.

1. God is not a being alongside other beings in the universe.

The first misunderstanding regarding the nature of God that we must avoid, according to Aquinas, is thinking that God is a being—an entity located in a particular place in the heavens above us. Commenting on this feature of Aquinas's thought, the theologian Robert Barron writes, "Because God is not namable even according to the most generic of categories, he cannot be circumscribed, defined, or grasped. Nor can he be in any sense *a being*, an individual, since this would make him comparable to other individuals."[12] This is not to suggest that Jesus Christ was not an actual historical figure or that Jesus was not divine. Rather, it is a Christian affirmation that God cannot be confined by either time or space. In other words, God is not a being. However, as Aquinas reminded us, it is much easier to understand what God is *not* rather than what God *is*. What is God if not a being? This question tests the very limits of our language and understanding.

It might be of some comfort to us to consider that it was this very question that bedeviled the great theologian of the early church, Augustine of Hippo. Before his conversion to Christianity, he conceived of God as a vast ocean and the universe like a sponge within that ocean saturated with the presence of God.[13] It was through his reading of Platonic philosophers that Augustine came to reject this idea that God is a refined material substance permeating the world, yet extending beyond the world in all directions. Once he was able to leap this intellectual hurdle, he no longer held that all reality was composed in some way of matter. There were immaterial realities (e.g., truth), and in fact, the highest form of reality was unchanging, omnipresent, and invisible.[14]

Aquinas also believed that God is an immaterial reality that is unchanging, omnipresent, and invisible, and it is for this reason that Barron speaks of "the strangeness of God." "The God who comes to us in Jesus Christ, who lifts us up beyond ourselves and moves us to salvation, the God of ecstatic self-offering, the God whose outreach of love is greater than we can think or imagine is very strange. That, it seems to me, is a valid one-sentence summary of Thomas Aquinas's doctrine of God."[15] God is "strange" because God is unlike any other reality we encounter in this life. This strangeness, however, should not be mistaken for aloofness. Barron notes "God's 'spirituality' or 'immateriality' does not imply God's distance from the world; on the contrary, it is precisely this quality of the divine being that enables God to be absolutely intimate and 'interior' to his creation. Because God is immaterial, God can 'become' one of her creatures, living in the depths of its being, luring it from within."[16]

2. God is not limited.

Aquinas recognized that we can only define things because they are limited in some way. We distinguish between horses and dogs, for example, although both are animals. Within the category of dogs, we recognize the difference between cocker spaniels and terriers, and then among terriers, between an airedale and a Jack Russell, and so on. God, however, is not limited, neither by time or space nor by any lack of knowledge, love, or power. For Aquinas, "there is no terminus or limit to [God's] perfection: He is supremely perfect."[17] What implications follow from this for our search for God?

The great twentieth-century Jesuit Karl Rahner made Aquinas's theories of human knowledge and the nature of God key components of his own theology. Our human knowledge of the world is not boundless. While this boundary—or to use Rahner's preferred expression, this horizon—exists, our minds constantly push the limits of our knowledge and understanding. There is a dynamism to our thought that carries us toward the horizon, but the horizon recedes as we approach it. As the theologian Robert Masson says of Rahner, "By conceiving God, who always exceeds our reach, as the horizon presupposed in the movement of knowing, freedom and love, Rahner provided a way for talking and thinking about God as 'mysterious,' that is to say, as a reality who is known, but only reflexively and indirectly—and perhaps not even consciously—as the ever receding horizon of the human spirit."[18] God is the unlimited background against which the horizon of our human understanding appears, and to which our love and understanding are constantly drawn.

Because of the unlimited nature of God, Rahner speaks of God as Mystery. God is, "the incomprehensible, impenetrable Mystery that can never be manipulated, and this he remains for all eternity."[19] In one of the many collections of prayers and meditations that he composed for a popular audience, Rahner communicates this sense of the unfathomable mystery of God: "All I know about You and about myself is that You are the eternal mystery of my life. Lord, what a frightful puzzle man is! He belongs to You, and You are the Incomprehensible—Incomprehensible in Your Being, and even more so in Your ways and judgments....You will still be the Incomprehensible, even when I see you face to face."[20]

This stress on both the unknowability of God and the limits of human understanding does raise troubling questions: Is the search for God futile? If God is unknowable, is the object of our search beyond our grasp? If human understanding is limited, are we capable of knowing God in this life? Aquinas and Rahner would both agree that we cannot *fully* understand God. As Aquinas states, "We cannot grasp what God is, but only what He is not and how other things are related to Him."[21] We can, that is, have partial, though reliable knowledge of God (1 Cor 13:12).

Where does that leave us? In his classic work *The Silence of St. Thomas*, the philosopher Josef Pieper offers the following assessment of our situation:

> It seems to me that St. Thomas's doctrine means that *hope* is the condition of man's existence as a knowing subject, a condition that by its very nature cannot be fixed: it is neither comprehension and possession nor simply nonpossession, but "not-yet-possession." The knowing subject is visualized as a traveller, a *viator*, as someone "on the way." This means, from one point of view, that the steps he takes have significance, that they are not altogether in vain, and that they bring him nearer to his goal. Yet this though has to be complemented by another: as long as man as "existing being" is "on the way," just so long is the "way" of his knowing uncompleted.[22]

Faith and hope, then, are central elements in Aquinas's theology, and as we will now see, love, too, is an essential component of the Christian's search for God.

3. God cannot will evil.

Aquinas holds that God cannot will evil.[23] Not only is this a truth of revelation for him, but he also argues that it is philosophically sound to hold that the highest form of reality should consist of the fullness of goodness, truth, and beauty. Since evil is a lack of a perfection, God could not will evil. Aquinas must then, however, confront the problem that some scriptural passages speak of God's hatred. In Deuteronomy, for example, Moses warns the Israelites not to adopt the religious practices of the Canaanites. "You must not do the same for the Lord your God, because every abhorrent thing that the Lord hates they have done for their gods" (12:31). Could a God who cannot will evil in any way "hate"?[24] Aquinas insists that such expressions must be taken metaphorically.[25] Without delving into the problem in detail, Aquinas acknowledges that we must discern which biblical passage are to be taken literally and which are not. This question that is absolutely critical in our search for God will persist throughout our entire investigation of Catholic theology.[26]

These philosophical and scriptural points, though certainly central to his case, might obscure the powerful affirmation Aquinas is making about the love of God. God cannot will evil because the love of God is "not only a true love, but also a most perfect and a most enduring love."[27] In other words, a perfect God loves perfectly. What is perfect love? "For this belongs properly to the nature of love," answers Aquinas, "that the lover will the good of the one he loves."[28] Aquinas cites the example of a man who likes someone because this person is useful to him or because he enjoys the friend's company. This man actually loves himself, and not the friend. "Again, for true love it is required that we will someone's good as [the other person's] good," not our own.[29] Following the fifth- or sixth-century spiritual writer known as Pseudo-Dionysius, Aquinas describes love as a "unitive power"—a power that draws the lover and the beloved into a deeper unity and intensity of love. "There is, therefore, in God not only a true love, but also a most perfect and a most enduring love."[30] The moral theologian Paul Wadell offers this description of Aquinas's compelling account of the love shared between God and humans:

> We who are children of God are called to be the friends of God. We are to love God not just in any way, but in friendship. It seems almost blasphemous to think of God this personally and intimately, but for Thomas it is the bedrock claim of the Christian moral life. He believes the unbelievable: we are called to an ever-deepening friendship with the God who is our happiness, a friendship of love given and received, a friendship in which each seeks the good of the other, and through love finally become one.[31]

The God depicted in Aquinas's *Summa Contra Gentiles* is unlike any other reality, a mysterious God of unlimited scope and unrestricted love.

JOHNSON'S USE OF THE WORK OF AQUINAS

Contemporary Catholic feminists are divided on the influence of Aquinas. Some regard him as a sexist thinker who perpetuated outmoded and oppressive attitudes about women.[32] Others see a richness in his thought, especially in his work on the Trinity, that speaks powerfully to our own theological, social, and political questions.[33] One of the leading feminist theologians in the latter group who incorporates much of Aquinas's thought into her own theology is Elizabeth Johnson. In Johnson's words, "I draw on themes and ideas from Thomas Aquinas…because I find these ideas dynamic, fresh, and helpful for thinking through my own intellectual questions."[34] In her work *She Who Is*, Johnson "attempts to braid a footbridge between the ledges of classical and feminist Christian wisdom."[35] Chief among those classical Christian sources of wisdom are Aquinas's views on the nature and mystery of God. Johnson believes that we can combine the classical beliefs of Aquinas with the insights of modern Christian feminism to craft a theology that is worthy of the God in whose image all human beings are created.

In her *She Who Is*, Johnson conducts her own search for right language about God. Her method is to mine scripture, tradition, and women's interpreted experience for resources to craft "a discourse about divine mystery that would further the emancipation of women."[36] For Johnson, such a discourse would not rely on exclusively male language about God (e.g., God as Father), but also would include female imagery (e.g., God as Mother), nature imagery (e.g., God as Fire) and relational imagery (e.g., God as Friend), to name but a few. She ultimately concludes that "SHE WHO IS can be spoken as a robust, appropriate name for God."[37] Johnson contends that her position is in keeping with the wisdom of classical Christian theology as found in the theology of Thomas Aquinas, especially in his appreciation for the incomprehensibility of God, the centrality of analogy in religious speech, and the need for having many names for God.

Johnson insists throughout *She Who Is* that the tendency to take literally male language about God needs to be checked with the constant reminder about the incomprehensibility of God. "In spite of ample testimony in the Scriptures and later tradition that the mystery of God is beyond all human comprehension, the exclusively male symbol of God is spoken in an uncritically literal way."[38] The wisdom of classical Christian theology, of which Aquinas is the preeminent representative, is that no "human concept, word, or image…can circumscribe divine reality, nor can any human construct express with any measure of adequacy the mystery of God who is ineffable."[39]

As we discussed earlier, the stress on the incomprehensibility of God raises the question of the possibility of human knowledge of God. If God is beyond our comprehension, can we have any assurance that our language about God is accurate? Here again Johnson follows Aquinas's lead, and defends the necessity and reliability of analogical speech about God. The very possibility of speaking about God accurately exists because humans are created by God. Because of this fundamental relationship between God and creation, "it is possible to speak positively of God, creator of all, through terms drawn from our knowledge of creaturely qualities, but always with the proviso that the reality of which we speak cannot be contained in this language."[40] Johnson, like Aquinas, believes that we strike this balance by categorizing our human statements about God as analogies.

Once we recognize the analogical character of our statements about God, the need for a variety of images of God becomes apparent. Because each image captures some dimension of the divine while at the same time obscuring others, a variety of images helps us expand and enrich our understanding of God. Johnson again approvingly quotes Aquinas, "From this we can see the necessity of giving to God many names."[41] Not only is it possible to have an abundance of images of God, it is preferable. "Absolutizing any particular expression as if it were adequate to divine reality is tantamount to a diminishment of truth about God."[42]

AQUINAS'S THREE INSIGHTS REVISITED

Earlier we extracted three insights into God's nature from Aquinas's work. Because he favored the negative way, we expressed them negatively: God is not a being alongside other beings in the universe; God is not limited; God cannot will evil. How does Johnson incorporate and expand upon these three insights in her own work?

Johnson reaffirms Aquinas's insight that God is not a being. A constant refrain in Johnson's theology is what Barron called "the strangeness of God." "Whether expressed by metaphorical, symbolic, or analogical theology, there is basic agreement that the mystery of God is fundamentally unlike anything else we know of, and so is beyond the grasp of all our naming."[43] On more than one occasion in *She Who Is*, Johnson reminds her readers of Augustine's admonishment, "If you have understood, then what you have understood is not God."[44] Because Johnson agrees with Aquinas that God is not a being that we can in any way define or quantify, she also endorses the negative way to God. "In the end, it is easier to say what God is not than what God is."[45] The most immediate implication of this for Johnson is that God is not a gendered being. Following Aquinas's suggestion that we give many names to God, Johnson includes in her list of proposed images the suggestion that we speak of God as Mother.

The second insight drawn from Aquinas—that God is not limited—led Rahner to speak of God as the ultimate Mystery. Johnson herself describes God as "illimitable mystery who…cannot be measured, manipulated, or controlled."[46] When our religious speech becomes literal rather than analogical, we fail to appreciate the mysterious quality of God's nature. When we lose sight of the mysterious nature of God, Johnson warns, we create a climate in which idolatry can take root. "Whenever one image or concept of God expands to the horizon thus shutting out others, and whenever this exclusive symbol becomes literalized so that the distance between it and divine reality is collapsed, there an idol comes into being. Then the comprehensible image, rather than disclosing mystery, is mistaken for the reality."[47] Johnson particularly fears this happens when we employ exclusively male language about God. Doing so "is theologically the equivalent of the graven image, a finite representation set up and worshipped as if it were the whole of divine reality. What is violated is both the creature's limitation and the unknowable mystery of the living God."[48]

This idolatry has social as well as theological consequences. Johnson insists that a patriarchal conception of God legitimates a patriarchal view of society. "The symbol of God functions. When the root metaphor for the divine in Christian discourse is patriarchal, then as the orienting focus of devotion...it inevitably sustains men's dominance over women."[49] In her review of *She Who Is*, the theologian Robin Darling Young takes issue with the suggestion that eliminating the exclusively male imagery for God would produce a more equitable social order for women. Young also questions whether the aim of theology should be the amelioration of social ills rather than the communication of "the entire body of Christian tradition in order that theology rightly develop and deepen."[50] Despite Young's deep disagreement with Johnson, she concedes that it "is also incontestable that male language of chief gods, or in the case of Christianity, the Godhead, can and has been used to justify everything summed up in the familiar term, 'sexism.'"[51] Despite their differences, then, Johnson and Young agree that the symbol of God can indeed "function" as a catalyst for creating, sustaining, or destroying the often unacknowledged assumptions that govern our social, political, and familial arrangements.

Johnson expands upon the third insight of Aquinas dealing with the love of God. Drawing on Aquinas (and Pseudo-Dionysius before him), she writes, "In the end, we are united to God as to an unknown, savoring God only through love."[52] She begins with agreeing with the fundamental insight of Aquinas. "We can only name God from creatures, argues Aquinas...and the human experience of love is so profoundly life-giving that it provides a key analogy for divine mystery. God is Love, and so penetratingly is this the case that love can be spoken of as the very essence of God."[53] Aquinas proceeded from here to speak of our "friendship" with God, but Johnson believes that he did not go far enough. While Aquinas eloquently develops the idea of our friendship with God, "God is never named a friend in return, and thus the mutuality inherent in the idea of friendship is not brought fully to expression."[54] If we extend the concept of friendship to describe God's own relationship to us, Johnson believes, then a productive avenue of thought about God opens up to us. Instead of believing that God is unaffected by the state of the world, we see a deeply compassionate (literally, "a suffering with") and loving God who shares in the grief of the broken-hearted and offers strength to the oppressed.

CONCLUDING THOUGHTS

What insights can we take away from our investigation of Aquinas and Johnson as we begin our search for God in Catholic theology?

First, the recognition of the incomprehensible nature of God, the premium placed on the negative way when thinking about God, and the indispensability of analogy when speaking about God remind us that God cannot be defined or confined by our words. The reality of God always surpasses our capacity to think or speak about God.

Second, with all of the qualifications just mentioned, we also recognize that we need to speak about God. It is a fire burning in our hearts and imprisoned in our bones (Jer 20:9). Of course, we also need to speak truthfully about God, but given the incomprehensible nature of God, can we ever be sure we are doing just that?

The French mathematician and philosopher Blaise Pascal (1623–62) popularized the idea that belief in either the existence or nonexistence of God is a wager. Pascal framed his discussion of the wager as a debate between theists and atheists. In a similar way, we can say that among theists there is a wager, not over the question, "Does God exist? but rather, "Who is God?" As we survey the images of God in scripture, sift through the ideas preserved in the Christian tradition, and apply our findings in various ways to our own day and age, we assign varying degrees of certainty to our findings. Over time, we may refine our understanding of God or perhaps significantly alter it, but in the end, there are some key beliefs about God that shape how we live each and every day of our lives. Because we can't know on this side of death whether our core beliefs about God are right, they represent our own personal wager on who God is.

Finally, our ideas about God shape how we view every facet of our existence. The link between our understanding of God and our moral lives is clear, but the connections do not end there. Our concept of God is the lens through which we view the very purpose of our lives. It frames how we view other people and the natural world in which we live. As Johnson asserts, "Inauthentic ways of treating other human beings go hand-in-glove with falsifications of the idea of God."[55] The love of God and the love of neighbor have always been inextricably linked in the Christian tradition. The search for God, then, is not merely a philosophical pursuit of truth, but a quest for a clarity of vision that allows us to see all things in our lives with the eyes of faith.

Discussion Questions

1. What is your image of God?

2. How much can humans know about the nature of God? How do we come to that knowledge?

3. Does the "negative way" help us get a better understanding of who God is?

4. What does it mean to say that God is not a being?

5. What evaluation do you give to Johnson's discussion of

God? Is it appropriate, in your view, to refer to God as Mother?

6. Complete the following: "The best analogy for understanding how God acts in the world is…."

7. What criticisms would you offer regarding Aquinas's or Johnson's view of God?

Suggested Readings

A brief summary of Johnson's theology can be found in the entry, "Elizabeth A. Johnson, CSJ (1941–)" by J'annine Jobling in Ian S. Markham, ed., *The Blackwell Companion to the Theologians*, vol. 2 (Malden, MA: Wiley-Blackwell, 2009). For a collection of essays devoted to Johnson's theology, see Phyllis Zagano and Terrence W. Tilley, *Things New and Old* (New York: Crossroad, 1999). For a study dealing with Johnson's treatment of the Trinity, see Patricia A. Fox, *God as Communion* (Collegeville, MN: The Liturgical Press, 2001). The U.S. Bishops' Committee on Doctrine issued a critique of Elizabeth Johnson's *Quest for the Living God* (New York: Continuum, 2007). The statement is available at http://www.usccb.org/doctrine/statement-quest-for-the-living-god-2011-03-24.pdf.

A good starting point for the massive body of literature on Aquinas is Fergus Kerr, *Thomas Aquinas: A Very Short Introduction* (Oxford: Oxford University Press, 2009). For Aquinas's thought on God, see Robert Barron, *Thomas Aquinas: Spiritual Master* (New York: Crossroad, 1996). For an in-depth study of Aquinas's view of God, see Gregory P. Rocca, *Speaking the Incomprehensible God* (Washington, DC: Catholic University of America Press, 2004).

2

THE BIBLE: HEARING GOD
Hugh of St. Victor and Sandra Schneiders

At most colleges and universities, an undergraduate majoring in physics may also be required to take an English course that might focus on British playwrights or a history major may be required to take a science course such as astronomy. While many in the academic world argue that we should increase the number and variety of these interdisciplinary requirements, most undergraduate programs introduce students to different ways of understanding the world and expose them to a wide range of perspectives on the perennial questions that humans confront. The distinctive mission of Catholic universities is to integrate the insights and methods of the various academic disciplines into the on-going intellectual and moral life of the church. One of the chief architects of this vision of Catholic education, Hugh of St. Victor (d. 1141), advised, "Learn everything; you will see afterwards that nothing is superfluous."[1] Hugh was also a great biblical scholar and spiritual writer, and so, for him, the pressing question was to integrate the various academic disciplines with the study of the Bible. This question continues to be important for Catholic scholars today who believe with Hugh of St. Victor that the Bible reveals God's will to us, but are fully cognizant of the challenges and questions such a claim entails. One such thinker is Sandra Schneiders, a Sister of the Immaculate Heart of Mary whose scholarly interests focus on the New Testament and Christian spirituality. Although both writers offer significantly different accounts of how the Bible should be read, they agree that when the Bible is properly interpreted, we can, in Hugh's words, hear "the voice of God speaking to [humans]."[2]

HEARING GOD SPEAK TO US THROUGH THE BIBLE

The early church thinker Origen of Alexandria (ca. 185–253) began a tradition of speaking about the need for the cultivation of our "spiritual senses" when reading the Bible. For example, the Psalmist encourages us, "O taste and see that the Lord is good" (Ps 34:8). Here, the Psalmist is metaphorically using the language of two of our bodily senses to refer to our experience of God. Just as our bodily senses allow us to gain knowledge of the visible world, our "spiritual senses" allow us to perceive the invisible God. Commenting on Matthew 5:8, "Blessed are the pure in heart, for they shall see God," Origen asks, "For what else is 'to see God in the heart' but to understand and know him with the mind?…So too we speak of hearing with the ears when we discern the deeper meaning of some statement."[3] Origen and the many spiritual writers who followed him recognized that just as we need to hone the skills necessary to appreciate the beauty of either a ballerina's pirouette or a second baseman's perfectly turned double play, we can develop over time the capacity to hear God speak through the Bible. The medieval thinkers labeled this kind of knowledge "connatural knowledge"—an intuitive grasp of what is being expressed. When coaches say that they had two or three players over the course of their coaching careers who "had an understanding of the game," they don't mean that those players knew every rule of the game. Rather, they are saying that the player anticipates how a play will develop and responds instinctively to the situation developing on the field or court. To search for God in the pages of the Bible, then, requires that we know how to "hear" the Word of God and not simply words about God.

BACKGROUND TO HUGH OF ST. VICTOR

The twelfth century of Western history was marked by a spike in population, increased food production, and the development of cities. Along with these changes came the rise of urban centers, the beginnings of universities, and a flurry of artistic and literary production. It was also a time of great religious fervor, inspired in large part by the efforts of the reform-minded Pope Gregory VII (d. 1085).[4] In 1108, a scholar by the name of William of Champeaux retired from his teaching post at the cathedral school at Notre Dame in Paris and relocated with a few of his students to a chapel dedicated to St. Victor on the left bank of the Seine.[5] There, they lived as "regular canons," clerics who lived according to the Rule of St. Augustine.[6] They modeled their own community on the example of the early apostolic community described in Acts (4:32–35) and dedicated themselves to prayer and study. After five years of leadership, William became bishop of Chalons-sur-Marne, but as the theologian Paul Rorem notes, "Before leaving St. Victor, he made one more decisive contribution there. William secured the approval of King Louis VI to charter St. Victor as a royal abbey including a school, indicating financial support; the king further entrusted the Victorines with the election of an abbot from within their ranks to be nominated to the bishop of Paris without needing separate royal approval."[7] Through William's influence, St. Victor achieved both financial security and freedom from interference in its governance by the political authorities. After William's departure in 1114, the community elected a canon named Gilduin as abbot. Gilduin would oversee the community's spiritual life and the expansion of its physical plant until his death in 1155. Hugh's entire career at St. Victor falls during the time of Gilduin's tenure. He arrived at St.

Victor shortly after Gilduin's election, became a prolific writer and respected spiritual director as well as the head of the school in 1133.[8] He died at St. Victor on February 11, 1141.

In the late 1120s, Hugh composed the *Didascalicon*, a blueprint of the ideal educational program that identified and sequenced the various subjects that should be pursued in order for students to attain the highest understanding of wisdom. Hugh crafted a comprehensive, yet distinctive curriculum that reflected the unique character of St. Victor. Where other schools only allowed clerics to attend, St. Victor was open to all students. Where other schools focused exclusively on "sacred learning" rather than "profane learning," Hugh combined them in the curriculum. Where the monastic schools fostered a life of prayer and the early universities fostered critical inquiry, Hugh sought to integrate what others would divide. Hugh placed all human knowledge into one of four categories: "the theoretical, which strives for the contemplation of the truth; the practical, which considers the regulation of morals; the mechanical, which supervises the occupations of this life; and the logical, which provides the knowledge necessary for correct speaking and clear argumentation"[9] Hugh's curriculum, therefore, included subjects ranging from geometry to fabric-making.

The study of these various disciplines served a greater spiritual purpose in Hugh's mind. In his next major work, *On the Sacraments of the Christian Faith*, this larger purpose comes into view. Here, Hugh situates human learning and the human condition within the sweep of human history stretching from creation to the end of time. Augustine spoke of six "ages" of humanity or six epochs in human history to correspond to the six days of creation. It is Augustine's framework that stands behind Hugh's distinction between God's two works in time: the work of foundation (i.e., creation), and the work of restoration. The secular disciplines (e.g., physics) describe the work of creation, while the study of scripture reveals God's work of restoration.[10] In the prologue to *On the Sacraments*, Hugh writes, "The work of foundation is that whereby those things which were not came into being. The work of restoration is that whereby those things which had been impaired were made better."[11] Hugh believed in the historical reality of the Fall of Adam and Eve. The Fall affects every aspect of the human personality: We have lost immediate awareness of God's presence; ignorance clouds our minds, and our desires are turned in all directions.[12] God, however, has not abandoned humanity, but rather has carried out what Hugh calls "works of restoration" through the events narrated in the Old Testament, the Incarnation of the Word in Christ Jesus, and in the church's sacraments. As Hugh notes, the true restoration of humanity consists in the "knowledge of truth and love of virtue,"[13] and the highest forms of both are found in the Bible.

HUGH OF ST. VICTOR ON READING THE BIBLE

Hugh stands in the long tradition of biblical scholars who believed that the Bible has more than one level of meaning. In Hugh's scheme, there are as many as three possible meanings to any biblical passage: history, allegory, and tropology. Hugh explains, "History is the narration of events, which is contained in the first meaning of the letter; we have allegory when, through what is said to have been done, something else is signified as done either in the past or in the present or in the future; we have tropology when through what is said to have been done, it is signified that something ought to be done."[14] By *history* Hugh means the *plain* meaning of the passage, which is not always to be equated with the *literal* meaning. Hugh certainly believed that Jesus' death on a cross was an event that occurred in history. However, when Jesus taught, "If your right eye causes you to sin, tear it out and throw it away" (Matt 5:29), clearly he clearly did not intend this to be a literal command, but was using a hyperbole that boldly instructed us to root the sources of evil out of our hearts. Hugh warns, "There are certain places in the divine page which cannot be read literally and which it is necessary that we construe with great judgment, so that we may not either overlook some things through negligence or, through misplaced diligence, violently twist them into something they were not written to say."[15]

In addition to the literal meaning, a person, event, or object can have allegorical meaning. The allegorical meaning refers to the significance a biblical passage has for Christian belief. The Victorine scholar Boyd Coolman labels it simply "the doctrinal sense" of a passage.[16] For example, the Old Testament passages about manna coming from heaven foreshadowed the Eucharist.[17] The holy city of Jerusalem was allegorically understood as referring to the soul or heaven. As we will see shortly, Hugh allegorically interpreted Noah's ark as a symbol for the church as both are vessels that save those who remain faithful to God.

The tropological meaning is the moral or spiritual meaning. As Coolman notes, "For Hugh, *tropologia* is a broader concept than the modern notion of morality. It embraces not only moral purification and formation, but also meditative illumination, prayer, and contemplative ascent to God."[18] In *Noah's Ark*, Hugh interprets the two wings that each seraph used for flying in Isaiah's vision (Isa 6:2) tropologically. "Those two wings with which the seraphim flew denote the tropological sense. For when through reading Holy Scripture we are prepared for doing good works, we are lifted up to higher things, as it were on wings."[19]

Hugh frequently compares the appropriate use of the three senses of scripture to the construction of a house. "In this question it is not without value to call to mind what we see happen in the construction of buildings, where first the foundation is laid, then the structure is raised upon it, and finally, when the work is all finished, the house is decorated by the laying on of color."[20] The foundation is history, the pieces of solid rock that are fitted together as a base in the earth that grounds the entire project; the allegorical expands and connects the various elements of construction as it rises toward the heavens. "Last of all, however, through the loveliness of morality, paint the structure over as with the most beautiful of colors."[21] Interpreting the Bible, like building a house, is a craft that requires skill, precision, and dedication. "It is necessary, therefore, so to handle the Sacred Scripture that we do not try to find history everywhere, nor allegory everywhere, nor tropology everywhere but rather that we assign individual things fittingly in their own places, as reason demands."[22] If we are successful in building such a structure in our own minds and hearts, then according to Hugh, we can hear the voice of God. As Grover Zinn, one of the foremost authorities on Hugh concludes, "Understood rightly, Hugh insists, the letter of the Scripture leads to the thing (*res*) that is the voice of God. Hence, understood in its deeper senses that are accessible through allegorical and tropological interpretations, Scripture does address divine matters and is, in fact, the voice of God speaking in a unique way to the reader."[23]

HUGH OF ST. VICTOR'S *NOAH'S ARK*

Hugh offers a grand synthesis of his scriptural, spiritual, and theological insights in the first of his major spiritual writings, *Noah's Ark* (*De Arca Noe Morali*). In the opening section we learn the genesis of the work.

When I was one day sitting with the assembled brethren, and replying to the questions which they asked, many matters came up for discussion. Finally the conversation was so directed that we began with one accord to marvel at the instability and restlessness of the human heart, and to sigh over it. And the brethren earnestly entreated that they might be shown the cause of these unstable movements in man's heart, and further particularly begged to be taught if such a serious evil as this could be countered by any skill or by practice of some discipline.[24]

The "discipline" that Hugh prescribed in response to his brothers' questions focused on a literal, allegorical, tropological consideration of the image of Noah's ark. Zinn writes, "The Ark becomes an allegorical and tropological symbol of a point of stability in the moving flux of time and in the chaotic conflict of desires engendered by love of the world."[25] If the ark symbolizes spiritual and moral peace and stability amid the chaos and confusion of the turbulent waters of the flood that fill life in this world, the solution to the human condition (i.e., "the instability and restlessness of the human heart") is be found by interiorizing the ark described in the pages of Genesis. "Now, therefore, enter your own inmost heart, and make a dwelling-place for God. Make Him a temple, make Him a house, make Him a pavilion. Make Him an ark of the covenant, make Him an ark of the flood; no matter what you call it, it is all one house of God."[26]

In keeping with his three-pronged approach to reading the Bible, Hugh begins by reviewing in great detail the design of Noah's ark as described in Genesis 6.

> Now the figure of this spiritual building which I am going to present to you is Noah's ark. This your eye shall see outwardly, so that your soul may be fashioned to its likeness inwardly. You will see there certain colours, shapes, and figures which will be pleasant to behold. But you must understand that these are put there, that from them you may learn wisdom, instruction, and virtue to adorn your soul.[27]

As noted in Genesis 6:15, the ark was three hundred cubits long, fifty cubits wide, and thirty cubits high. Hugh, unlike earlier respected interpreters, did not believe that the shape of the ark was that of a truncated pyramid (Origen) or that of a box (Augustine).[28] Instead, he based his reconstruction of the ark on both the biblical text and the methods of shipbuilding practiced in his day. Hugh concluded that the ark must have had a rectangular hull with a roof, and that the sides of the roof closed to within a cubit's (a biblical unit of measurement) length at the top. The ark had five decks. The lowest deck collected the animals' waste. Food and other provisions were stored on the second deck. The wild animals were kept on the third floor, while the tame animals were housed on the fourth. On the top deck, humans and birds coexisted. The two lowest levels may well have been submerged below the water line. There was a door built into the hull outside the third deck at sea level. There was also a window in the roof of the ark. On the outer wall of the hull, space was allowed for nests, and there were passages built into the hull allowing amphibians to move back and forth between the dry deck and the sea.

Hugh then offers an extended allegorical interpretation of the ark as representing the church and various elements of the ark's design symbolizing some characteristic of the Christian community. In his allegorical treatment of the ark's width, Hugh reflects the common ancient and medieval belief in the sacred significance of certain numbers. Hugh writes, "The Church is herself the ark, which her Noah, our Lord Jesus Christ, the Helmsman and the Haven, is guiding through the tempests of this present life."[29] The ark's length of three hundred cubits symbolizes the periods of time from creation to the end of time. "The fifty cubits' breadth denotes all believers everywhere, who are established under one Head, that is Christ. For fifty is seven time seven—that is, forty-nine, the number that means the total sum of all believers—*plus* one, which means Christ, who is the Head of His Church and the goal of our desires."[30] The ark's height of thirty cubits corresponds, by Hugh's reckoning, to the thirty books of the Bible.[31] The proportions of the ark, Hugh notes, conform to those of the human body, which is fitting given that the Church is the Body of Christ. "But the fact that the length of the ark is six times its width and ten times its height provides us with an allegorical figure for the human body in which Christ appeared, for it is itself His body."[32]

In Hugh's tropological interpretation, "the ark of the flood is the secret place of our own heart."[33] Hugh, therefore, attaches a spiritual meaning to the materials used to construct the ark, the dimensions of the ark, and the floor plan of the ark. Where the literal ark is made of wood and the allegorical ark is comprised of believers, the interior ark is constructed with "pure and profitable thoughts."[34] Just as God instructs Noah to coat the interior and exterior timbers of the ark with pitch or tar to prevent the ship from taking on water, Christians must seal their hearts so that the love carried within them will not dissipate, so that they will treat all those they meet on life's journey with gentleness. The dimensions of the literal ark likewise correspond to the ways we must expand our hearts and minds. As Rorem explains, "The 'length' of three hundred cubits is our consideration of the marvelous salvation history God is working from beginning to end; the width is the wideness of heart in contemplating the lives of the faithful, and the height corresponds to the high knowledge of the scriptures."[35] The door and window in the ark represent paths by which we leave the state of inner contemplation. Just as the animals pass to and from the ark through the door, we go out to the world through our actions. Just as the birds take flight through the window at the top of the ark, our thoughts turn our attention elsewhere. Some thoughts are like the raven that did not return to the ark after its release, preferring worldly concerns to inner stability. Other thoughts are like the dove that returned with joy to the ark. The floor plan of the ark consists of five stories, two decks below the water level and three above, which for Hugh are, in ascending order, knowledge, good works, and the love of God. On the first story we study the Scriptures and the exemplary lives of the saints. When we acquire the virtues that we admire in others, then we have moved to the second story. When we "strive to show inwardly before the eyes of God whatever good appears in [us] outwardly to human sight, then [we] have gone up into the third storey."[36] This highest state is characterized, above all, by love. The pillar in the middle of the ark that supports the various floors is the tree of life, Christ himself who unites heaven and earth.

In the closing chapter of *Noah's Ark*, Hugh returns once again to his grand scheme of God's plan of restoration. In our fallen state, our minds are distracted and our desires are misplaced.

"Everyone, then, is subject to a kind of flood of concupiscence in his own heart, from which nobody can be released save by the ark of faith....It is indeed a dangerous tempest that goes on inside us."[37] The ark provides safe passage and ensures the eventual restoration of what God created. We will once again hear the voice of God. "Before he sinned, the first man had no need for God to speak to him outwardly, for he possessed an ear within his heart by which he could hear God's voice after a spiritual manner. But when he opened his outward ear to listen to the serpents's guile, he closed his inward ear to the voice of God."[38] To regain our spiritual sense of hearing, we must enter into the silence of the ark of our heart. There, as we meditate upon the Scriptures, we can once again hear the voice of God.

For Hugh of St. Victor, entering the symbolic world of the Bible is like stepping into a magnificent temple where the voice of God echoes through the chambers. Through prayer and study we learn to listen more carefully and discern more clearly the Word that God speaks to us in the silence of our hearts. Hugh's deep reverence for the Bible as well as his own intimate knowledge of its contents enabled him to craft a compelling spiritual and theological account of the Christian life. Twenty-first century biblical theologians who see great wisdom in Hugh's writings immediately confront a problem. Hugh lived before Galileo or Darwin, so he most likely assumed that the sun revolved around the earth and that humans first appeared when God created Adam and Eve. In Hugh's day, slavery had not been abolished; women were commonly denied fundamental political rights, and mental illness was often attributed to demonic forces. Because those who resisted change in these areas often used the Bible in defense of their position, today's theologians work with a heightened sense of the possibility that the Bible is being misused.

The image to depict the practice of biblical theology today might well be that of a town hall meeting. The people who are gathered there are all deeply concerned about the welfare of their community and have come to debate a controversial proposal for a new town ordinance. Questions are raised, and statements of support and opposition are expressed. The tone of the debate varies: Most times it's cordial, but on occasion it turns acrimonious. At one point, someone leaves the meeting in protest. For some in the town, the meeting is nothing more than an exercise in political posturing; for others, it is the messy, but necessary means for discerning the will of the people. If this image fairly represents the state of biblical scholarship, then the challenge for contemporary Catholic biblical scholars who see great value in Hugh's spiritual reading of the Bible is to craft an approach to the Bible that addresses the legitimate concerns and objections of those in both the church and the academy while also assisting them in the search for God through biblical study.

Sandra Schneiders, professor emerita of the Jesuit School of Theology of Santa Clara University, has undertaken that very challenge. Like Hugh of St. Victor, Schneiders is a member of a religious order and a biblical scholar. She has written extensively on the Bible (especially the Gospel of John), spirituality, and the religious life. In one of her major works, *The Revelatory Text*, Schneiders develops her own method of biblical interpretation by entering into critical dialogue with some of the leading theorists in the field of hermeneutics (theories of interpretation) in the theological, philosophical, and literary worlds. She was especially concerned with the role that the Bible has played "in causing and legitimating the oppression of women in families, churches, and societies."[39] We will first explore some of the key theoretical issues that Schneiders addresses in *The Revelatory Text* and then apply her method to the story of the Samaritan woman at the well (John 4:1–42).

THE BIBLE AS "CONVERSATION BETWEEN GOD AND HUMANITY"

In the Preface to the second edition of *The Revelatory Text*, Schneiders comments that when the French edition was being prepared, the publishers realized that there was no exact equivalent of the English title. They finally settled on *Le Text de la Recontre* (*The Text of the Meeting*), which alludes to the "meeting tent" where "the Lord used to speak to Moses face to face, as one speaks to a friend" (Exod 33:11). Schneiders notes, "This wonderful French rendering, in effect, supplies the key to the proper understanding of the title. It intends to suggest that the biblical text is, potentially, and through the process of interpretation, a place of meeting, the locus of encounter and conversation between God and humanity."[40] If we claim that the Bible is a place of conversation, one in which God speaks to us and we, in turn, bring our questions and concerns to God, then we must clarify what we mean when we make certain theological claims about the Bible. This discussion is by its nature technical and involves such weighty issues as the *inspiration* of the Bible, the *inerrancy* of the biblical teachings, and the claim that the Bible is God's unique *revelation* to humanity. The traditional line of reasoning followed along these lines: If God *inspired* the biblical authors to write what they did, then the Bible must be *inerrant* on matters that are essential to the faith. The proper faith-response of Catholics is the free and full assent of their intellects to the eternal truths that comprise God's *revelation*.

Inspiration: Where the traditional claims emphasize that the uniqueness of the Bible rests upon the fact that God inspired its authors to write what they did, Schneiders argues that the concept of inspiration applies generally to human experience and not exclusively to the Bible. "The influence of the Spirit of God (which is what we mean by inspiration) is not limited to the Bible any more than the presence of God is limited to the Church.... Experience has established that many classics of the Christian tradition mediate the encounter with God. They are indeed inspired; they are not, however, biblical."[41] Instead of the "quasi-dictation model" assumed by ancient and medieval theologians, Schneiders proposes that we understand the concept of inspiration far more broadly.[42] Several moments in the history of a text account for its inspired quality.

The first is when the testimony of a witness or the collective memory of a community is committed to writing. Because any text is produced during a specific historical period, proper interpretation requires historical knowledge of that era. Because it is also a literary work, the interpreter must be aware of literary genres (e.g., history, myth, etiology), symbolism, and allusions. Following the lead of the philosopher Paul Ricoeur, Schneiders sees the transition from oral discourse to a fixed written form as critically important in terms of a text's meaning.[43] Not only is the memory preserved, but also the text now stands apart from the author. The text's meaning is no longer defined simply as "what the original author intended," but includes other valid meanings that can be discovered by later readers.

The second element that needs to be taken into consideration in the process of biblical interpretation is the history of its interpretation in the life of a community. This history is important because it shapes how a community understands the meaning of a text. By highlighting one passage in a gospel rather than another, or by elevating the importance of one set of writings within the canon over another (e.g., Paul's Letters rather than Matthew's Gospel), interpreters within a tradition arrive at different understandings of what "the central message" of the Gospel or New Testament is. This history of interpretation is a double-edged sword in that it can preserve powerful spiritual insights or it can blind us to certain elements in the biblical stories. Feminist scholars often speak of the need to hear the voices suppressed by a tradition of interpretation. Elizabeth Johnson writes, "Almost all theology in the Christian tradition, including liberation theology done from the perspective of the poor and oppressed, has been done by male theologians. In our day we are witnessing the phenomenon that all over the world the 'other half' of the human race, women, are waking up to their own dignity and *finding their own voice*" (emphasis added).[44]

The third element in biblical interpretation is the reader who brings his or her own experiences, preconceptions, and views about the world to the text. The meaning of the text for Schneider is not something frozen in time, but arises when readers steeped in a particular tradition grapple with the text from their own unique perspectives, their own social, economic, and political circumstances. Schneiders wants to go the middle way between those who say that the text has one and only one meaning and those who say that a text can mean anything we want it to mean.

> Believing readers are not interested simply in theoretically possible meanings of the text (even valid ones), but in the "real meaning" intended by God [as the Vatican II document *Dei Verbum* says] "for the sake of our salvation." Even readers sufficiently sophisticated to know that "real meaning" need not mean one fixed semantic message but can embrace multiple enriching and valid interpretations are convinced that the biblical text is not a Rorschach ink-blot that merely constellates the subjectivity of the viewers.[45]

Inerrancy: Given her position on inspiration, it follows that Schneiders does not share the traditional belief in the inerrancy of the Bible. Although it is true that there are "evident factual and even theological and moral errors in the Bible," this is not even the most important theological argument against the concept of biblical inerrancy. "An inerrant scripture admits of only one response, namely, unqualified intellectual assent accompanied by absolute moral submission. In other words, the notion of inerrancy in scripture is the end of a fine thread that, if followed, leads to a conception of God as an absolute, authoritarian monarch whose will is clear and who brooks no dispute."[46] Schneiders concludes "that propositions such as the 'inerrancy' of Scripture need to be either completely reformulated or abandoned."[47]

Revelation: Schneiders insists that revelation is not primarily propositional in nature (i.e., the declaration of truth claims to which we give intellectual assent), but interpersonal (i.e., the invitation to enter into a relationship with God).[48] The revelation occurs when the invitation is accepted. "It is more correct to say that the Bible is (potentially) revelatory than to say that it is revelation."[49] This, for Schneiders, does not diminish the importance of the Bible as a source of revelation for Christian living. The "Bible enjoys a privileged position among the multiple actualizations of revelation....[It] grounds and governs the ongoing revelatory experience of Christians in succeeding ages."[50]

Schneiders's theological proposals create a different set of assumptions about the Bible than what we saw in Hugh of St. Victor's writings, and consequently, generate a different method for determining the meaning of biblical passages. First, in Schneiders's use of the term, to say a gospel is "inspired" is to make an affirmation of faith based on the reader's experience of the gospel's revelatory power. "To affirm that this book is divinely inspired is to profess to have experienced it as uniquely disclosive of the divine, which grounds the affirmation that it is influenced by God in some special way."[51] The Bible, in other words, is labelled "inspired" because it is "inspiring" in a uniquely powerful way. On the issue of inerrancy, while Hugh certainly did not regard all the passages in the Bible to be literally true, the occasional discovery of a literally impossible passage did not hurt the credibility of the Bible; rather, the interpreters simply looked for a deeper spiritual meaning. For Augustine, for example, the appearance of light in the creation story (Gen 1:3) before the creation of the sun (Gen 1:16) was logically impossible, but spiritually instructive. For Schneiders, the problem of error runs deeper than it does for Hugh, and it is not so easily overcome. Suspicion will therefore play a more prominent role in the process of biblical interpretation endorsed by Schneiders. Third, when Schneiders rejects the propositional theory of revelation, revelation becomes less a matter of believing divinely disclosed faith tenets or obeying divinely ordained moral commands, than it does of entering into a relationship that consists of "the ever-developing guiding influence on our thought and action of an ever-deepening familiarity with God in Jesus."[52] This, in turn, produces a wide variety of responses on the part of the biblical readers. More specifically, "the commands of Jesus are not specific moral injunctions but the coordinates of a way of life whose particular realizations will vary enormously from person to person, culture to culture, and age to age."[53]

AN INTERPRETATION THAT "MAKES THE TEXT SPEAK"

In many ways, though Schneiders and Hugh begin with significantly different presuppositions about the Bible, they both aim for the same goal: a reading of the Bible that transforms the reader through participation in the divine power communicated through the text. We do so, according to Schneiders, when we arrive at an interpretation that "makes the text speak."[54] Taking our lead from Schneiders's theological points, we can make the text speak when our interpretation of the Bible is fruitful, critical, and transformative.

An interpretation is "fruitful" when it sparks the imagination of readers and produces an abundance of inspiring insights into the biblical story. Schneiders insists, "Texts are susceptible of endless new interpretations as different interpreters, with different questions and different backgrounds, interrogate the text about its subject matter....No answer, that is, no interpretive result, will be *the* final and definitive interpretation of the text."[55] Schneiders cites the examples of historical events (e.g., World War II), major works of painters (e.g., the *Mona Lisa*), and great plays (e.g., *Hamlet*) to illustrate how the history of interpretation continually brings new questions to bear on the meaning of events or artistic works. They are examined through different lenses and with the passage of time different meanings are attached to them. Written works have a "surplus of meaning that make multiple valid interpretations of a significant text not only possible but inevitable and, indeed, desirable."[56]

A critical reading of the Bible makes judgments about the content of the message being presented in the biblical text itself or in the history of its interpretation. "Criticism is the process of systematically sifting the text for error and deceit."[57] Readers in the modern age, believing that any text reflects the interests of the individual or group who produced it, bring varying degrees of suspicion to their reading. For Schneiders, modern feminism represents a contemporary example of this type of critical engagement with the biblical text. "It is the realization that the biblical text itself is ideologically biased against women that has raised the question that underlies all feminist criticism: can the biblical text function as revelatory text, as locus of salvific encounter with God, for women once their feminist consciousness has been raised?"[58]

Schneiders believes that despite whatever limitations the biblical text may have, it still possesses the power to transform those who enter into critical dialogue with it. "Biblical interpretation reaches its ultimate goal," writes Schneiders in a later piece, "when it actually promotes and nourishes the transformation of the reader (whether the individual or the community) in relation to God, self, world and society."[59] When Christians, for example, read the New Testament and "live in the world projected by the text," the scriptures can become for the reader a "transformative encounter with the living God."[60] On this point, Hugh of St. Victor and Sandra Schneiders are in complete agreement.

A CONCLUDING ILLUSTRATION

Schneiders concludes *The Revelatory Text* by offering her own interpretation of the story of Jesus and the Samaritan woman at the well in John 4:1–42.[61] Here we can see how her theory translates into practice. The story, which only appears in

John's Gospel, is set at Jacob's well in Samaria. The Samaritans and Jews had a tense relationship dating back to the sixth century BC. The Jews who returned from the Babylonian exile did not regard the Samaritans, who were descendants of Israelites who had married non-Jewish neighbors, as authentic Jews. The Samaritans eventually built their own Temple on Mt. Gerizim as a rival to the Temple in Jerusalem. As the story begins, Jesus' disciples have gone into town to buy provisions and Jesus, alone with the unnamed Samaritan woman, asks her for a drink of water from the well. What follows is a conversation between Jesus and the woman that revolves around the rich symbolism of water. During the course of their discussion, the woman realizes the identity of Jesus as God-in-the-flesh, signified by Jesus referring to himself by the divine name, "I am" (John 4:26; see Exod 3:14). The mores of the day frowned upon social interaction between a man and a woman unrelated to him by kinship or marriage. This, coupled with the Jewish antipathy toward the Samaritans, accounts for the disciples' shock when they return and find Jesus speaking with the Samaritan woman. The woman leaves her water jar at the well and returns to her town to announce that she has seen the Messiah. At the conclusion of the story, many of the townspeople go to Jesus and come to believe that he "is truly the Savior of the world" (John 4:42).

Schneiders has argued that a method of interpretation should be judged by its ability to produce fruitful, critical, and transformative readings of the biblical texts. First, Schneiders believes that a feminist approach highlights elements in the story that have been overlooked or obscured by the Christian tradition. One of the most immediate consequences of this approach is to acknowledge that women (Mary, John 2; the Samaritan woman, John 4; and Martha and Mary, John 11) play a significant role in disclosing the identity of Jesus in John's Gospel.[62] The most dramatic example of this is Mary Magdalene, who is the first one to meet the Risen Lord and is the one who informs the disciples of this fact (John 20:18). The Bible also has several stories of women who play important roles in the history of Israel who meet men at wells (Rebekah, Gen 24; Rachel, Gen 29; Zipporah, the wife of Moses, Exod 2).[63] Schneiders also takes issue with traditional interpreters who believe that the woman is a prostitute or a woman with questionable morals based on the following exchange:

> Jesus said to her, "Go, call your husband, and come back." The woman answered him, "I have no husband." Jesus said to her, "You are right in saying, 'I have no husband'; for you have had five husbands, and the one you have now is not your husband. What you have said is true!" (John 4:16–18).

Schneiders argues that this interpretation overlooks the image of the unfaithful spouse as a common prophetic denunciation of idolatry or unfaithfulness (Hos 2:2). The woman at the well represents the Samaritan people, and Jesus stands as their loving Bridegroom (John 3:29–30). Schneiders writes, "In summary, the entire dialogue between Jesus and the woman is the 'wooing' of Samaria to full covenant fidelity in the New Israel by Jesus, the New Bridegroom."[64] This interpretation casts the woman in a far more positive light as a symbol of Jesus' loving outreach to all peoples of the world. It is also by her proclamation of the good news that many of the Samaritans come to believe that Christ is, indeed, the Savior of the world.

Schneiders also applies the standard historical-critical tests to the story. For example, Schneiders does not believe that this episode actually occurred during the ministry of Jesus. For Schneiders, this story addresses the situation of the community that produced John's Gospel that was comprised of many Samaritan converts. One of the issues that divided them was the place of the proper worship of the Lord. Jesus states that worship of God is not a matter of going to either Jerusalem or Mt. Gerizim, but rather that "the hour is coming, and is now here, when the true worshipers will worship the Father in spirit and truth, for the Father seeks such as these to worship him" (John 4:23).

Lastly, according to Schneiders, when we enter into the world depicted in this scene from John's Gospel, we step into a world "essentially characterized by an astonishing, even shocking, inclusiveness. Jesus goes to Samaria, the land of the hated 'other,' to confront and to heal the ancient divisions and to integrate into the New Covenant not those who were merely ignorant of, but those who had been unfaithful to, the Old Covenant."[65] If we allow ourselves to enter into this "meeting tent" and hear God speaking to us, we can then speak and act in loving ways to the world in which we live.

Discussion Questions

1. Do you believe that God speaks to us through the biblical writings?

2. Are there many possible meanings of any given biblical passage? How do we know we are not reading into the Bible meanings that aren't there?

3. Is Hugh of St. Victor's interpretation of the story of Noah's ark convincing? Why or why not?

4. What is your interpretation of the story of Noah's ark?

5. Is the Bible inerrant? What implications for reading the Bible follow from your answer?

6. What are the similarities and differences between Hugh's approach to the Bible and Schneiders's approach? What are the strengths and weaknesses of each of them?

7. What is your evaluation of Schneiders's interpretation of the story of the Samaritan woman at the well?

Suggested Readings

For two very good introductions to the theology of Hugh of St. Victor, see Paul Rorem, *Hugh of St. Victor* (Oxford: Oxford University Press, 2009); and Boyd Taylor Coolman, *The Theology of Hugh of St. Victor: An Interpretation* (New York: Cambridge

University Press, 2010). One of the most respected of authorities on Hugh is Grover A. Zinn, Jr. See his *"De gradibus ascensionum*: The Stages of Contemplative Ascent in Two Treatises on *Noah's Ark* by Hugh of St. Victor," in John R. Sommerfeldt, Larry Syndergaard, and E. Rozanne Elders, eds., *Studies in Medieval Culture V* (Kalamazoo, MI: Western Michigan University, 1975), 61–79. For background on the Victorine tradition, see Steven Chase, *Contemplation and Compassion* (Maryknoll, NY: Orbis Books, 2003); chapter 3 of Beryl Smalley, *The Study of the Bible in the Middle Ages* (Notre Dame, IN: University of Notre Dame Press, 1964); and chapter 9 of Bernard McGinn, *The Growth of Mysticism* (New York: Crossroad, 1996).

Schneiders added a new preface to the second edition of *The Revelatory Text* (Collegeville, MN: The Liturgical Press, 1999). For a collection of essays devoted to the spiritual theology of Sandra Schnieders, see Bruce H. Lescher and Elizabeth Liebert, eds., *Exploring Christian Spirituality* (Mahwah, NJ: Paulist Press, 2006), which also includes a bibliography of Schneiders's works on pages 215–23. For a nice summary of Schneiders's approach to biblical interpretation, see Susanne M. DeCrane, *Aquinas, Feminism, and the Common Good* (Washington, DC: Georgetown University Press, 2004), 4–17. For a review symposium on Schneiders's *The Revelatory Text*, see *Horizons* 19, no. 2 (1992): 288–302. See also Schneiders's address to the Catholic Theological Society of America, "Living Word or Dead(ly) Letter" in Paul Crowley, ed., *Proceedings of the Forty-Seventh Annual Convention* 47 (1992): 45–60; and her Anthony Jordan lectures published as *Beyond Patching* (Mahwah, NJ: Paulist Press, 1991). For a helpful guide to the Gospel of John, see Judith Schubert, *The Gospel of John: Question by Question* (Mahwah, NJ: Paulist Press, 2008).

3

PHILOSOPHICAL THEOLOGY: THINKING ABOUT GOD
Erasmus of Rotterdam and Eleonore Stump

Sometimes when we read the Bible our search for God grinds to a halt. Certain biblical passages confound us. When Israel's first king, Saul, sins yet again, the Bible simply notes, "And the Lord was sorry that he had made Saul king over Israel" (1 Sam 15:35). The modern reader cannot help but wonder, "Can the Lord be 'sorry' for something? Doesn't that imply God didn't know in advance that Saul would sin?" This process of rigorously thinking about God in light of a scriptural passage, liturgical practice, or religious belief moves us into the field of philosophical theology.[1] Broadly speaking, a scholar in the field of Christian philosophical theology subjects a particular Christian belief or practice to "rational scrutiny" as defined by a particular school of philosophical thought. In this chapter, we focus our attention on two highly influential works of philosophical theology in the Catholic tradition: the sixteenth-century humanist Erasmus of Rotterdam's discussion of free will and the contemporary philosopher Eleonore Stump's treatment of petitionary prayer.

INTRODUCTION TO ERASMUS

Desiderius Erasmus of Rotterdam (1466/67–1536), who gar-
nered international attention with his witty satires of clerical
immorality and ineptitude, was along with his older brother
Pieter born the son of a priest who had entered into a relationship with the daughter of a local physician.[2] The boys began
their education in the town of Gouda and then in Deventer. It
was in Deventer that Erasmus came into contact with the
Brethren of the Common Life, a religious group committed to
the development of a lay spirituality marked by "interior fervor
and simple faith."[3] Tragedy befell the boys when an outbreak of
the plague claimed their mother's life in 1483 and their father's
life the following year. The boys' guardians encouraged them to
enter religious life. In 1485, the brothers entered religious life as
Augustinian canons, Erasmus in the town of Steyn and Peter in
the town of Sion. Steyn was a mixed blessing for Erasmus. He
began his lifelong interest in Latin and classical writings, but he
was not fond of the regulated life of the Augustinians. After his
ordination in 1492, he became secretary to the bishop of Cambrai
who had his eye set on becoming a cardinal. When the bishop's
plans for career advancement faltered, Erasmus moved to Paris
where he studied theology for nearly five years, but found the
scholastic theology being taught there overly abstract and unin-
teresting. In order to support himself, Erasmus tutored students.
One of those students, William Blount, took Erasmus to England
where he met and befriended Thomas More and John Colet who
encouraged him to pursue biblical studies and the study of
Greek. Erasmus began to travel extensively throughout Europe,
and in 1500, he published *Adages*, a collection of proverbs drawn
from classical sources. The historian Erika Rummel describes
Adages as "Erasmus's ticket of admission to the circle of the
humanists."[4] Erasmus remained a prominent figure in that circle
until his death in 1536. In addition to publishing critical editions
of the works of early church thinkers, Erasmus also produced a

new critical edition of the Greek New Testament accompanied by a new Latin translation and annotations in 1516. He also penned a number of satirical works that enjoyed a wide readership, most notably *The Praise of Folly* in 1549. Though he was a vocal critic of the church, Erasmus also opposed Martin Luther, and it is his conflict with Luther over the question of free will that will be the focus of our investigation.

ERASMUS AND CHRISTIAN HUMANISM

Renaissance humanists believed that the future of human civilization depended on how thoroughly we retrieved the riches of our past. They were utterly convinced that from art and architecture to oration and playwriting, the greatest Greek and Roman achievements represented the pinnacle of excellence that all succeeding generations of thoughtful individuals should aspire to attain. Cicero was not merely a great *Roman* thinker and orator, but a great *human* thinker and orator. The teachings of the ancient philosophers addressed the abiding questions of truth, virtue, and happiness that are essential for human fulfillment. A humanistic education, therefore, teaches students how to appreciate that which is truly valuable, to deliver compelling discourses, and to compose works of profound insight into the human condition.

As a Christian humanist, Erasmus saw an underlying harmony among many of the insights of Plato, Seneca, and Plutarch, and the gospel preached by Jesus. Erasmus belonged to the tradition of Christian thinkers who saw in pagan thinkers not an absence of revelation, but a participation in the Reason (*Logos*) with which God created the human race. This is why Erasmus can refer to "the divinely inspired Plato"[5] and have a character in one of his colloquies (discourses) exclaim, "Saint Socrates, pray for us!"[6] In the same colloquy, another character takes issue with the distinction between "sacred" and "profane" writers.

On the contrary, whatever is devout and contributes to good morals should not be called profane. Of course Sacred Scripture is the basic authority in everything; yet I sometimes run across ancient sayings or pagan writings— even the poets'—so purely and reverently expressed, and so inspired, that I can't help believing their authors' hearts were moved by some divine power. And perhaps the spirit of Christ is more widespread than we understand, and the company of saints includes many not in our calendar.[7]

Though placed on one of his character's lips, this position reflects Erasmus's own Christian humanism.

In keeping with his humanistic outlook, Erasmus commonly referred to the "philosophy of Christ." In 1516, Erasmus published the *Paraclesis* as a preface to his Greek and Latin edition of the New Testament. In it he offers a plea for Christians to study the New Testament because it is there that we find the philosophy of Christ in its purest form.[8] Erasmus notes that "it is not pleasing to renew at the present time this complaint, not entirely new but, alas, only too just—and perhaps never more just than in these days—that when men are devoting themselves with such ardent spirit to all their studies, this philosophy of Christ alone is derided by some, even Christians, is neglected by many, and is discussed by a few, but in a cold manner (I shall not say insincerely)."[9] Rather, says Erasmus, Christians should know the books of the New Testament so well that "the farmer [would] sing some portions of them at the plow, the weaver hum some parts of them to the movement of his shuttle, the traveler lighten the weariness of the journey with stories of this kind!"[10] Unlike the teachings of many philosophers, the philosophy of Christ pertains not to abstruse topics, but rather to personal transformation. "Indeed, this philosophy easily penetrates into the minds of all, an action in especial accord with human nature. Moreover, what else is the philosophy of Christ, which He himself calls a rebirth, than the restoration of human nature originally well formed?"[11]

In the same year that he published the *Paraclesis*, Erasmus produced *The Education of a Christian Prince*, which he dedicated to the future Charles V. In contrast to Machiavelli's *The Prince* that appeared three years earlier, Erasmus argued that a prince should love philosophy so that he can rule with wisdom and beneficence. Erasmus makes it clear, however, what type of philosopher he has in mind. "Further, you must realise that 'philosopher' does not mean someone who is clever at dialectics or science but someone who rejects illusory appearance and undauntedly seeks out and follows what is true and good. Being a philosopher is in practice the same as being a Christian; only the terminology is different."[12] Erasmus had little time for pretentious philosophers who did not recognize that a true philosopher is the one who loves wisdom and lives a life of simple virtue. He had even less time for pretentious theologians whose trade involved offering hair-splitting distinctions rather than the simple life of piety. In *The Praise of Folly*, Erasmus displays his scorn for the scholastic theology that he encountered in Paris. Theologians "are so closely hedged in by two rows of [magisterial definitions], conclusions, corollaries, explicit and implicit propositions, they have so many '*holes they can run to*,' that Vulcan himself couldn't net them tightly enough to keep them from escaping by means of distinctions, with which they can cut all knots as cleanly as the fine-honed edge of 'the headman's axe'— so many new terms have they thought up and such monstrous jargon have they coined."[13]

As Erasmus published his Greek and Latin editions of the New Testament, a young German Augustinian monk was delving into his own study of the Bible. In 1517, Martin Luther posted his Ninety-Five Theses on the church door in Wittenberg, beginning the Protestant Reformation. While Erasmus and Luther shared a deep devotion to the Scriptures and were both keenly aware of the need for church reform, they had different temperaments and their relationship to the Catholic Church would take divergent paths.

Where Erasmus certainly ruffled the feathers of many prelates (When a papal legate complained on behalf of Pope Clement VII to Erasmus about him eating meat on Friday, Erasmus replied, "My heart is Catholic but my stomach is Protestant."), he lived and died as a loyal member of the Catholic Church.[14] When Pope Leo X issued a formal declaration known as a "bull" of excommunication against Luther in 1520, Luther responded by publicly burning it. Luther then composed his rebuttal (*Assertio*) to the each of the forty-one charges of heresy that Leo cited in his bull. It was Luther's response to article thirty-six that caught Erasmus's eye. In it Luther denied the existence of human free will. On both humanistic and theological grounds, Erasmus rejected Luther's position and entered into the fray by publishing *On the Freedom of the Will* (*De libero arbitrio*) in 1524.

ERASMUS ON FREE WILL

The question of how God could work through the free actions of an individual without violating that person's freedom has concerned philosophers and theologians for centuries. The philosopher and theologian Vincent Brummer poses the problem as follows:

Some [philosophers and theologians, such as J. Burnaby] would go so far as to say that "the power of God's love takes effect in human history in no other way than through the wills and actions of men in whom that love has come to dwell." But in what sense can we claim that God acts "through the wills and actions of men"? If God were to bring about our actions, do we not thereby cease to be agents of these actions and become rather the tools by means of which God performs *his* actions? If on the other hand a human person were to remain the originator of his own actions (as he must if they are to be ascribed to him), how can these actions then also be ascribed to God as though they were *his*? In brief, does it make sense to ascribe the same action to two different agents?[15]

The twentieth-century Anglican philosopher and theologian Austin Farrer did, indeed, speak of the "double agency" of the human will and the divine will. Echoing Paul's own declaration that "it is no longer I who live, but it is Christ who lives in me" (Gal 2:20), Farrer writes that "the more it is God, the more it is I; and the more it is I, the more it is God."[16] In whatever way this paradox is expressed, it requires at its core a cooperation of the human will with the divine will. As Farrer notes, "When we make our own will the prolongation of God's will for us and in us, then we know God."[17]

Erasmus begins his short discourse by acknowledging that the Bible contains verses that both support and undermine the belief that humans have "free choice," which he defines as "a power of the human will by which a man can apply himself to things which lead to eternal salvation, or turn away from them."[18] In addition to other passages, Erasmus cites Wisdom 15:14–17 in support of free will. "It was he who created humankind in the beginning, and left them in the power of their own free choice. If you choose, you can keep the commandments, and to act faithfully is a matter of your own choice. He has placed before you fire and water; stretch out your hand for whichever you choose. Before each person are life and death, and whichever one chooses will be given."[19] We were endowed with the divine gift of free will, and because it is truly free, it can be used or misused to bring about either good or evil. There are likewise verses scattered through the Bible that could be used to marshal the claim that God, not humans, make the decisions about what happens in this world. For example, in the story of the ten plagues in the Book of Exodus, the Israelites who demand their release are met with stubborn resistance from the Pharaoh. Then we learn that it was not the Pharaoh himself who was responsible for this reaction. "But the Lord hardened the heart of Pharaoh, and he would not listen to them, just as the Lord had spoken" (Exod 9:12).

What would be the point of God doing this? We read a few verses later, "But this is why I have let you live: to show you my power, and to make my name resound through all the earth" (Exod 9:16). The Pharaoh is actually God's instrument to show the people that God's power cannot be thwarted.

Erasmus, in keeping with his humanistic and Catholic interest in the work of the ancient Christian writers, carves out a place for free will in the execution of God's will in this world. He writes that "some of the orthodox Fathers distinguish three stages of human action: the first is thought, the second will, the third accomplishment. In the first and third they give no place for the workings of free choice; our soul is impelled by grace alone to think good thoughts, and by grace alone is moved to perform what it has thought. Yet, in the second phase, that is, in consenting, grace and the human will act together, but in such a way that grace is the principal cause, and the secondary cause our will."[20] Erasmus argues that we attribute all to God out of humility and respect, but in actuality we do contribute our own will when we cooperate with God. "But since our own efforts are so puny, the whole is ascribed to God, just as a sailor who has brought his ship safely into port out of a heavy storm does not say: 'I saved the ship' but 'God saved it.' And yet his skill and his labor were not entirely useless."[21] We can also turn our will away from doing God's will. Following the interpretation given by the early church thinker Origen of Alexandria, Erasmus argues that in the case of Pharaoh, it was not God who hardened his heart as much as the Pharaoh himself by his persistent refusal to repent.[22]

Erasmus's argument involves a number of issues in philosophical theology, not least among them questions about the origin of evil and the omnipotence of God, but we will focus instead on the nature of God. The humanities professor Albert Rabil notes, "The attributes which Erasmus emphasizes throughout are the notions of God as loving, persuading, promising, truthful in fulfilling his promise. And each of these calls to mind a human response." Rabil continues, "A loving God is one who persuades;

he does not compel. God invites everyone but forces no one. Man's response is therefore a matter of free choice."[23] God's love and human freedom are two sides of the same coin. Without a loving God and a free human being, what sense can we make of the mercy of God and the need for human repentance? Erasmus asks rhetorically, "Who will be able to bring himself to love God with all his heart when He created hell seething with eternal torments in order to punish his own misdeeds in his victims as though he took delight in human torments?"[24] The Reformation scholar Roland Bainton sees this emphasis in Erasmus's work most clearly displayed in his commentary on the parable of the prodigal son. Erasmus writes:

> When the prodigal came to himself he arose. Now to arise is the first step in salvation. "And while he was a great way off he father saw him." He who had the greater love did first espy the other. The father saw the lad who had departed so insolently, now ragged, famished, filthy and weeping. The father saw him and had compassion and ran. The boy had prepared a speech. He would say, "Father, I have sinned against heaven and before thee, and I am no longer worthy to be called thy son. Make me as one of thy hired servants." But before he had even started to speak his father fell on his neck and kissed him. Now in the natural love of this father for his son behold the goodness of God, who is far more clement to sinful man, if only he repent and despise himself, than any father toward his son, however, tenderly he may love him.[25]

"This," Bainton writes, "is the essence of Erasmus."[26]

LUTHER'S RESPONSE TO ERASMUS

Sixteen months after Erasmus's discourse appeared, Luther completed his response, *On the Bondage of the Will* (*De Servo Arbitrio*). As one might expect, there are a number of lines of argumentation that Luther pursues in his criticism of Erasmus. For example, Luther rejects Erasmus's claim that scripture is obscure and filled with strong arguments on both sides of the issue, and that it might be a question best left unanswered. Luther's chief complaint is that Erasmus neglects to highlight the role that the death and resurrection of Christ plays in terms of justification by faith, the relationship between faith and good works, and God's election of the saved. We will turn our attention not to these aspects of the Erasmus-Luther debate, but to the philosophical and theological issue of the nature of God. Where Erasmus centered his discussion around the love of God for the errant sinner who repents, epitomized by the prodigal son, Luther stresses God's absolute foreknowledge.

For Luther, the philosophical issue is quite simple: God's foreknowledge precludes the possibility of human free will.[27] "I admit that the question is difficult, and indeed impossible, if you wish to maintain at the same time both God's foreknowledge and man's freedom. For what could be more difficult, nay more impossible, than to insist that contradictions or contraries are not opposed, or to find a number that was at the same time both ten and nine?"[28] Erasmus argues for a compatibility between God's foreknowledge and human free will; Luther, by contrast, sees a zero-sum proposition in which credit given to one party necessarily involves a loss of credit to the other. "Thus God's foreknowledge and omnipotence are diametrically opposed to our free choice, for either God can be mistaken in foreknowing and also err in action (which is impossible) or we must act and be acted upon in accordance with his foreknowledge and activity....This omnipotence and the foreknowledge of God, I say, completely abolish the dogma of free choice."[29] Critics of Luther would insist that God can know what free choices humans will make in the future without God having determined those choices in advance.

Where Erasmus believes that the concept of free will offers genuine hope to the repentant sinner, Luther sees the omnipotence of God as the cornerstone of the Christian faith. The

Lutheran scholar Gerhard Forde writes, "If God does not rule by his immutable necessity, who, Luther asks, will believe his promises?…Faith is created and sustained by the promises of God, not by the efforts of free choice."[30]

Luther argues, "Therefore, Christian faith is entirely extinguished, the promises of God and the whole gospel are completely destroyed, if we teach and believe that it is not for us to know the necessary foreknowledge of God and the necessity of the things that are to come to pass. For this is the one supreme consolation of Christians in all adversities, to know that God does not lie, but does all things immutably, and that his will can neither be resisted nor changed nor hindered."[31]

INTRODUCTION TO ELEONORE STUMP'S "PETITIONARY PRAYER"

When philosophically considering the practice of prayer, we are forced to confront our most fundamental beliefs regarding the nature and activity of God. If we accept the traditional view that God is all-knowing, all-loving, and all-powerful, then questions arise at every turn.[32] If, for example, God is all-knowing, then we might wonder whether prayer is necessary since we can't inform God about something that God doesn't already know. If God is all-loving, then asking God to help a loved one might seem pointless since a loving God would always act in the best interests of humans regardless of whether we asked God to do so or not. Finally, if God is all-powerful, we might wonder if God is able to change events that have already occurred.[33] For example, if a family heard on the news that a ship carrying friends of theirs sank off Nova Scotia and that half of the passengers perished and the other half were rescued and were now safely on shore, would it make sense for the family to pray to God that their friends are among those passengers who survived?

In this section, we will focus on an influential essay on petitionary prayer by the philosopher Eleonore Stump. Stump examines the logic and theology that underlie the traditional Christian belief that in certain cases God responds to prayers of petition and brings about states of affairs in the world that would not have arisen had the prayers not been offered. Before turning to the argument itself, we need to offer three points of clarification. First, when we qualify the statement, "God answers prayers" with "in certain cases," it seems to terribly weaken the original assertion. Philosophers who support Stump, however, would first make the provision that we are dealing with prayers that are asking for things that do not violate the goodness of God.[34] We are not considering cases where someone prays for harm to come upon an innocent person whom he or she despises for some reason. Second, when we argue that God brings about a state of affairs in response to the prayer, we cannot simply mean by that a change in the attitude of the one who prays. The nineteenth-century religious thinker Søren Kierkegaard wrote that "prayer does not change God, but it changes the one who offers it."[35] This conception of prayer frequently appears along with the belief that God has a plan for each and every person, and prayer is our submission to that plan. We see this displayed most poignantly in Jesus' own prayer in the Garden of Gethsemane, "Abba, Father, for you all things are possible; remove this cup from me; yet, not what I want, but what you want" (Mark 14:36). While it is undoubtedly true that prayer changes the one who prays, Stump is arguing the stronger case that a new state of affairs arises in the world and not merely in the heart of the individual. Third, Stump is not claiming that this new state of affairs must be an instantaneous miraculous event in which God acts unilaterally in the world. Unlike the story of Elijah on Mt. Carmel in which Elijah prays and God sends down fire from heaven (1 Kgs 18), prayers can be answered through the ordinary workings of humans helping each other.

STUMP'S ARGUMENT IN "PETITIONARY PRAYER"

Stump acknowledges that many philosophical attempts to find a compatibility between God's omniscience or immutability and the practice of prayer get us tied up in knots. For example, if we begin with the immutability of God, then we might conclude that prayer is futile. "Before a certain petitionary prayer is made, it is the case either that God will bring about the state of affairs requested in the prayer or that he will not bring it about. He cannot have left the matter open since doing so would imply a subsequent change in him and he is immutable. Either way, since he is immutable, the prayer itself can effect no change in the state of affairs and hence is pointless."[36] Stump, therefore, proposes a different route: one that conceives of the divine-human relationship in terms of friendship. In order to convey the idea that "God loves [humans] and wants to be loved in return," the biblical authors describe our relationship with God as husband and wife, father and son, and even as one friend to another (John 15:12–15).[37] When we think of friendship with God, however, we would reasonably wonder how a genuine friendship can exist between "an omniscient, omnipotent, perfectly good person and a fallible, finite, imperfect person."[38] In any unequal relationship, the disadvantaged partner (1) "can be so overcome by the advantages or superiority of this 'friend' that he becomes simply a shadowy reflection of the other's personality, a slavish follower who slowly loses all sense of his own tastes and desires and will," or (2) "become spoiled in the way that members of royal family in a ruling house are subject to. Because of the power at their disposal in virtue of their connections, they often become tyrannical, willful, indolent, self-indulgent, and the like."[39]

How then could we guard against these two dangers? Here, Stump offers some examples to help clarify the conditions that would be necessary in order for a genuine friendship to exist between two unequal parties.

Suppose a teacher sees that one of his students is avoiding writing a paper and is thereby storing up trouble for himself at the end of the term. And suppose that the student *asks* the teacher for extra help in organizing working time and scheduling the various parts of the work. In that case I think the teacher can without any problem give the student what he needs, provided, of course, that the teacher is willing to do as much for any other student, and so on.[40]

If the student did not ask for the teacher's help and the teacher took it upon him/herself to call the student, then the teacher would be meddling. If, however, a friend of the student approached the teacher, expressed his/her concern for the struggling student and asked the teacher to please speak with the student, the teacher could do so. "If the teacher now goes to help Jim and is rudely or politely asked 'What right have you got to interfere?' he'll say, 'Well, in fact, your friend came to me and *asked* me to help.'"[41] Stump contends that the act of asking for help for oneself, or even the act of a friend asking on someone else's behalf provides a sufficient protection against the dangers that she outlines at the start of her essay. "Prayer acts a kind of buffer between man and God. By safeguarding the weaker member of the relation from the dangers of overwhelming domination and overwhelming spoiling, it helps to promote and preserve a close relationship between an omniscient, omnipotent, perfectly good person and a fallible, finite, imperfect person."[42] Just as a teacher can offer to help a student who is struggling academically if the student requests help (provided the teacher will assist all students in a similar situation who make the same request), God can rightfully respond to prayers of petition.

STUMP AND THE SEARCH FOR GOD

Stump's argument raises two critically important questions in our search for God: "Who is God?" and "How does God act in our lives?" In this way, the often maddening philosophical investigations yield some very practical insights into the nature and activity of God.

"Who is God?" Stump would certainly agree with Erasmus that God is not a tyrant.[43] Stump's entire argument assumes that God respects human freedom. She insists that "orthodox Christianity is committed to claiming that the advent of God's kingdom on earth, in which all people freely love God, would *make* the world better than it would otherwise be. But I think that it is not possible for God to make the world better in this way, because I think it is not possible for him to *make* men *freely* do anything."[44] Brummer makes a similar point in his work *What Are We Doing When We Pray?* The very nature of personal relationships demands that both parties in the relationship are autonomous beings. "A can *offer* his fellowship to B but cannot *cause* B to return it. On the other hand, B cannot return A's fellowship, unless A has *offered* it to him first. In this way personal relations presuppose not only that both partners are personal agents, but that each acknowledges the personal agency of the other as well as his own dependence on the other for establishing the relation."[45] Applying this understanding of personal relationships to God, Brummer concludes, "God [fulfills] most of our needs and desires without our having to ask him. If, however, he were to [fulfill] *all* our needs and desires in this way, we would be like [potted plants] on his window-sill and not persons with whom he has a personal relationship."[46]

Not all philosophers have been persuaded by Stump's contention that the practice of petitionary prayer accords with the orthodox understanding of God. The philosophy of religion professor Michael J. Murray offers the following helpful summary of the opposing position:

We can think of the goods God might provide for us as falling into two categories: (a) basic goods which are required to ensure that our long-term quality of life is not significantly diminished and (b) discretionary goods which serve simply to enhance an already acceptable quality of life. While it seems reasonable to suppose that God might sometimes withhold discretionary goods...it also seems reasonable that he could never do so when it comes to basic goods. The problem, of course, is that religions that believe in petitionary prayer usually highlight the fact that one ought to pray (even especially) for basic goods. Thus, while [certain philosophical arguments make sense] of some types of petitionary prayer, [they] do not make sense of the sort advocated by most major theistic traditions.[47]

Does it make sense, in other words, to say that those who are starving should pray to an all-loving God for food? The philosopher David Basinger doesn't think so. He argues that "just as I don't think that a parent could justifiably withhold basic human care or minimum shelter from a child until requested in order to foster appreciation of the parent as a provider, so I don't believe that God could justifiably withhold life-saving or life-sustaining intervention until requested to foster better appreciation of God's role as provider or to teach us something about his nature or to keep from spoiling us."[48]

"How does God act in our lives?" The general answer to this question that we find in Stump's article involves the principle of "mediation." As the theologian Richard P. McBrien explains, "Catholicism holds...that the encounter with God is a mediated experience but a real experience, rooted in the historical and affirmed as real by the critical and systematic judgment that God is truly present and active here or there, in this event or that, in this person or that, in this object or that."[49] Does this mean that God never comes to us in a direct, unmediated fashion (e.g., mystical union) or even in an uninvited way (e.g., Saul on the road to Damascus)?[50] Stump's position doesn't exclude such occurrences, but they are clearly not the focus of her argument. Instead, she suggests that God's presence is mediated to us through the concern of family and friends, and the cooperative efforts of people whom we may never meet.

Stump considers the case of St. Monica's fervent prayer on behalf of her son St. Augustine. Looking back on his life prior to his conversion, he writes in the *Confessions*, "For nearly nine years were yet to come during which I wallowed deep in the mire and the darkness of delusion. Often I tried to lift myself, only to plunge the deeper. Yet all the time this chaste, devout, and prudent woman...never ceased to pray at all hours and to offer you the tears she shed for me."[51] While it is problematic to assert that Monica's prayer were *necessary* for Augustine's eventual conversion, Stump argues, it would be equally wrong to assert that they were inconsequential to the outcome. God's power and goodness may have well brought Augustine to Christianity apart from the prayers offered by Monica, but it is possible "to argue that God would have saved Augustine without Monica's prayers but not in the same amount of time or not by the same process or not with the same effect."[52]

Stump's entire argument is in many ways an extended reflection on the Lord's Prayer. She sees a similarity, for instance, between the state of affairs desired in the first three petitions of the Lord's Prayer and the state of affairs necessary for the success of many large-scale activities undertaken by humans. "One man can't put out a forest fire, but if everyone in the vicinity of a forest fire realized that fact and on that basis decided not to try, the fire would rage out of control."[53] In a similar way, the request for God's name to held as sacred by all people, for God's kingdom of justice and peace to reign on earth, and for God's will to govern all human decisions is not a request involving only one's self or one's friends, but people we will never meet. It is a prayer for a state of affairs that requires a deep abiding spiritual awareness of the unity of the human family. As the title character in *Doctor Zhivago* put it, "You in others—this is your soul."[54] Our soul, our point of contact with God, is the loving bond between ourselves and our seen and unseen neighbors.

For Erasmus and Stump, the search for God does not bypass the rigorous demands for philosophical precision when analyzing our most cherished Christian beliefs and practices. Yet in the midst of these logical dissections of the concepts of free will and petitionary prayer, we find a reaffirmation of the simple truths taught by Moses and Christ long ago: "I have set before you life and death, blessing and curses. Choose life so that you and your descendants may live, loving the Lord your God, obeying him, and holding fast to him." (Deut 30:19b–20a). "Is there anyone among you who, if your child asks for a fish, will give a snake instead of a fish? Or if the child asks for an egg, will give a scorpion? If you then, who are evil, know how to give good gifts to your children, how much more will the heavenly Father give the Holy Spirit to those who ask him!" (Luke 11:11–13).

Discussion Questions

1. Would reading the great Greek and Roman playwrights and poets shed light on how to live a Christian life? Why? Why not?

2. Did God "harden the heart" of Pharaoh (Exod 9:12)? If so, was the Pharaoh free? If not, what does this expression mean?

3. If God knows the future, can we can alter its course by our actions?

4. Does praying to God on our own behalf alter God's action in our lives? Does praying to God on behalf of others alter God's action in their lives?

5. What are some specific examples of God's mediation in the world?

Suggested Readings

For three helpful introductions to Erasmus, see Erika Rummel, *Erasmus* (New York: Continuum, 2004); James McConica, *Erasmus* (New York: Oxford University Press, 1991); and James D.

Tracy, *Erasmus of the Low Countries* (Berkeley, CA: University of California Press, 1996). See also chapter 2 of Carter Lindberg, ed., *The Reformation Theologians* (Malden, MA; Blackwell, 2002). For background on Erasmus, see chapter 9 of Lewis Spitz, *The Religious Renaissance of the German Humanists* (Cambridge, MA: Harvard University Press, 1963). For Erasmus's "philosophy of Christ," see chapter 7 of Cornelis Augustijn, *Erasmus: His Life, Works, and Influence*, translated by J. C. Grayson (Toronto: University of Toronto Press, 1991).

For two very helpful overviews on the philosophical analysis of prayer, see Harriet Harris, "Prayer," in Charles Taliaferro and Chad Meister, eds., *The Cambridge Companion to Christian Philosophical Theology* (Cambridge, MA: Cambridge University Press, 2010); and Scott A. Davidson, "Petitionary Prayer," in Thomas P. Flint and Michael Rea, *The Oxford Handbook of Philosophical Theology* (Oxford: Oxford University Press, 2009). Vincent Brummer's *What Are We Doing When We Pray?* (London: SCM Press, 1984) is an excellent treatment of the question. For articles arguing for and against the logic of petitionary prayer, see chapter 9 of Michael L. Peterson and Raymon J. VanArragon, *Contemporary Debates in Philosophy of Religion* (Malden, MA: Blackwell, 2004).

4

THEOLOGICAL ANTHROPOLOGY: DESIRING GOD

Bernard of Clairvaux and M. Shawn Copeland

The first three chapters of Genesis set the stage for the entire biblical narrative. Creation and fall, temptation and sin, hostility and death: These are the elements introduced at the very outset of the biblical story and they shape every scene that follows right through to the final scene in the Book of Revelation. These very same dynamics are at play in any comprehensive Christian theological system of thought, and the understanding of the human person offered in that exploration is called a "theological anthropology." An adequate Christian theological anthropology must account for the human capacity for deep communion with God and a profound love of neighbor as well as for the potential for painful inner turmoil and senseless brutality toward others. In this chapter, we will focus on the theological anthropology of the towering figure of twelfth-century Christian history, the Cistercian Bernard of Clairvaux (1090–1153) and one of the most influential Catholic theologians dealing today with issues of race and gender, M. Shawn Copeland.

INTRODUCTION TO BERNARD OF CLAIRVAUX

Bernard of Clairvaux is one of the most complex figures in all of church history. He was a vowed cloistered monk, but circumstances and papal summons required that he travel extensively throughout Europe. He composed some of the most moving passages on love in the Christian tradition, but preached passionately for the Second Crusade.[1] His fasting left him gaunt in physical appearance, but his powerful presence could strike fear in the hearts of princes and prelates alike. This key figure in the Cistercian monastic reform of the twelfth century was also a keenly perceptive analyst of the human personality and highly esteemed spiritual guide. Out of his rich life, we will focus almost exclusively on his spiritual writings, especially his work *On Loving God*.

Bernard's own life and the early history of the Cistercians are deeply intertwined. Bernard was born in 1090 in the lower nobility near Dijon in Burgundy, France. He received a solid education and was well trained in Latin, but about these years we know very little. In 1113, at the age of twenty-three, Bernard and thirty others, including his uncle and brothers, entered the monastery at Citeaux.[2] Citeaux, the motherhouse of the Cistercians, had been founded in 1098. The Cistercians were a reform movement within the Benedictine order. When local nobles and other outside influences began interfering in the internal governance of the Benedictine monasteries, a new monastery was established at Cluny in 909 that reported directly to the pope. Cluny then became a model for other monasteries, and by 1100, three hundred monasteries had followed Cluny's lead.[3] As time passed, some monks believed that the Clunaic monasteries themselves were in need of reform, and so in 1098, Robert, abbot of the monastery in Molesme, left and founded a new monastery in the marshes of Citeaux (in Latin, *Cistercium*). The monks at Molesme appealed to the Rome to order Robert to return and he complied, leaving Alberic as abbot at Citeaux. He was succeeded by an important figure in the young Cistercian movement, Stephen

Harding, who welcomed Bernard and his thirty companions to the struggling monastery in 1113. Stephen must have quickly recognized Bernard's gifts because in 1115 he sent him to found a monastery in Clairvaux. Bernard would go on to found more than sixty more monasteries throughout his career.

During his tenure as abbot of Clairvaux, Bernard was embroiled in many controversies that drew him away from the monastery. In his first public role, Bernard participated at the Council of Troyes (1128), which produced the regulations for the newly established Knights Templar, a religious institute charged with guarding pilgrims in Jerusalem. In 1130, at the death of Pope Honorius II, a disputed election for his successor resulted in a schism between the supporters of Innocent II and Anacletus. Bernard campaigned among princes and cardinals on behalf of Innocent II who finally prevailed after the death of Anacletus in 1138. Soon after Innocent II secured the papal throne, Bernard began his public controversy with the theologian Peter Abelard, securing a condemnation of Abelard's teachings at the Council of Sens in 1140. In 1146, the first Cistercian pope Eugene (Eugenius) III enlisted the help of Bernard in promoting the disastrous Second Crusade. Bernard spent the next year and a half enlisting the support of both the general public and the nobility for the cause.[4]

In the midst of his intensely active life, Bernard also found time to compose several important works. The grand project that occupied Bernard's time and attention beginning in 1135, but which remained unfinished at the time of his death was Bernard's *Sermons on the Song of Songs*. In this biblical love song between a bride and groom, Bernard found the perfect allegory for the mutual exchange of love between God and each soul (and between God and the church as a whole). However, none of Bernard's works better reflects the paradoxical unity in his personality between his deep love of the monastic life and his political skill at dealing with the very highest levels of power than *On Loving God*.

The idea for *On Loving God* originated with a letter Bernard composed in the early 1120s for the monks at the Grand

Chartreuse, the motherhouse of the Carthusian Order. The Carthusians were founded by Bruno who for a time lived with some other monks in the forests near Molesme, where he received spiritual direction by Robert of Molesme. In 1084, Hugh, the bishop of Grenoble, gave Bruno the land on which the Grand Chartreuse still stands, a thousand feet up in the Alps. There, the Carthusian monks continue to live lives centered on solitude and personal prayer.[5] Bernard developed the ideas in the letter in greater depth in *On Loving God*, which he wrote in response to a request by Aimeric (Haimeric), a cardinal deacon in the church of Rome. Aimeric was later to become the papal chancellor "during which period he was the most influential politician in the papal curia," according to the historian Ian Stuart Robinson.[6] Whether addressing himself to secluded monks perched high in the Alps or a powerbroker with the ear of the pope, Bernard speaks directly and perceptively about the drives and desires of the human heart and the path from self-centeredness to a genuine love of self in God.

BERNARD'S THEOLOGICAL ANTHROPOLOGY

Bernard McGinn and John Sommerfeldt, two highly re-spected authorities on Bernard, agree that the key to Bernard's spiritual theology is his theological anthropology.[7] At the center of Bernard's theological anthropology is the biblical claim that humans are created in the image and likeness of God. Like many of his theological predecessors, Bernard distinguished between "image" and "likeness."[8]

A general consensus emerged among twelfth-century theologians, reports the Trappist scholar Michael Casey, "which affirmed that the 'image' was the permanent and fundamental affinity with God enjoyed by human beings; the 'likeness' was the waxing and waning conformity with this basic orientation to God. Thus 'imagehood' could not be lost, but it could be obscured and deformed through the loss of 'likeness.'"[9] This "permanent and fundamental affinity with God" accounts for our free will, intellect, and immortal soul. As the ancient Greeks taught, "like is known by like," so our knowledge and love of God requires some similarity or "natural kinship" (Sermon 80) between human nature and the nature of God.

Bernard, however, also takes seriously the biblical story of the Fall. Borrowing the imagery of Augustine, Bernard says that our wills are "bent" or curved in on ourselves rather than directed toward God. Bernard explains that, "the soul which does not desire or have a taste for heavenly things, but clings to earthly things, is clearly not upright but bent, but it does not cease to be great, and it always retains its capacity for eternity" (Sermon 80). In other words, though the image is preserved, the likeness has faded. The soul has fallen into a "region of unlikeness" where it has become like faded gold. "The gold laments that it has grown dim, but it is still gold; its pure color is faded, but the base of the color is not altered. The simplicity of the soul remains unshaken in its fundamental being, but it is not seen because it is covered by the disguise of human deception, pretence, and hypocrisy" (Sermon 82).[10]

Regaining the likeness intended by God requires not a denial of our desires, Bernard insists, but rather a harnessing of our desires and the redirection of them toward God.[11] As Casey notes, the human being "is made for love and only God himself is large enough to be able to satisfy the immense craving for love which the human heart experiences. Being made in the image of God signifies that the person has a capacity for God which cannot be filled by anything else. And until such time as he is fully invaded by divine charity, he remains imperfect."[12] If we direct that "immense craving for love" to God, insists Bernard, we will be like the prodigal son who returned from his state of debasement in a foreign land (i.e., "the region of unlikeness") to the intimate love of his father.[13] The path of that return is charted by Bernard in his work *On Loving God*.

ON LOVING GOD

On Loving God is a compact work, but its sweep is broad, encompassing the entire span of a person's spiritual journey. It reminds us of a speech someone might deliver at the end of a retirement dinner given in his or her honor. For example, a man who enjoyed a long and rewarding career in teaching might reflect that when he began his career he related to the students as an older brother, then as an uncle, then as a father, and finally as a grandfather. In this simple observation, he captures his entire forty-year career. Reflecting further on his time in the classroom, he may offer some perspective on those aspects of teaching that he found to be of lasting importance, those aspects that seemed important at one time but now seem insignificant, and those aspects that challenged him at various times throughout his career. In a similar way, Bernard's work divides the Christian spiritual journey into four stages, and identifies love as the virtue that is of lasting importance for the Christian, and self-interest as the constant challenge to loving God and neighbor as we should.

Bernard's *On Loving God* arose from his countless hours reading and praying the Scriptures. Not only does it abound with quotations and allusions from the Psalms, the foundational texts for most of the monk's public and private prayer, and the Song of Songs, Bernard undoubtedly had several other passages in mind. Clearly, Christ's teaching that the greatest commandment is to love the Lord your God with all your heart, soul and mind, and your neighbor as yourself exerted tremendous influence on his thought. (Matt 22:37–39). The Gospel and Letters of John are all filled with teachings on the love of God. Chief among them is the simple, yet profound insight that God is love (1 John 4:8) and that "those who abide in love abide in God, and God abides in them" (1 John 4:16). In the Gospel of John, following the washing of the disciples' feet, Jesus commands them, "Just as I have loved you, you also should love one another" (John 13:34). In his First Letter to the Corinthians, Paul offers one of the most eloquent passages on the priority of love: "If I speak in the tongues of mortals and of angels, but do not have love, I am a noisy gong or a clanging cymbal. And if I have prophetic powers, and understand all mysteries and all knowledge, and if I have all faith, so as to remove mountains, but do not have love, I am nothing" (1 Cor 13:1–2).

Given the rich abundance of biblical passages devoted to love, it is clear that Bernard is right to single out love as the chief virtue of the Christian life, but Bernard is far too keen an observer of the human spirit not to recognize that *saying* that we should love God and neighbor in an utterly selfless manner, and actually *doing* it are two different things entirely. As Paul himself acknowledges in his Letter to the Romans, "I do not understand my own actions. For I do not do what I want, but I do the very thing I hate" (7:15). Bernard is also very attuned to the conflicting desires that fill our hearts. Because we do not desire only the noblest things in life, we do not love in the right way, but through the grace of God we can transform our desires and properly love God, neighbor, and self. Each of the four stages, then, identifies a way of loving that follows from the state of our desires. His scheme consists of four stages, each representing a higher form of love: the love of self for the sake of the self; the love of God for the sake of the self; the love of God for the sake of God; the love of self for the sake of God.

The human journey to God begins for Bernard in "carnal love" by which he means a self-centered existence. "Since nature has become more fragile and weak, necessity obliges a man to serve it first. This is carnal love by which a man loves himself above all for his own sake."[14] When dealing with "carnal love," Bernard often quotes Paul, "But it is not the spiritual that is first, but the physical, and then the spiritual" (1 Cor 15:46). Bernard's clear-eyed assessment of the human condition is that we begin as persons driven by self-interest, with a deep desire to have our wants and needs satisfied. When we were infants, we cried when we were hungry or cold or when we needed to be changed. He maintains, "Our love advances by fixed degrees, led on by grace, until it is consummated in the spirit."[15] What is consummated in the spirit, however, begins with the body.

The spiritual journey that every Christian undertakes mirrors the early disciple's own journey with Christ. Each begins with a love focused on the fleshly or earthly realities, and culminates in a love of the spiritual or heavenly realities. In Sermon 20 of his commentary on the Song of Songs, Bernard sees "carnal love" as the first step in the love of Christ. Here, Bernard uses the word *carnal* to refer to the humanity of Christ, to the events in his life as the Incarnate Word of God. "I think this is the principal reason why the invisible God willed to be seen in the flesh and to converse with men as a man. He wanted to recapture the affections of carnal men who were unable to love in any other way, by first drawing them to the salutary love of his own humanity, and then gradually to raise them to a spiritual love."[16] The Ascension marks the transition in the lives of the disciples to this higher form of love. Bernard continues, "I think Paul had reached this level when he said: 'Even if we once knew Christ in the body, we know him thus no longer' [2 Cor 5:16]. Perhaps this was also true of the Prophet [i.e., Jeremiah] who said: 'A Spirit before our face is Christ the Lord.' [Lam 4:20]."[17] Just as Christ ascends from a bodily existence to a purely spiritual one, according to Bernard, the Christian's love must elevate from the carnal to the spiritual.[18] This, however, should not cast our carnal love of Christ in a negative light. As Casey notes, "a 'carnal' love for Christ, a sentimental attachment to the person of Jesus through an imaginative dwelling on his mysteries is not unusual. It is a beginning, in many cases, a necessary beginning, but it is transcended in the process of spiritual growth."[19] In the same way, according to Bernard, a love of self for the sake of the self is a necessary beginning for us, but one that with the grace of God can be transcended.

The second and third stages both deal with our love of God. For Bernard, how we love God, in turn, shapes how we love our neighbor. While Bernard does not devote a great deal of time in

On Loving God to the second stage itself, he does discuss in some detail the changes in our thinking that accompany our transition from the first to the second stage. We grow increasingly aware of the fact that our very being and our continued existence is dependent upon God. "He who made nature protects it, for nature was created in a way that it must have its creator for protector. The world could not subsist without him to whom it owes its very existence."[20] We also realize that in order to fulfill our own needs we must cooperate with our neighbors. In doing so, we become aware of the rights of others. The command to love our neighbor as ourselves begins to turn our concerns away from an exclusive focus on own selves.[21] "Thus carnal love becomes social when it is extended to others."[22] In the third stage, as we increasingly approach God with our needs we begin "to taste and discover how sweet the Lord is."[23] We find our delight in honoring God rather than in satisfying our own needs, that is, we come to love God for God's own sake rather than for what God can give us. It parallels the experiences of students who begin volunteering at a nursing home or food pantry so that they can add it to their resumes, but discover along the way that they care deeply about the people they serve. When we love God for God's own sake, then we can love others in the same way God loves them, that is, not for one's own benefit, but rather with a genuine interest in the welfare of the ones we love.

In the fourth stage, the individual loves oneself solely for the sake of God. As Bernard explains in his letter to the Carthusians that is attached to *On Loving God*, "In some wondrous way he forgets himself and ceasing to belong to himself, he passes entirely into God and adhering to him, he comes one with him in spirit."[24] Bernard is not claiming that we are absorbed into God's nature, but that there is a deep and abiding union of the person's free will and the will of God.[25] In this deep union of wills, humans find their true fulfillment and happiness.

The satisfaction of our wants, chance happiness, delights us less than to see his will done in us and for us, which we implore every day in prayer saying: "...your will be done on earth as it is in heaven...." O pure and sacred love! O sweet and pleasant affection! O pure and sinless intention of the will, all the more sinless and pure since it frees us from the taint of selfish vanity, all the more sweet and pleasant, for all that is found in it is divine.[26]

Bernard acknowledges that these fleeting mystical experiences are rare in this life. He alludes to his own such experience in Sermon 74 on the Song of Songs.

I tell you that the Word has come even to me—I speak in my foolishness—and that he has come more than once (2 Cor 11:17). Yet however often he has come, I have never been aware of the moment of his coming. I have known he was there; I have remembered his presence afterward; sometimes I had an inkling that he was coming. But I never felt it, nor his leaving me (Ps 120:8)....But when the Word has left me, and all these things become dim and weak and cold, as though you had taken the fire from under a boiling pot, I know that he has gone.[27]

How, then, does Bernard's analysis of the human person and his "road map of spiritual development" help us in our search for God?[28] When we reflect on Bernard's description of the fourth stage of love, we realize that the immensity of human desire also reveals the unfathomable depth of God's love. No matter how deep our cravings, the love of God fulfills them, and not only for a moment in time, but for all eternity. In his work *On Consideration,* which Bernard wrote for his fellow Cistercian Pope Eugene III, Bernard reflects upon "the length, breadth, height, and depth" of God (Eph 3:18).[29] God's "length" refers to the eternal nature of God, because it knows no limit in time or space. The breadth of God symbolizes God's love for all people. God's "height" is God's power over all of creation, and God's "depth" refers to depth of God's wisdom. The fullness of God's being, love, power, and wisdom surpasses all human understanding. So great is the love of God that even those in heaven desire it and it alone. "Is there any conclusion to [the] seeking of God? For the Scripture says, 'Seek his face always.' It is my belief that, even when he is found, there will be no halt to the seeking" (Sermon 84).[30]

INTRODUCTION TO M. SHAWN COPELAND'S THEOLOGICAL ANTHROPOLOGY

As we move from Bernard's *On Loving God* to M. Shawn Copeland's *Enfleshing Freedom*, we are struck by the significant and undeniable differences between their works. Bernard's theology draws heavily on the monastic theology of the West. Copeland, by contrast, develops her theological anthropology through an analysis of first-person accounts of freed slaves, the songs of Billie Holiday, and the novels of Toni Morrison. Bernard downplayed the innovation in his work, stressing instead its deep continuity with the leading figures in Western theology (e.g., Augustine). Copeland is far more suspicious of ancient (and medieval and modern) accounts of human nature by leading Western theologians and philosophers, detecting in many of their influential works a failure to recognize the full humanity of members of a certain race, gender, or social class.[31] Perhaps most glaring of all is the different perspective Bernard and Copeland have on pride. For Bernard the term describes an unappealing human trait, an unhealthy attachment to the self that prevents us from humbly submitting to the authority of God in our lives. For Copeland, pride connotes joyous liberation from the constraints imposed on us by others, and an affirmation of our own identity and self-worth. Despite these obvious and deep differences, there is much that unites Bernard and Copeland, and it is their common ground that we will explore.

COPELAND'S *ENFLESHING FREEDOM*

Copeland, presently a professor of theology at Boston College, once related to an interviewer her experience of learning about the Holocaust at the age of twelve.

> My concerns have been, probably since I was twelve years old, expressed under the rubric of theological anthropology, that is, what does it mean to be human? What does it mean to be human from a Christian point of view? What does it mean to be human in the kind of social setting in which we live? I think my first question about this was a time when in the seventh grade I had nothing to do one summer and I wanted to go to summer school to learn French and do world history. And so my mother let me and I learned about the Shoah [i.e., the Holocaust], and it struck me quite forcibly that people who have a great disregard for human life, if they can stigmatize you and identify you and if they are in charge, they can make laws which can eradicate you.[32]

Commenting on that interview, the theologian Christopher Pramuk writes, "It would not be a stretch, I think, to measure the whole of her theological career in view of this early, troublesome awakening....From the beginning, her work has sought to unmask the thought-systems that would allow for the stigmatizing, identifying, and eradicating of whole groups of persons—persons deemed different, inferior, dangerous. Indeed, her theological vocation may be described as a defense of the vulnerable, not only from invisibility in society, but from evils that render them *all-too-visible* in the body public: that is, racism, sexism, and classism."[33] In *Enfleshing Freedom*, Copeland offers us a clear statement of this theological vision by focusing our attention on the ways in which black women's bodies have been viewed and treated in Western history.

Copeland's *Enfleshing Freedom* is in many ways an extended reflection on various types of bodies: the physical body, the social body, the body of believers comprising the church, and the Eucharist as the Body of Christ. Taking her cue from the work of the anthropologist Mary Douglas, Copeland sees a deep connection among the various bodies that define who we are. The social body assigns certain meanings to the race and gender of the physical body. The identity of the church (the Body of Christ) and the practice of sharing the Eucharist (the Body of Christ) shape one another. The Eucharist can either affirm the unity of the church or challenge the church to live more fully the unity that the Eucharist celebrates. In order to understand or critique a society's or church's set of beliefs or practices we must examine the meanings attached to each of these bodies at a particular time and place. Theological anthropology, insists Copeland, is less a matter of positing some timeless essence of human nature, and more a close and careful reflection on the experiences of persons who are marginalized or exploited by the social powers of the day.

The acknowledgment that meaning is so heavily dependent on the perspectives of groups raises an important, albeit theoretical, question about theological anthropology, which Copeland confronts in the first chapter of *Enfleshing Freedom*. If meaning is socially constructed, is any one group's perspective truer or better than another group's? If so, what is that standard that stands separate and apart from time and remains untouched by human manipulation? If such a perspective doesn't exist, then is any one perspective better (and not merely different) than another? This admittedly technical question has important consequences for the kinds of discussions about race and gender that Copeland undertakes in the text. "Taking black women's bodies as a prism, this work considers the theological anthropological relation between the social body and the physical body."[34] This attention to the experience of black women as the prism through which theology is done is the hallmark of the movement known as "womanist theology."

Copeland steers a middle course between two approaches in theological anthropology. In the first approach, Western thinkers have often assumed that there is a universal human "nature" or "essence." In practice, however, thinkers often did not regard women and people of color as being capable of a full embodiment of that nature. The ideas of the Enlightenment thinkers Kant, Hume, and Hegel regarding race, for example, "served to reinforce proslavery attitudes, to sustain racial segregation and discrimination."[35] Liberation movements have had to dislodge the prevailing cultural stereotypes about race and gender before they could bring about social change. This, in turn, has generated a host of theologies focused on the experiences of particular groups. In affirming their own alternative interpretation of their own identity, these groups have insisted that there is no one overarching "interpretive framework" that determines the identity and social standing of all persons. This second approach, commonly labelled "postmodern," calls for a plurality of meanings and interpretations based a variety of perspectives. The concern is that if meaning is in the eye of the beholder, then the oppressor's account of a social situation is no better or worse than the victim's account of the same situation. While Copeland herself accepts the postmodern claim that any description of body, race, and gender "is never innocent, never ahistorical, and never divorced from power," she does not surrender the traditional belief that there are common features shared by all human beings.[36] "The black struggle for authenticity is coincident with the human struggle to *be* human and reveals *black-human-being* as a particular incarnation of universal finite human being."[37]

In chapter 2, Copeland introduces her explicitly theological concerns. Copeland derives from the creation story in Genesis three central convictions about the human person: "(1) that human beings, created in the image and likeness of God (*imago Dei*), have a distinct capacity for communion with God; (2) that human beings have a unique place in the cosmos God created; and (3) that human beings are made for communion with other living beings." Because no other "Christian teaching has been more desecrated by slavery than the doctrine of the human person or theological anthropology," Copeland believes that a careful study of the social mechanisms that made slavery possible sheds light on current attitudes that legitimate various forms of oppression and discrimination in our own day and age.[38] The struggles of slaves to preserve their dignity and assert their own identity also speak powerfully to the question of what it means to be a human person created in the image of God.

While Copeland acknowledges that speaking about "theological anthropology in terms of black female embodiment may seem overly concrete," she believes that this specificity actually puts into sharper focus the universal human "struggle to achieve and exercise freedom in history and society." The focus on the body (rather than the human essence, soul, or mind) reminds us that "the body is the medium through which the person as essential freedom achieves and realizes selfhood through communion with other embodied selves."[39] A social group's treatment of the bodies of an entire class of people reflects that group's deeply entrenched convictions about who is "a human person." The oppressive mechanisms of slavery, from the violent seizure of humans to the separation of children born into slavery from their mothers, all rely upon the objectification of black women's bodies "as objects of property, of production, of reproduction, of sexual violence." By regarding bodies as property, as objects, as instruments of labor, and so on, slaveholders saw their slavers as commodities to be bought and sold rather than persons to be respected. By refusing to internalize this devaluation, slaves testified to the tenacity of the human spirit, to the inexhaustible yearning for freedom in mind, body, and spirit. Their struggles enable to us to see that to be a human subject is to be a person "who consciously and intentionally in word and deed assumes and affirms her or his own personhood and humanity. This affirmation means that a human subject cannot consent to any treatment or condition that is intended to usurp the transcendental end or purpose for which human beings are divinely created."[40]

In contrast to an oppressive society that stigmatizes and dehumanizes (which Copeland labels "the empire") stands the

Kingdom of God preached by Jesus that unites and uplifts. The empire segregates; the Kingdom unifies. The empire esteems the powerful; the Kingdom attends to the impoverished and marginalized. The empire wounds; the Kingdom heals. Jesus not only preached about the Kingdom but demonstrated it by eating at the same table with those regarded as sinful or unclean (Mark 2:15–17). In our own day and age, contends Copeland, economic and political forces continue the empire's policies of exclusion. "Globalization, the dominative process of empire, now cannibalizes the bodies, the labor and creativity, and the sexuality and generativity of global 'others.' In sacrilegious antiliturgy, the agents of empire hand over red, yellow, brown, white, black, and poor bodies to the tyranny of neo-liberal capitalism, to the consuming forces of the market." In the current empire, just as in the Roman Empire of the first century in Christian history, "Jesus of Nazareth calls us to break bonds imposed by imperial design, to imagine and grasp and realize ourselves as his own flesh, as the body of Christ."[41]

Copeland believes that by failing to confront "the dynamics of domination" that made slavery possible, much of Western theology lost the critical edge needed to challenge the forces of domination, colonialism, and imperialism. In the past fifty years, however, new theologies have emerged that have rightly refocused attention on "the exploited, despised, marginalized poor masses." These new approaches have rekindled a sense of solidarity with children born HIV positive, refugees fleeing genocidal regimes, and victims of human trafficking. This shift in perception "entails recognition of the humanity of the 'other' as human, along with regard for the 'other' in her (and his) own otherness." Such a realization moves us away from the categories and perceptions of the empire and toward the vision of the Kingdom that Christ proclaimed. "Solidarity preserves the universality of love… and affirms the interconnectedness of human beings in common creatureliness. Humanity is no mere aggregate of autonomous, isolated individuals. Humanity is one intelligible reality—multiple, diverse, varied, and concrete, yet one."[42]

In the final chapter, Copeland offers a powerful reflection on the integral role the Eucharist plays in nourishing us with the presence of Christ, calling us to greater communion with our neighbors, and opening our eyes to the ways in which we as a church have failed to live as the Body of Christ. In a searing image, Copeland describes the lynching tree as a symbol of the cross. Both are wooden instruments of execution that aim to terrorize the spirit of all those who look upon it. "Eucharistic solidarity orients us to the cross of the lynched Jesus of Nazareth, where we grasp the enormity of suffering, affliction, and oppression as well as apprehend our complicity in the suffering, affliction, and oppression of others."[43] With this realization comes a call to action. As Copeland notes in a separate work, "there are social as well as sacramental consequences to the Eucharist. For to be one in Christ Jesus is to reject those systems of living that deprive women and men of human and political rights, that oppress the poor, that suppress women, that authorize racism, that promote discrimination against men and women because of their fear of their sexual orientation, that obstruct the self-determination of the peoples of the world."[44]

BERNARD AND COPELAND: COMMON GROUND

Despite the many differences between Bernard's *On Loving God* and Shawn Copeland's *Enfleshing Freedom*, the two share three key elements in their understanding of the human person. First, each human person, created in the image of God, has an inviolable dignity that all other humans must acknowledge and respect. Bernard identifies three God-given "nobler gifts" that each person possesses: dignity, knowledge, and virtue. A person's dignity consists in having free will; knowledge is the awareness that "that this dignity is in him but that it is not of his own making" and a person's virtue "is that by which man seeks continuously and eagerly for his Maker and when he finds him, adheres to him with all his might."[45] Slavery is the supreme denial of a human's dignity, but even slavery could not extinguish the yearning to free the mind, spirit and body.

Second, the desires of the individual person or groups of people are unstable and subject to tremendous misdirection. When Bernard and Copeland speak of "the region of unlikeness" or "empire," both are naming the forces at work within ourselves and in the wider society that blind us to the truth about ourselves, our neighbors, and God. It is for this reason that both writers emphasize the on-going need for conversion.

Third, both emphasize the transformative power of human and divine love. Bernard's famous four-stage analysis and description of the spiritual life is a testament to the transformative power of God's love. Copeland's survey of the same process begins in oppression and ends in solidarity. In her 2007 Madeleva Lecture in Spirituality, "The Subversive Power of Love," presented at St. Mary's College in Indiana, Copeland chronicled the life of Henriette Delille, the foundress of the Sisters of the Holy Family. Copeland describes Delille's spiritual journey in language that is reminiscent of Bernard's. "God's passionate love dismantled and abolished the horizon that heretofore had shaped her concern and interest, drew her ever more deeply into the divine self, opened, expanded, and flooded her heart. God's passionate love transformed not only what she desired, but her very desiring self. Her deepest desire was fulfilled, 'for being in love with God [is] the ultimate fulfillment of [our] capacity for self-transcendence.'"[46]

Bernard and Copeland both carry out the search for God through reflection on human experience. In the opening Sermon in his *Sermons on The Song of Songs*, Bernard notes that it is fitting that we call the biblical book "The Song of Songs" rather than "a song of steps." He explains, "This sort of song only the touch of the Holy Spirit teaches (1 Jn 2:27), and it is learned by experience alone. Let those who have experienced it enjoy it; let those who have not burn with desire, not so much to know it as to experience it."[47] Copeland turns our attention to the same deep yearning in the lyrics of the spiritual, "Oh Freedom."

> On Freedom! Oh, Freedom! Oh Freedom, I love thee!
> And before I'll be a slave, I'll be buried in my grave
> And go home to my Lord and be free![48]

Though Bernard refers to a song springing from spiritual joy and Copeland highlights a song borne from physical oppression, the search for God requires that we listen attentively to both and carry each of them in our hearts.

Discussion Questions

1. What specific claims are we making about human beings when we assert that humans are created in the image of God?

2. Is human desire misdirected? If so, can it be altered over time?

3. Are children selfish? If so, do we genuinely move beyond that selfishness or simply disguise it better as we age?

4. Why do humans love God? Why should humans love God? How do your responses compare to Bernard's?

5. What would it mean to love ourselves for the sake of God?

6. Is there a single "nature" or "essence" to all human beings? What role do gender and race play in our experiences as human beings?

7. Which groups are not accorded full human dignity in our own day and age?

8. What would be a specific meaningful expression of human solidarity today?

Suggested Readings

For a helpful introduction to Bernard's thought, see Dennis E. Tamburello, *Bernard of Clairvaux* (New York: Crossroad, 2000); John R. Sommerfeldt, *The Spiritual Teachings of Bernard of Clairvaux* (Kalamazoo, MI: Cistercian Publications, 1991); and Charles Dumont, *Pathway of Peace* (Kalamazoo, MI: Cistercian Publications, 1999). See also chapter 5 of Bernard McGinn, *The Growth of Mysticism* (New York: Crossroad, 1996); and chapter 3 of William Harmless, *Mystics* (New York: Oxford University Press, 2008). For Bernard's theological anthropology, see Michael Casey, *Athirst for God* (Kalamazoo, MI: Cistercian Publications, 1988).

For an introduction to Copeland's theology, see Christopher Pramuk, "'Living in the Master's House': Race and Rhetoric in the Theology of M. Shawn Copeland," *Horizons* 32, no. 2 (2005): 295–331. For Copeland's theological anthropology, see her chapter in Serene Jones and Paul Lakeland, eds., *Constructive Theology* (Minneapolis, MN: Fortress Press, 2005), 97–116; and her "The New Anthropological Subject at the Heart of the Mystical Body of Christ," *CTSA Proceedings* 53 (1998): 25–47. See also Copeland's, *The Subversive Power of Love* (Mahwah, NJ: Paulist Press, 2009).

PART TWO

The Critical Clue

5

CHRIST I
(HISTORICAL APPROACH):
SEEING GOD
Alfred Loisy and John Meier

In the first four chapters, we dealt with issues that are an integral part of our search for God. Given the nature of God, is it even possible for us to speak about God? In what way does God speak to us through the Bible? Does rational inquiry help us clarify our thinking about God? In what ways does human desire turn us toward or away from God? While each of these questions is important in its own right, each also brings a necessary perspective to the central Christian affirmation about God: Jesus Christ is the definitive revelation of God in human history. For Christians, Christ is the critical clue in our search for God. In John's Gospel, Jesus says to Philip, "Whoever has seen me has seen the Father" (14:9). There is a double meaning attached to "seeing" in the Bible. In addition to its literal sense, "seeing" also means "understanding" as is the case when we say, "I see what you mean." The verse in John's Gospel plays off this double meaning. In both this chapter and the next, we will explore two senses of "seeing" the person of Jesus. We can "see" Jesus as a historical figure who lived in a particular place at a particular time, or we can "see" Jesus in light of the church's faith regarding his human and divine natures. In this chapter, we will take the first approach and examine how two Christian scholars, Alfred Loisy (1857–1940), writing in the first decade of the twentieth century, and the contemporary biblical scholar John Meier, writing in the last decade of the twentieth century, describe the historical figure Jesus of Nazareth using the accepted historical methodology of their day.

THE CAREER OF ALFRED LOISY

In May 1881, a young scholarly priest left parish work to return to the Institut Catholique in Paris to continue his theological studies, with a special concentration in Hebrew. Before Loisy left for summer vacation, Louis Duchesne, the professor of history at the Insitut gave him a gift, a critical edition of the New Testament by the German scholar Constantin von Tischendorf. Reflecting back on this moment in his life, Loisy writes, "When we parted for vacation in the summer of 1881, he put into my hands the volume of Tischendorf's classical edition of the New Testament containing the Gospels, that I might gain some idea of the processes of textual criticism [the comparison of different manuscripts to establish the most accurate text]. But I went beyond his intention, not satisfying myself with observing the various readings of the manuscripts, but comparing the Gospel narratives with one another. I was astounded, the farther I progressed, never to have noticed the contradictions before."[1] Loisy was convinced that "the narratives of the birth of Christ in Matthew and Luke must have arisen from distinct sources, and are not capable of being reconciled so as to make consistent history."[2] Not only did Loisy's discovery raise thorny historical questions in his mind, but the larger questions regarding the divine inspiration of the Bible and the authenticity of certain passages also troubled Loisy.[3]

Throughout his career, Loisy engaged the problems that he confronted in the summer of 1881. As he did so, first in his teaching and then in articles in scholarly journals and books, his proposals increasingly drew him into conflict with church officials. In 1893, Pope Leo XIII issued an encyclical *Providentissimus Deus* that criticized the methods of biblical interpretation being advocated by Loisy. Cardinal Richard of Paris assembled the board of governors of the Institut who voted to have Loisy removed from his post.[4] Loisy became chaplain at a school for girls run by the Dominican nuns in the Neuilly, a suburban of Paris where he continued his research and published articles under the pen name of A. Firmin. Loisy left the school in 1900 when he received a government appointment as a lecturer at the Sorbonne, a position that carried both scholarly prestige and an independence from church control.[5] In the same year, the distinguished German Lutheran theologian Adolf von Harnack published a series of lectures under the title *What is Christianity?* When the work appeared in French translation in 1902, Loisy offered his rebuttal in *The Gospel and the Church*. Loisy's popular work was quickly denounced by Cardinal Richard. The tension between Loisy and Richard escalated, and in 1903, Leo XIII's successor, Pope Pius X, placed five of Loisy's books on the Index of Forbidden Books. Loisy resigned his position at the Sorbonne and retired to the countryside. Pius X condemned the movement that had come to be called Modernism (and the father of the movement was widely believed to be Loisy himself) in two statements in 1907: first in his syllabus *Lamentabli sane exitu,* and later in his encyclical *Pascendi Dominici gregis.* In March of the following year, Loisy was excommunicated. His academic career, however, continued at the College de France from 1909 to 1932. Loisy died in 1940.

LOISY'S METHODOLOGY

The obvious question that arises is: Why was Loisy excommunicated? In order to answer this, we need to situate his work within the theological context of late-nineteenth- and early-twentieth-century Catholic theology. In his 1879 encyclical *Aeterni Patris,* Leo XIII mandated that the philosophy of Thomas

Aquinas be taught in all seminaries. Leo believed that Aquinas's philosophy not only provided a solid basis for Catholic theology, but also offered a defense against what Leo saw as the errors of modern philosophy.[6] In the late nineteenth century, the theological texts commonly used in seminary courses were manuals that moved methodically from one proposition to the next. The traditional Catholic philosophical-theological synthesis offered in these texts ran somewhat as follows. Jesus, fully conscious of his divinity, taught a body of truths regarding salvation and commissioned the apostles to guard this deposit of faith. The four evangelists, under the inspiration of the Holy Spirit, recorded the actual words and deeds of Christ in the four Gospels. Christ established the Church and its seven sacraments and entrusted the bishops and their legitimate successors to govern the Church until the end of time. These ideas mutually supported each other, and taken together upheld the common traditional theological claims that there are no contradictions among biblical books; the central teachings of Christ were codified by the last apostle's death, and the current structure of church hierarchy existed from the time of the early church.

Loisy challenged this synthesis by distinguishing between theological beliefs that are justified on the basis of faith and historical claims that are justified by a critical examination of the available sources. This second approach, Loisy argued, was more in keeping with the scientific spirit of his day. Where traditional theology sees its task as preserving the complete truth that was delivered in the past, science proceeds by trial and error as it strives to arrive at a more complete understanding of the truth at some point in the future. Theologians and historians, Loisy insisted, approach their subject matter differently.[7] Theologians accept certain propositions on faith; historians bracket their beliefs about supernatural reality. Where the believer may in faith attribute a certain event to the direct involvement of God, the historian seeks to understand events in purely naturalistic terms. These two approaches, therefore, result in two different ways of reading the Gospels. The historian reads the Gospels as he or she would read any other document from antiquity. The descriptions of events are checked against other historical documents, artifacts, or archaeological findings. The stories are compared with the conventional literary forms of the day, and so on. The theologian reads the Gospel in light of the beliefs presented in the creeds of the church. The historian's claims will, therefore, necessarily be more modest and the explanations more cautious than those expressed by traditional theologians.

When Adolf von Harnack's *What is Christianity?* achieved instant popularity (fifty thousand copies were sold the first year), Loisy believed it was the perfect opportunity to advance his own case for the acceptance of the historical study of the Gospels in Catholic circles.[8] In his autobiography, Loisy later explained:

> On the one hand, my reasoning in opposition to Professor Harnack implied a criticism of Gospel sources more radical at several points than that of the Protestant theologian; and on the other hand, my defense of the Roman Church against certain judgments of the learned author implied at the same time the abandonment of those absolute theses which are professed by the Scholastic theology touching the formal institution of the Church and its sacraments by Christ, the immutability of its dogmas, and the nature of its ecclesiastical authority. Thus I did not confine myself to a criticism of Professor Harnack, but paved the way, discreetly yet definitely, for an essential reform in Biblical exegesis, in the whole of theology, and even in Catholicism generally.[9]

In the opening chapter of *What is Christianity?*, Harnack declared that it was his intent to offer a historical analysis, not a dogmatic defense of Jesus' teachings and their subsequent transmission throughout the Christian tradition. "What is Christianity? It is solely in its historical sense that we shall try to answer this question here; that is to say, we shall employ the methods of historical science, and the experience of life gained by studying the actual course of history."[10] In Loisy's mind, he accepted the rules of engagement set forth by Harnack and entered into the fray confident that his own position would prevail.

LOISY'S *THE GOSPEL AND THE CHURCH*

We need first to delineate the limits of our investigation. First, Harnack's *What is Christianity?* covers three areas: "the Gospel of Jesus Christ," the "impression [Jesus] himself and Gospel made upon the first generation of his disciples," and "the leading changes which the Christian idea has undergone in the course of history." Loisy responds to Harnack's observations in each of the three areas, but we will focus almost exclusively on the first of them. Second, Harnack and Loisy focus almost exclusively on the Synoptic Gospels (Matthew, Mark, and Luke) as the sources for the historical Jesus. Harnack writes, "Everything that we know, independently of these Gospels, about Jesus' history and his teaching, may be easily put on a small sheet of paper, so little does it come to. In particular, the fourth Gospel, which does not emanate or profess to emanate from the apostle John, cannot be taken as an historical authority in the ordinary meaning of the word." Third, Harnack and Loisy agree that the three Synoptic Gospels are not "historical works" in the sense of providing a neutral biography of Jesus. Not all passages, therefore, are given equal historical weight. Furthermore, not all passages are equally expressive of the essential message of Jesus. Harnack writes, "Truly the historian's task of distinguishing between what is traditional and what is peculiar, between kernel and husk, in Jesus' message of the kingdom of God is a difficult and responsible one."[11] This image of separating the kernel from the husk has been intimately associated with the theology of Harnack ever since he penned this line. We will compare how the results of Loisy's historical investigation differ from those of Harnack in three important areas: Jesus' teaching regarding the Kingdom of God, the significance of the titles assigned to Jesus in the Gospels, and the relation between the Jesus of history and the Christ preached in the Christian tradition.

JESUS AND THE KINGDOM OF GOD

Nineteenth-century biblical scholars agreed that Jesus' preaching centered on the concept of the kingdom of God. Generally speaking, these scholars offered two alternative understandings of what Jesus meant by "the kingdom of God." Some understood the kingdom to be an ethical ideal, a human community ruled by love. The second group of scholars believed that Jesus was part of the Jewish tradition of apocalyptic thought who spoke of the kingdom as a dramatic and sudden overturning of the present order by God. Typically, apocalyptic communities believe that they stand at the moment in history when the old order is passing away and the imminent arrival of the kingdom is expected. Complicating the matter is the fact that Jesus sometimes speaks of the kingdom as a future event (Luke 11:2) and at other times he speaks of it as a present reality (Luke 17:20–21). Harnack offers his assessment: "The kingdom of God comes by coming to the individual, by entering into his soul and laying hold of it. True, the kingdom of God is the rule of God; but it is the rule of the holy God in the hearts of individuals; *it is God himself in his power.*"[12]

Loisy believes that Harnack misrepresents Jesus' teaching regarding the kingdom. The kingdom is not "personal and already present," but collective and imminent, yet still to come. "Nowhere does [Christ] identify the kingdom with God, and God's power acting in the heart of the individual."[13] The crucial passage is Luke 17:21, which Harnack translates as, "[The kingdom] is not here or there, it is within you."[14] Loisy contends, "The most natural meaning would be 'the kingdom of God is in the midst of you,' and it is perhaps in this way that the writer understands it, unless he has simply wished to say, that the kingdom will come when it is least expected, and before there is time to announce that it has appeared in this place or in that." In contrast to Harnack's view that the coming of the kingdom is an event in the heart of each individual, Loisy insists, "It is in the first place collective, the good of the kingdom being destined for all who love God, and of such a nature that all can enjoy it in common, and so well that their happiness cannot be compared to anything so fitly as to a great festival.... It regards, and can only regard, the future, as befits its nature of hope; and this future is not the fate of the individual in the world, but the renewal of the world, the restoration of humanity in eternal justice and happiness."[15]

· JESUS AS SON OF GOD AND MESSIAH

Harnack's interpretation of the titles "Son of God" and "Messiah" follows from his claim, "*The Gospel, as Jesus proclaimed it, has to do with the Father only and not with the Son.*" Coupled with this is Harnack's belief that "the whole of Jesus' message may be reduced to these two heads—God as the Father, and the human soul so ennobled that it can and does unite with him." When Jesus referred to himself as the Son of God, he was giving expression to his own intimate awareness of the truths he wanted his hearers to grasp. "The consciousness which he possessed of being *the Son of God* is, therefore, nothing but the practical consequence of knowing God as the Father and as his Father." Harnack based his view in large part on Matthew 11:27: "All things have been handed over to me by my Father; and no one knows the Son except the Father, and no one knows the Father except the Son and anyone to whom the Son chooses to reveal him." For Harnack, "Messiah" is essentially an equivalent title for "Son of God." Despite the fact that there was a wide variety of expectations of what type of figure the Messiah would be, it still remained the most natural title for his fellow Jews to assign to Jesus "for it is in the Messiah's activity that God Himself comes to His people." The title "Messiah" declares that Jesus was not only the most effective preacher of the Gospel, *"he was its personal realization and its strength, and this he is felt to be still."*[16]

Loisy takes issue with Harnack's interpretation of the titles "Son of God" and "Messiah." "The gospel conception of the Son of God is no more a psychological idea signifying a relation of the soul with God than is the gospel conception of the kingdom. There is absolutely nothing to prove it; and even the text quoted does not say that Jesus became the Son because He was the first to know God as the Father." The verse, Loisy insists, identifies Christ with the wisdom of God and is thus referring to the relationship of Jesus to the Father, not Jesus' own consciousness. Loisy also contends that Harnack's interpretation of the title "Messiah" reflects Harnack's own desire to detach Jesus' message from its particular historical context, fearing that any historical particularity would undercut its universality. To do so would be to confuse the task of the historian with that of the theologian. Loisy stresses the need to root Jesus and his message in the context of Judaism. "The Gospel, appearing in Judea and unable to appear elsewhere, was bound to be conditioned by Judaism. Its Jewish exterior is the human body, whose Divine Soul is the spirit of Jesus. But take away the body, and the soul will vanish in the air like the lightest breath."[17]

THE HISTORICAL JESUS IN THE CHRISTIAN TRADITION

Harnack's description of the task of the historian as one of separating the kernel from the husk suggests that there is a pristine message of Jesus that is either preserved or corrupted throughout the course of Christian history. On the whole, Harnack regards the developments in the Christian tradition, especially in its institutional forms, as distortions. Loisy, by contrast, insists that it is only through tradition that we know Jesus. "Whatever we think, theologically, of tradition, whether we trust it or regard it with suspicion, we know Christ only through tradition, across the tradition, and in the tradition of the primitive Christians." Loisy sees the tradition as a legitimate unfolding of the vital impulse that is at the heart of all living beings. In this way, the metaphor that captures the relationship of Jesus to the tradition is a seed to a tree. Loisy asks:

> Why not find the essence of Christianity in the fulness and totality of its life, which shows movement and variety just because it is life, but inasmuch as it is life proceeding from an obviously powerful principle, has grown in accordance with a law which affirms at every step the initial force that may be called its physical essence revealed in all its manifestations? Why should the essence of a tree to be held to be but a particle of the seed from which it has sprung, and why should it not be recognized as truly and fully in the complete tree as in the germ?

In the same way a seed develops into a mature tree, the preaching of Jesus develops over time into the organized body of believers. "Jesus foretold the kingdom, and it was the Church that came; she came, enlarging the form of the gospel, which it was impossible to preserve as it was, as soon as the Passion closed the ministry of Jesus."[18]

It was this organic understanding of Christian belief that caught the eyes of Cardinal Richard in Paris and church officials in Rome. "The conceptions that the Church presents as revealed dogmas are not truths fallen from heaven, and preserved by religious tradition in the precise form in which they first appeared," Loisy declared. This was both a response to Harnack and a challenge to his Catholic colleagues. "Till now, Catholic theologians have been especially preoccupied with the absolute character that the dogma derives from its sources, the Divine revelation, and critics have hardly noticed the relative character that its history makes manifest. The efforts of a healthy theology should be directed to a solution of the difficulty, presented by the unquestionable authority faith demands of dogma, and the variability, the relativity, the critic cannot fail to perceive in the history of dogmas and dogmatic formulas."[19] How can followers of Christ believe certain things to be absolutely true when we know from history that everything changes? Over a century has passed since Loisy posed this question and it remains with us.

LOISY AND THE UNANSWERED QUESTION

Like a lawyer making an opening statement before the jury, Loisy states his case against Harnack in the opening chapter of *The Gospel and the Church*. "The essence of the gospel can only be determined by a critical discussion of the gospel texts, the most sure and most clearly expressed texts, and not those *whose authenticity or whose meaning may be doubtful* (emphasis added)." Loisy believes that Harnack is guilty on both counts: His case is built on texts that may not be authentic and whose meaning is doubtful. Over the course of his book, Loisy develops his case regarding the second charge at great length. He goes on at great length to challenge Harnack's interpretation of certain passages. He does not, however, expound on the first. What does Loisy mean when he says that Harnack builds his argument on texts that may not be authentic? Specifically referring to the two passages that are central to Harnack's argument (Matt 11:27, Luke 17:21), Loisy comments that both passages "might well have been influenced, if not produced, by the theology of the early times."[20] His definition of *authenticity* then comes into focus. Some sayings attributed to Jesus in the Gospels may, in fact, be products of the early church. If this position is correct, then the question that immediately arises is: "How do we know which sayings of Jesus in the Gospels are from the historical Jesus himself and which ones are from the early church?" Loisy does not pursue this question in his case against Harnack, but in time, it would occupy a prominent place in Catholic biblical theology and continues to be on the docket of biblical scholars to this day.

Loisy was not unaware of the question that he did not pursue. His earlier work on the Pentateuch led him to conclude that, contrary to the traditional view, Moses was not in fact the author of the first five books of the Bible. He also attended the 1882 lectures of Ernst Renan, who offered controversial positions on Christ's identity in his own hugely popular work *The Life of Jesus*.[21] Why, then, did Loisy not pursue his line of reasoning regarding the authenticity of certain sayings attributed to Jesus in the Gospels? The answer may well be that the Catholic Church at the turn of the twentieth-century simply wasn't ready for that discussion. The late Raymond Brown, one of the great luminaries of American Catholic biblical scholarship, breaks down the twentieth-century Catholic thought into three periods. "The first period (1900–1940) was dominated by the rejection of modern biblical criticism, an attitude forced on the Church by the Modernist heresy."[22] The critical turning point came, according to Brown, when Pius XII issued his encyclical *Divino Afflante Spiritu*. In this second period (1940–70), "methods of scientific biblical criticism that had hitherto been forbidden" were now approved for use by Catholic biblical scholars.[23] In the third period, Brown predicted, the implications of these new methods for Catholic theology and church life would be felt. John Meier, who co-authored a book with Brown in 1983, is one of the leading Catholic biblical scholars working in this third period.[24] In his multivolume work *A Marginal Jew*, Meier deals directly with the very issues that Loisy skirted in *The Gospel and the Church*.

While Catholic biblical scholars at the turn of the twentieth century were not yet dealing with the historical question of the authenticity of the sayings attributed to Jesus in the Gospels, their Protestant counterparts had been struggling with that issue for more than a century. As the question of the historical reliability of the Gospel stories was debated in nineteenth-century Protestant thought, various responses emerged. The general intent of scholars involved in this "quest for the historical Jesus" was to reconstruct the life of "the historical Jesus" from the Gospel stories. A few short years after Loisy published *The Gospel and the Church*, the Protestant theologian Albert Schweitzer produced his bombshell work *The Quest of the Historical Jesus*. Schweitzer offered a devastating critique of the major works in the "quest for the historical Jesus." Despite their expressed commitment to objectivity, the various authors "discovered" the Jesus that they consciously or unconsciously set out to find. These so-called objective histories told the reader more about the author's view of Jesus than the actual Jesus of history. Scholars found Schweitzer's analysis so profound that it was not until mid-century that the legitimacy of the quest was once again raised by leading scholars. The "old quest" that Schweitzer had demolished was over, but a "new quest" began, one that first identified the criteria that could be reasonably applied to the Gospels to determine the probability that a particular saying or action attributed to Jesus in the Gospels is historically accurate.

CRITERIA OF AUTHENTICITY: *A MARGINAL JEW*, VOLUME ONE

In the first volume of *A Marginal Jew*, Meier dedicates a chapter to the question, "How do we decide what comes from Jesus?" Meier lists ten criteria that he will use, but groups them into five "primary criteria," and five "secondary (or dubious) criteria." The first of the five primary is "embarrassment." "The criterion of 'embarrassment' (so Schillebeeckx) or 'contradiction' (so Meyer) focuses on actions or sayings of Jesus that would have embarrassed or created difficulty for the early Church."[25] The logic of this criterion is simple and straightforward: If a verse in the Gospel is "embarrassing," then it is unlikely that the evangelist invented it. The baptism of Jesus by John is a case in point. Not only would a sinless Jesus not require baptism, but by submitting to John's baptism, Jesus seems to accord him the superior role. Likewise, after Jesus delivers a discourse about the events preceding the end time, his disciples ask him when the end will come. Jesus' replies in a way that Christians, especially those who live after the formulation of the doctrine of the Trinity, find confusing, "But about that day or hour no one knows, neither the angels in heaven, nor the Son, but only the Father" (Mark 13:32).

The second criterion, discontinuity, "focuses on words or deeds of Jesus that cannot be derived either from Judaism at the time of Jesus or from the early Church after him."[26] It is important to note that this criterion gives us a sampling of highly unique features of Jesus' ministry, but is unable to offer positive statements about what Jesus shared with the Jews who lived before him and the Christians who lived after him. For example, this criterion will not yield a great deal of material about their common practice of prayer. What does stick out, however, is that Jesus and his disciples, unlike Jews and Christians, do not fast during Jesus' public ministry (Mark 2:18–20).

The third criterion, multiple attestation, highlights passages that are found in independent sources or different literary forms. The general scholarly consensus is that Mark was the first Gospel written. Because Matthew and Luke follow the essential story line in Mark, there are collectively known as the Synoptic Gospels. There are, however, passages that appear in both Matthew and Luke that do not appear in Mark. Scholars hypothesize that there may have been a written or oral source known to Matthew and Luke, but that was not available to Mark. This material is labeled Q from the German word *Quelle*, which simply means "Source." There are stories unique to Matthew that are simply labeled M material (the coin for the Temple tax in the mouth of a fish Matt 17:24–27 = M) and the same holds true for Luke (the parable of the Prodigal Son in Luke 15:11–32 = L). Sources for John are more difficult to determine. Not only are there many stories that are unique to John (e.g., the wedding feast of Cana, John 2:1–11), the style of writing is noticeably different than that found in the Synoptics. An example of a concept that has multiple attestation in the Gospel sources is the kingdom of God. Despite the fact that "the kingdom of God" is not a central theme in Old Testament writings, "the phrase is found in Mark, Q, special Matthean tradition, special Lucan tradition, and John, with echoes in Paul, despite the fact that 'kingdom of God' is not Paul's preferred way of speaking."[27]

The fourth and fifth criteria are coherence and "criterion of rejection and execution." These two come into play after the first three criteria have been applied. Once a certain number of saying or actions have withstood the first three criteria, other passages that cohere with the preliminary findings can be considered for addition. The criterion of rejection and execution "directs our attention to the historical fact that Jesus met a violent end at the hands of Jewish and Roman officials and then asks us what historical words and deeds of Jesus can explain his trial and crucifixion as 'King of the Jews.'"[28]

The five secondary criteria introduce factors that are relevant, but not decisive in determining the historical reliability of a given saying or action attributed to Jesus in the Gospels. The Gospels were written in Greek, but Jesus spoke Aramaic, so expressions that preserve "Aramaic vocabulary, grammar, syntax, rhythm, and rhyme in the Greek version of the sayings of Jesus" have an increased likelihood of coming from Jesus himself. Second, Jesus lived in Palestine, not Antioch or Rome, so "sayings of Jesus that reflect concrete customs, beliefs, judicial procedures, commercial and agricultural practices, or social and political conditions in 1st-century Palestine have a good chance of being authentic."[29] Third, some scholars believe that if a story is filled with vivid details rather than broad generalities about the persons and setting involved, then this may suggest an eyewitness to the event gave the account. Meier sees this criterion as having very limited value. Fourth, if the editorial hand of an evangelist is detected in a story, the chances of historical authenticity diminish. Lastly, Meier cautions against ruling in advance if the burden of proof falls on the critic arguing for the authenticity of a saying of Jesus or on the critic arguing against a saying's authenticity. Instead, Meier concludes, we may in some cases determine that the evidence is unclear or inconclusive.

APPLYING THE CRITERIA TO A SAYING OF JESUS

In volume two of *A Marginal Jew*, Meier focuses on the role of John the Baptist, Jesus' preaching about the kingdom of God, and the miracle stories. We will focus first on Meier's application of the criteria to the saying of Jesus, "But if it is by the finger of God that I cast out the demons, then the kingdom of God has come to you" (Luke 11:20, with its parallel in Matt 12:28). This verse is the subject of much scholarly debate because, as Meier and many other scholars interpret it, Jesus proclaims the kingdom as a present and not a future reality. While there is a scholarly consensus that the concept of the "kingdom of God" was central to the preaching of Jesus, there is much debate over what exactly Jesus meant by it. "Kingdom of God" is a biblical shorthand for the full realization of God's kingly rule of the world. For apocalyptic thinkers, the phrase became an expression of hope and eager anticipation of the time when God would dramatically and suddenly overthrow the foreign nations that oppressed those who remained faithful to God during times of persecution. The arrival of the kingdom of God would be a day of vindication and judgment. It would also be preceded by signs and wonders (Mark 13). In some cases, it was believed that these signs had been revealed to a prophet of a former era (e.g., Daniel). This expectation of the imminent arrival of the kingdom can be found in some sayings of Jesus. "Truly, I tell you, there are some standing here who will not taste death until they see that the kingdom of God has come with power" (Mark 9:1). If all of Jesus' sayings spoke about the kingdom's imminent arrival, then Jesus would be classified an an apocalyptic messenger. That is why Luke 11:20 is so significant. If this is an authentic saying of Jesus, then his preaching can not be neatly placed in the category of apocalyptic preaching. Rather, Jesus would be making the startling claim that in his ministry the kingdom of God in some way has arrived.

The first step that Meier takes is to determine if the saying existed independently in the oral tradition or if it was part of a larger unit. In the Gospels of Matthew and Luke, the saying appears in the midst of a controversy over the source of Jesus' power that enables him to expel demons. The Pharisees (Matt) or some in the crowd (Luke) say that Jesus' power comes not from God, but from Satan or Beelzebul. Jesus counters by saying that such a claim is patently false because Satan would not cast out Satan, a kingdom divided against itself would never stand. Rather, to plunder a strong man's house, the robber must bind the man. The parallel to this is Mark 3:23–27, which Matthew and Luke incorporate into their own Gospels, but Mark does not have the verse in Luke 11:20 and Matthew 12:28. Meier concludes, therefore, that this Q saying existed independently of the exorcism story in which Matthew and Luke have placed it.

The second step would be to determine the original wording of the saying because there are slight variations between the saying in Matthew and Luke. As found in Matthew's Gospel, the saying reads: "But if it is by the Spirit of God that I cast out demons, then the kingdom of God has come to you." The saying in Luke uses the expression "the finger of God" rather than "the Spirit of God." Because Luke frequently speaks of the Spirit of God, it seems strange that he chooses not to use it here. Meier reasons, "It is unlikely that, without some pressing reason, Luke would replace one of his favorite theological words and symbols with the unusual phrase 'finger of God.'" For this reason, Meier concludes that "the finger of God" is actually more likely the original wording. If this is correct, then we must ask what that expression meant. The most logical source would be the story of the plagues in Exodus. The first two plagues, water turning to blood and an overabundance of frogs, interestingly were duplicated by the magicians of Egypt. In third plague the dust of the earth becomes a swarm of gnats. The Egyptian magicians are unable to duplicate this feat and report to the Pharaoh, "This is the finger of God" (Exod 8:15, in NRSV 8:19). The meaning of the expression "the finger of God" in Luke becomes clearer. "At the very least, Jesus is indicating by the phrase that he places himself alongside Moses and Aaron, genuine messengers from God who were empowered by him to perform symbolic miracles connected with Israel's liberation from slavery. By implication, Jesus is now doing the same; his authorization and power to perform miracles, specifically, liberating exorcisms, come from the God of Israel, not from demons."[30]

In the final step in his analysis, Meier applies the criteria that he outlined in volume 1 to the saying attributed to Jesus in Luke 11:20. Meier argues that the verse enjoys a high probability of being historically accurate based on the criteria of continuity and coherence. In terms of its discontinuity, "the linking of 'the kingdom of God' with a verb meaning 'to come' in a direct affirmation is unknown in the OT, in ancient Judaism before Jesus, and in the rest of the NT outside the Gospel sayings of Jesus."[31] A further argument can be made on the basis of discontinuity of the unique use of expression "the finger of God." "Significantly, the phrase is never used in the description of exorcisms performed by disciples of Jesus or by early Christians. Hence it is very difficult to assign this saying to Christian writers or prophets instead of Jesus himself."[32] In terms of coherence, Matthew and Luke both situate the saying within the context of Jesus' sharp retort to the suggestion that his powers come from Satan. "But no one can enter a strong man's house and plunder his property without first tying up the strongman; then indeed the house can be plundered" (Mark 3:27). "Without using the key phrase 'kingdom of God,' Mark 3:27 proclaims the same basic reality [as Luke 11:20]: through Jesus' exorcisms the God of Israel is even now exercising his rule in the end time by breaking the power of Satan and/or demons and thus liberating his people."[33]

APPLYING THE CRITERIA TO THE STORY OF JESUS WALKING ON WATER

The story of Jesus walking on water appears in two independent traditions in the Gospels. The first account is found in Mark 6:45–52, which Matthew repeats and expands to include a story of Peter also walking on water (Matt 14:22–33), and the second appears in John 6:16–21. Luke omits the story. Meier reports, "What is especially intriguing about the independent agreement between Mark and John is that it extends not just to this one story but to a whole primitive pattern or grid of stories about Jesus' ministry in Galilee."[34] This suggests that the story was an early composition, and not a later Christian addition arising from conflicts with opponents from outside the church.

The second task is to determine the original version of the story. Mark and John differ on some points: geography (the destination is Capernaum in John and Bethsaida in Mark) and the reaction of the disciples (the disciples in Mark are "astounded," while the disciples in Matthew pay homage to Jesus; and in John, Jesus does not appear actually to board the boat with the disciples). One of the more puzzling features of this story is that in Mark we read that Christ "intended to pass them by" (6:48). To complicate matters a little more, there seems to have been a connection made between the story of the feeding of the multitude and the story of Jesus walking on the water. If we do not understand the first, then we will not comprehend the second: "Then he got into the boat with them and the wind ceased. And they were utterly astounded, for they did not understand about the loaves, but their hearts were hardened" (Mark 6:51–52). Even though the Gospel of John was written later, Meier argues, "I think that John's version of the story is on the whole more primitive than Mark's."[35] Meier cautions us that when we are comparing accounts among Gospels, we must not assume that the Gospel that was written later (John) cannot contain material that actually predates the composition of the very first Gospel (Mark).

There are several Old Testament passages that might shed some light on this mysterious episode. The most important of them are the descriptions of God in Job as the one "who alone stretched out the heavens and trampled the waters of the Sea" (9:8) and, as found in the Greek translation of the Old Testament, the one who "walked upon the deep waters of the abyss" (38:16).[36] Similar expressions of God's activity are found in the prophet Habakkuk, "You trampled the sea with your horses, churning the mighty waters (3:15). These verses and others like them (e.g., Sir 24:5) reflect ancient mythological conceptions of God's creation as the subduing of the waters of chaos. It is for this reason that Meier categorizes the walking on the water as an epiphany story, a story dealing with the sudden and mighty manifestation or appearance of God's power. This also, argues Meier, helps explain the odd comment in Mark that "he meant to pass them by." In the Sinai story when Moses asks to see God's face, God replies that while that is not possible, God's presence will "pass by" (Exod 33:19, 22) Moses on the mountain. In this light, then, "The action of 'passing by' has nothing to do with withdrawing from others' view so as to protect one's transcendence and mystery."[37] Further supporting this interpretation are the words of Jesus reassuring the disciples, "It is I; do not be afraid" (John 6:20) that recall the revelation of the divine name to Moses at the burning bush (Exod 3:14).

The decisive judgment for Meier comes in the third step when he applies the criterion of coherence to the story. Despite the multiple attestation of the account, Meier does not believe it coheres with the miracles that have a greater claim for authenticity. "Almost all the miracles that have some claim to go back to an event in Jesus' life have two things in common: (a) Other miracles help someone who is in dire need or mortal danger: e.g., the gravely ill, the blind, the paralyzed, lepers ostracized from society, and demoniacs deprived of a normal, peaceful life. (b) These miracles focus on helping the person in need and on proclaiming the coming of the kingdom; they do not focus on Jesus' person and status or seek his self-glorification." The walking-on-water story does not cohere with the general thrust of the miracles being either manifestations of the power of God's kingdom breaking into the world or fulfillments of prophecies. Rather than playing a supportive role, the allusions to the Old Testament, in Meier's view, take center stage in the story of Jesus walking on the water. "When the OT material, especially the OT portrayal of Yahweh, enters so massively into a NT miracle story, we have a fairly good indication that we may be dealing with a theological creation of the early church." Meier's own suggestion is that story may have originated in the early church's reflection on the practice of the Eucharist in light of the miracle of the feeding of the multitudes. This, Meier reasons, might help explain the connection made between both stories early in the tradition. "The story of the walking on the water reflects the fact that, for the early church, the eucharist was the ritualized experience of an epiphany of the risen Jesus, coming to a small group of believers laboring in the night of the present age; once again he gave courage and calmed fears simply by announcing his presence."[38]

Given the self-imposed limits under which historians work, their work will not answer questions of faith such as, "Was Jesus the Son of God?" The task of the historian is subject the Gospels to the same historical scrutiny as would be applied to another other documents from the ancient world. Even within these parameters, historians uncover the early church's proclamation of the arrival of the long-awaited Messiah who inaugurated the coming of the kingdom of God. If we can see through the lens of modern historical criticism what that moment meant to those who lived in the generations immediately following the time of Christ, then we might gain a clearer sense of how to live that good news in our own day and age. In terms of how this might help in our search for God, we will let Loisy have the last word. "The most Divine thing in the world is not the crash of the thunder, nor the light of the sun, nor the unfolding of life; it is beauty of soul, purity of heart, perfection of love in sacrifice, because this is the sovereign gift of God to man, the grandest work of manifestation of God in the universe."[39]

Discussion Questions

1. How historically accurate are the Gospels? What implications follow from your answer for how we should read them?

2. Is there an "essence" to the Gospel? If so, what is it?

3. How significant are the findings of historians for how we read the Gospels?

4. What do you think Loisy meant when he wrote, "Jesus foretold the kingdom, and it was the Church that came…."?

5. Are Meier's criteria reasonable for determining the probability that a saying or action attributed to Jesus is authentic?

6. What is meant by the saying of Jesus, "But if it is by the Spirit of God that I cast out demons, then the kingdom of God has come to you" (Matt 12:28)?

7. Did Jesus walk on water? Anticipate objections and respond.

Suggested Readings

Philip Kennedy devotes a chapter each to Harnack and Loisy in his *Twentieth-Century Theologians* (London: I.B. Tauris, 2010). For Loisy, see Harvey Hill, *The Politics of Modernism* (Washington, DC: The Catholic University of America Press, 2002). For an overview of modernism, see Introduction I and II in Darrell, Jodock, ed., *Catholicism Contending with Modernity*

(Cambridge, MA: Cambridge University Press, 2000); and Gerard Loughlin, "Catholic Modernism," chapture 24 in David Fergusson, ed., *The Blackwell Companion to Nineteenth-Century Theology* (Malden, MA: Wiley-Blackwell, 2010).

For a discussion of the historical-critical method of biblical interpretation, see Joseph Fitzmyer, *The Interpretation of Scripture* (Mahwah, NJ: Paulist Press, 2008). For an overview of the recent trends in research on the historical Jesus, see Mark Allan Powell, *Jesus as a Figure in History* (Louisville, KY: Westminster John Knox Press, 1998); and Ben Witherington, *The Jesus Quest* (Downers Grove, IL: InterVarsity Press, 1995).

6

CHRIST II
(DOGMATIC APPROACH):
UNDERSTANDING GOD
Cyril of Alexandria and
Gerald O'Collins

"In the fifteenth year of the reign of Emperor Tiberius, when Pontius Pilate was governor of Judea, and Herod was ruler of Galilee, and his brother Philip of the region of Ituraea and Trachonitis, and Lysanias ruler of Abilene, during the high priesthood of Annas and Caiaphas, the word of God came to John son of Zechariah in the wilderness" (Luke 3:1–2). In this passage from Luke's Gospel, we can see where the interests of historians and theologians overlap and where they diverge. For the historian, this passage provides a great deal of historical background on Jesus' contemporary John the Baptist. This historical data, if determined to be credible, provides the context for understanding who this son of Zechariah and Elizabeth was. For the theologian, however, John's identity extends beyond whatever historical reconstruction can be made by scholars today. John, in the context of Christian faith, is the one who prepared the way for the Messiah. In the same way, historians and theologians have different frames of reference for describing the identity of Jesus. In the previous chapter, we examined the historical approach to

Christology. Now we turn to the dogmatic approach, which takes as its starting point the claim that Jesus Christ was both fully human and fully divine. The official promulgation of this dogma came at the Council of Chalcedon in 451 with the declaration that Jesus Christ was "one person in two natures." In this chapter, we will examine the work Cyril of Alexandria (378–444), who helped pave the way for Chalcedon, and Gerald O'Collins, a contemporary Jesuit theologian who argues for continued relevance of the Chalcedonian formula for understanding the nature of God as revealed in Christ Jesus.

BACKGROUND TO CYRIL OF ALEXANDRIA

Cyril was by all accounts a hard-nosed and self-assured bishop who also wielded much political clout in Alexandria. His uncle Theophilus became archbishop of Alexandria when Cyril was only seven. Cyril received an excellent education and rose in the ranks of the church. When his uncle died in 412, Cyril succeeded him as archbishop. Backed by the imperial policy of Theodosius I, Cyril initiated repressive measures against dissident Christians, Jews, and pagans in Alexandria. Cyril also had a contentious relationship with Orestes, the Roman prefect of the city. One of the most notorious events to occur during Cyril's tenure as archbishop was the murder of the pagan philosopher Hypatia who supported Orestes. An angry mob of Christians pulled her from her carriage, dragged her to the cathedral where they stoned her and dismembered her body, even burning some of her remains. The murder of Hypatia blemished the reputation of the entire church of Alexandria and scholars to this day lay varying degrees of blame for its occurrence at the feet of Cyril.

Not only did Cyril play a prominent role in the local politics of Alexandria, he also exerted a great deal of influence in the international church. Five major sees emerged in the early church: Rome, Antioch, Alexandria, Constantinople, and Jerusalem. There were competing theological traditions in Antioch and Alexandria that often resulted in disputes between the two churches. Alexandria and Constantinople tangled over which enjoyed greater authority in matters of church governance. Alexandria enjoyed a well-deserved and long-standing reputation of being a leading intellectual center in the Roman world, while Constantinople boasted of being the seat of the emperor. This underlying tension fueled the controversy between Cyril in Alexandria and Nestorius in Constantinople that we will explore in this chapter.

Cyril's career must also be seen in the context of the internal disputes that racked the church over the issue of Christology (the understanding of Christ's identity). One of the most hotly contested issues in the early fourth century involved two figures from the Alexandrian church, Arius and Athanasius. Arius had argued that if Christ was God, then when Jesus walked on earth and prayed to the Father, there would have been two Gods. Since we can't have two Gods, Jesus must have been "the Son of God," great in power, but not co-eternal with the Father. Athanasius countered by taking as his starting point the foundational Christian claim that Christ is the Savior of the World who gives us eternal life. Since no mere human being can give eternal life, Christ must be "of the same substance" as the Father. In the first ecumenical council (a meeting of the bishops of the entire church) at Nicaea in 325, the bishops sided with Athanasius. They composed the now familiar Nicene Creed. This decision created two further questions for the church. First: How can we preserve monotheism while affirming the divinity of the Father and the Son (and the Holy Spirit)? This trajectory led to the doctrine of the Trinity. Second: How can Christ be fully human and fully divine without compromising one or the other element? This is the question of Christology that occupied many of the church's best and brightest minds from the Council of Nicaea in 325 to the time of the fourth ecumenical council held in Chalcedon in 451.

NESTORIUS SPARKS A DEBATE

Soon after his elevation to the office of archbishop in 428, Nestorius stepped into a hornet's nest in the church at Constantinople. A group within the church approached Nestorius with a question concerning the proper title for Mary: Was Mary rightly called the Mother of God (*Theotokos*)? When he stated that the proper title for Mary should be the Mother of Christ (*Christotokos*), not only had Nestorius entered into a theological debate, but he had also angered a number of influential members of both the church and the imperial court. Not long after offering his opinion on the question of Mary being called *Theotokos*, one of his priests who had accompanied him from Antioch preached a sermon in the cathedral denouncing the title. About a month later, a rebuttal was given by a bishop Proclus whose sermon in the cathedral was met with thunderous applause. Proclus also had the support of Pulcheria, the emperor's older sister. In the following spring, Nestorius gave a series of lectures in which he denounced the use of the title *Theotokos*. Not only did Nestorius encounter opposition within the capital city, but word also spread to Cyril in Alexandria who felt he needed to address the matter.

While this controversy is ostensibly about Mary, it is ultimately a question about the relation between the humanity and divinity of Christ. Nestorius was originally from Antioch and educated there under Theodore of Mopsuestia (350–428) who, like other Antiochene theologians, spoke of an "association" or "conjunction" between Christ's humanity and divinity. Theodore's predecessor, Diodore of Tarsus, even spoke of Christ as being two Sons—the Son of God and the Son of Man. Diodore was also one of the leading critics of his fellow Syrian Apollinarius who espoused a position that is more commonly associated with the theologians in Alexandria. Apollinarius taught that in Christ, the word of God had replaced his human mind or "rational soul."[1] The common thread that runs throughout Diodore,

Theodore, and Nestorius's writings was their adamant rejection of any position that seemed inspired by Apollinarius who, in their view, undercut the full humanity of Christ. Jesus experienced hunger, thirst, and suffering, and perhaps more importantly, he also serves as the model for Christians struggling with temptation.[2] Nestorius feared that calling Mary the Mother of God implied an Apollinarian Christology and therefore opposed it.[3]

When Nestorius publicly denounced the use of the title *Theotokos*, he also offered his own understanding of the Christology taught at the Council of Nicaea. Christ, according to Nicaea, is "of the same substance as the Father." In the words of John's Gospel, "In the beginning was the Word [*Logos*, Gk.], and the Word was with God, and the Word was God" (1:1) and in Christ, "the Word became flesh and lived among us" (1:14). Mary is not the Mother of God, argued Nestorius, for the simple reason that a "creature did not produce him who is uncreatable. The Father has not just recently generated God the Logos from the Virgin (for 'in the beginning was the Logos,' as John [John 1:1] says… [The Holy Spirit] formed out of the Virgin a temple for God the Logos, a temple in which he dwelt."[4] Jesus himself referred to his body as a temple and spoke of its destruction (John 2:19). Just as the word did not come into being at a moment in time, neither did the word die at Golgotha. Following the important christological teaching in the Letter to the Philippians (which will appear frequently in this chapter) that Christ "though he was in the form of God, did not regard equality with God as something to be exploited, but emptied himself, taking the form of a slave, being born in human likeness" (2:6–7), Nestorius takes Paul to be saying that Christ had two distinct natures, one human and one divine. Paul "takes the term *Christ* to be an expression which signifies the two natures, and without risk he applies to him both the style 'form of a slave,' which he took, and that of God. The descriptions are different from each other by reason of the mysterious fact that the natures are two in number."[5]

The difficult theological issue confronting Nestorius was how to best describe the relationship between the two natures of Christ. Nestorius asserted that it would be a mistake to claim the human flesh of the person Jesus Christ was divine.

> That which was formed in the womb is not in itself God. That which was created by the Spirit was not in itself God. That which was buried in the tomb was not in itself God. If that were the case, we would manifestly be worshipers of a human being and worshipers of the dead. But since God is within the one who was assumed, the one who was assumed is styled God because of the one who assumed him. That is why the demons shudder at the mention of the crucified flesh; they know that God has been joined to the crucified flesh, even though he has not shared its suffering.[6]

While Nestorius states that God is "joined" to the flesh of Jesus, his critics believed that Nestorius's language did not adequately express the unity of the two natures.

Nestorius concludes his address, "Hear Paul proclaiming both the eternity of the Only Begotten's deity and the recent birth of the humanity, and the fact that the dignity of the association or conjunction has been made one. 'Jesus Christ,' he says, 'is the same yesterday and today and forever' [Heb 13:8]. Amen."[7] Here, Nestorius speaks of the "association" or "conjunction" between the two natures; elsewhere, he says that there is a "mixture" of the two natures.[8] Whatever expression he uses, however, he is careful to maintain the distinction between the divine and human natures of Christ.

CYRIL RESPONDS TO NESTORIUS

Cyril's response to Nestorius began with veiled references to him in his Festal Letter (a letter written for Easter) for 429 and in his "Letter to the Monks of Egypt," but quickly turned to an exchange of letters between them, and culminated soon thereafter with Cyril's demand that Nestorius renounce his position or face the disciplinary action of his fellow bishops. In his second letter to Nestorius, Cyril speaks of the unity of the two natures of Christ. "While the natures that were brought together into this true unity were different, nonetheless there is one Christ and Son from out of both." Cyril introduces an expression in the letter that would figure prominently in proceedings and pronouncements of the Council of Chalcedon in 451. Cyril insists that there is a "hypostatic union" between the two natures. *Hypostasis* was one of several key Greek terms in the christological debates of the early church. As the historian Philip Jenkins explains, "*Hypostasis* is a complex word but can be translated as 'individual realty.' The word suggests 'underlying' and could have an architectural sense, implying the foundation of a house."[9] In his third letter to Nestorius, Cyril compares the unity of Christ's two natures to the unity of body and soul in the human being. "The one and only Christ is not twofold even though he is understood as compounded out of two different elements in an indivisible unity, just as a man is understood as consisting of soul and body and yet is not twofold but rather is one from out of both. No, we think correctly and so we must maintain that both the manly as well as the godly sayings were uttered by one subject."[10] Cyril repeatedly emphasizes that all actions of Christ, from the very human act of speaking with his friends to the miracles themselves, are attributed to a single subject. Attached to this third letter were twelve anathemas (propositions to be rejected by anyone claiming to be orthodox in belief) presented to Nestorius for his acceptance. The third anathema reflected the "single subject" Christology endorsed by Cyril: "If anyone divided the hypostases of the One Christ after the union, connecting them only by a conjunction in terms of honour or dignity or sovereignty, and not rather by a combination in terms of natural union, let him be anathema."[11]

Nestorius would not accept the propositions attached to Cyril's Third Letter, so a church council would need to settle the dispute.[12] Cyril had earlier written Pope Celestine who gave Nestorius ten days to recant or be excommunicated. Now he wrote to the emperor Theodosius II asking for a council and in November 430 the emperor announced that the council would meet in the city of Ephesus next Pentecost, June 7, 431. The council was plagued by infighting between factions, the oppressive summer heat, and delays in the arrival of the delegations from Antioch and Rome. By June 22, John of Antioch still had not arrived, so they began the proceedings without him. Though he was in Ephesus, Nestorius did not participate, having failed to comply with Celestine's earlier order. When John finally completed the six-hundred-mile journey and arrived in Ephesus on June 26, he was angered that the council had begun without him. (The delegation from Rome did not arrive until July 10.) John and his delegation convened a separate council, and chaos loomed as the original council deposed Nestorius, while John's council deposed Cyril and Memnon, the bishop of Ephesus. When the original council's report was delivered to Nestorius, he refused to accept it. Though Theosodius's representative ordered that the bishops not leave the city until the issue had been resolved, one bishop wore a disguise and smuggled the letter out of Ephesus in his cane. When he received contradictory reports from Ephesus, the emperor sent a high-ranking official, Count John, to act on his behalf. When Count John arrived, he placed Cyril, Memnon, and Nestorius under arrest while the emperor sorted things out. When the dust had finally settled, Nestorius was deposed as bishop of Constantinople and was exiled to a monastery in Antioch; Cyril returned to Alexandria where he remained bishop; and in 433, representatives from both Antioch and Alexandria ended their feud when they agreed to a statement of belief known as the Formula of Reunion, which was foundational to the dogmatic statements issued at the Council of Chalcedon in 451.

CYRIL'S *ON THE UNITY OF CHRIST*

A few years after the Council of Ephesus Cyril composed *On the Unity of Christ*, a work that not only provides one of the most complete statements of his Christology, but is also a valuable source for clues in our search for God. Early in *On the Unity of Christ*, which is written in the form of a dialogue between two characters simply designated "A" and "B," the debate over the use of the title *Theotokos* for Mary is revisited. "B" poses the central question in the debate. "If we are to preserve the immutability and unalterability as innate and essential to God, in what sense, then, should we say that the Word has become flesh?"[13] Both "A" and "B" assume that God, by definition, must be unchanging. How, then, could the unchanging God undergo the process of birth? How could an unchanging God *become* anything? Drawing on the hymn from Philippians ("[Christ Jesus], though he was in the form of God, did not regard equality with God as something to be exploited, but emptied himself, taking the form of a slave…" [2:6–7]), "A" replies that "he is said to have undergone a birth like ours, while all the while remaining what he was…. He was God in an appearance like ours, and the Lord in the form of a slave. This is what we mean when we say that he became flesh, and for the same reasons we affirm that the holy virgin is the Mother of God."[14]

If we do not proclaim that Mary is *Theotokos*, claims "A," then the entire Christian account of salvation is destroyed. "In short, [God] took what was ours to be his very own so that we might have all that was his. 'He was rich but he became poor for our sake, so that we might be enriched by his poverty' (2 Cor 8:9). When they say that the word of God did not become flesh, or rather did not undergo birth from a woman according to the flesh, they bankrupt the economy [the plan] of salvation, for if he who was rich did not impoverish himself, abasing himself to our condition out of tender love, then we have not gained his riches, but are still in our poverty…."[15] When Cyril speaks of the riches of God being imparted to us through Christ, he is thinking primarily of the gift of eternal life or incorruptibility. "He is from God, from on high, and naturally God, yet he came down to our condition in a strange and unusual manner, and was born of the Spirit, according to the flesh, so that we too might abide in holiness and incorruptibility like him. Clearly grace came upon us from him, as from a new rootstock, a new beginning."[16] Through Christ, who is by nature the Son of God, we become sons and daughters of God by adoption (Rom 8:15). This is for Cyril the good news of Christianity, and without it, the gospel loses its power.

We can see the central role eternal life plays in Cyril's overall thought when we notice that Cyril speaks of God, Christ, and the Eucharist all as "Life." In his *Commentary on John's Gospel*, Cyril paraphrases Jesus's statement, "On that day you will know that I am in the Father, and you in me, and I in you" (14:20) as, "I, being Life by nature...[joined] you through Myself unto God the Father, Who is also Himself by nature Life."[17] In *On the Unity of Christ*, Cyril speaks of Christ as the one "who as God is Life and Life-Giver," and later when commenting on the Bread of Life discourse in John 6, Cyril asks rhetorically, "And how could the flesh of anyone ever give life to the world if it has not become the very flesh of Life, that is him who is the Word of God the Father?"[18] Just as the divinity of Christ is central to Cyril's thought, "[t]he Eucharist lies at the heart of Cyril's piety," says the patristics scholar Norman Russell.[19] Russell continues, "Foreshadowed in the manna of the desert and the paschal lamb, the Eucharist enables the believer to participate corporeally in Christ as intimately as the earthly body of Christ participated in the Word."[20] When we grasp the unity of the Father who created the universe, the Son who recreated us in the image of God, and the Holy Spirit who nourishes us through the Bread of Life, suggests Cyril, we begin to arrive at a partial, yet genuine understanding of the nature of God.

While the Council of Chalcedon remains the church's standard for theological statements regarding the identity of Jesus

Christ, some theologians worry that the categories of thought underlying the decrees of Chalcedon are no longer meaningful for contemporary Christians. The theologian Roger Haight comments, "A common criticism of Chalcedon is that its doctrine, like the theological mode of thought that generated it, has abandoned Jesus as he is portrayed in the synoptic gospels. It deals with Jesus in the abstract or general metaphysical categories of nature, person, substance, and being. When this kind of language controls the subject matter, it compromises an imaginative focus on Jesus of Nazareth."[21] Where earlier theologians accepted the divinity of Christ and then sought to safeguard his human nature, Haight continues, today Christians take Jesus' humanity as their starting point and then seek to understand how he could also be divine. Because we pose different christological questions and think in different terms than those used at Chalcedon, Haight concludes, we need to develop a new framework in which the truths of Chalcedon can be expressed in a way that contemporary Christians find intelligible and meaningful.

In contrast to Haight, the theologian Gerald O'Collins does not believe the language of Chalcedon has lost relevance for contemporary Christians, and while a reformulation of the Chalcedonian doctrine is certainly possible, most modern attempts to do so typically undercut either the full humanity or full divinity of Christ. From the 1960s to the present, O'Collins has published extensively in the area of Christology.[22] While O'Collins has argued in various works that the "one person in two natures" formulation offers a faithful rendering of the identity of Christ as proclaimed in the New Testament, we will focus specifically on the defense of Chalcedon that he offers in his 2002 work *Incarnation*.[23]

WHAT CHALCEDON CLAIMED
ABOUT THE INCARNATION

The very first step in O'Collins's argument is to clarify and defend the christological definition of Chalcedon. In any earlier work, *Interpreting Jesus*, O'Collins declares, "We can reasonably express the essential message of Chalcedon as follows: 'The human is so united with the divine in Christ, that the *one* Christ can be confessed to be both truly God and truly man.'"[24] A definition such as this is necessary in order to account for the wide range of statements about Jesus scattered throughout the New Testament. Reflecting his humanity, Jesus grows tired (John 4:6), weeps at the loss of his friend (John 11:35), and becomes "distressed and agitated" (Mark 14:33). Reflecting his divinity, Jesus is without sin (Heb 4:15), able to raise the dead, and born of a virgin. In the opening chapter of *Incarnation*, O'Collins cites three passages that highlight Christ's divinity. First, the opening verses from the hymn in Paul's Letter to the Philippians declares that Christ Jesus "though he was in the form of God, did not regard equality with God as something to be exploited, but empties himself, taking the form of a slave, being born in human likeness. And being found in human form, he humbled himself and became obedient to the point of death—even death on a cross" (Phil 2:6–8). Second, the opening of the Letter to Hebrews, drawing on the Jewish wisdom tradition, proclaims, "He is the reflection of God's glory and the exact imprint of God's very being, and he sustains all things by his powerful word" (Heb 1:3). Third, O'Collins cites one of the most important verses in the early church's christological debates, "And the Word became flesh and lived among us, and we have seen his glory, the glory of a father's only son, full of grace and truth" (John 1:14). This verse is the basis for the doctrine of the Incarnation: the word of God enters human history and takes on flesh in the person of Jesus Christ.

O'Collins takes issue with thinkers in the modern age who have used the word *incarnation* in an extended sense of being a general truth about the spiritual potential of all human beings. In this view, all humans have a spiritual component to their personality, which has been variously described by various religious, philosophical, and poetic traditions, and those who embody that spiritual consciousness in an exemplary way (e.g., the founders of the world's major religions) can be said to be "incarnating" that Ultimate Reality. Proponents of this approach contend that such an approach allows for interreligious dialogue and avoids "unacceptable religious exclusivism, an arrogant claim that, having been founded by the incarnate Son of God, Christianity is superior and unique."[25] This understanding of incarnation, counters O'Collins, fails to correspond to the New Testament claims about Christ as the "one incarnation of the Son of God who with self-giving love took on a fully human existence to live, die and rise for the full and final welfare of all human beings and their world."[26]

EXPLORING CHALCEDON

The question at the heart of Chalcedon's definition is the relationship between the human and divine natures of Christ, but before moving to that issue, O'Collins tackles one crucial preliminary issue. "The personal pre-existence of the Word or Son of God is a necessary presupposition for any orthodox belief in the incarnation or the Word 'becoming flesh.'"[27] Again O'Collins distinguishes between the traditional meaning of *preexistence* and the extended meaning that some modern thinkers attach to it. *Preexistence* in this extended sense argues that Christ metaphorically preexisted in the mind of God in the history of Israel. O'Collins rejects this extended meaning of *preexistence* for the same reason that he rejected the extended meaning of *incarnation*. In O'Collins's view it simply does not accurately represent the claims made in both the New Testament and the creeds. "Belief in Jesus divinity stands or falls with accepting his *personal* pre-existence within the eternal life of the Trinity," O'Collins writes elsewhere. He adds, "This belief is not to be confused with false ideas about some pre-existence of his created humanity."[28]

O'Collins contends that preexistence provides the necessary connection between the Old Testament's account of creation and the New Testament's proclamation of salvation. Without compromising their strict monotheistic beliefs, various Old Testament writers spoke of various personifications of God's activity, such as the word of God and the wisdom of God, being present at creation (Ps 33:6; Prov 8:23–31). When writing to the Corinthian church about the resurrected and exalted Christ, Paul states that "for us there is one God, the Father, from whom are all things and for whom we exist, and one Lord, Jesus Christ, through whom are all things and through whom we exist" (1 Cor 8:6). By using this type of language, argues O'Collins, Paul and the Christians at Corinth "acknowledge the *person* of Jesus Christ to have pre-existed and collaborated in the work of creation, a role the OT Scriptures had attributed to those *personifications* of divine activity, Word and Wisdom."[29] According to Christian belief, this same Christ, now glorified, will return at the end of time. "Both in his earthly lifetime and in his risen life, what occurred at the incarnation persists—for the salvation of human beings who are already touched by his power and will meet him in glory when he 'comes to judge the living and the dead.'"[30] Without preexistence, O'Collins concludes, the unity of the divine activities of creation, redemption, and consummation is shattered.

An acceptance of Christ's preexistence leads logically to question of how Christ's human and divine natures could exist without confusion in one person. O'Collins poses the question in the following way:

How can the same individual be both human and divine? Divinity and humanity constitute and disclose seemingly incompatible ranges of characteristics. Divinity involves a purely spiritual, all-powerful, all-knowing, omnipresent, eternal and unlimited way of being. Humanity involves a material and temporal existence that is spatially located and limited in power and knowledge.[31]

Many thinkers, both critics and supporters of Christianity, have found the concept of two natures existing in a single person to be a contradiction that must either be rejected outright or modified in some way. O'Collins believes that the charge that it is a logical contradiction (as say a four-sided circle) can be avoided if we keep in mind that each of Christ's natures is a separate "frame of reference." O'Collins argued in an earlier work, the first edition of his work *Christology*, "It would be a blatant contradiction in terms to attribute to the same subject at the same time *and under the same aspect* mutually incompatible properties. But that is not being done here. With respect to his divinity Christ is omniscient, but with respect to his humanity he is limited in knowledge. Mutually exclusive characteristics are being simultaneously attributed to him but not within the same frame of reference."[32]

This move has not gone unchallenged. The theologian John McIntyre charges that O'Collins's "frame of reference" argument has failed to deal adequately with the problem of the two natures. McIntyre reasons that O'Collins's statement could be taken in one of two ways, neither of which solves the problem. "Either, on the one hand, the 'explanation' of the incompatibility in question amounts to a restatement of the problem, namely, that within the divine frame of reference, or in his divine nature as the old language would have it, Jesus Christ is omniscient, and within the human frame of reference, in his human nature, he is limited in knowledge."[33] This still does not deal with the heart of the matter because it does not address the question of how the two frames of reference relate to one another. "Or, on the other hand, if there is not to be constant incompatibility between two such diverse natures, then the other option is that alternation takes place between the two frames of reference."[34] The idea that Christ would alternate between his human nature and divine nature recalls the controversy that engulfed Nestorius.

In the second edition of *Christology*, O'Collins argues that the goal of his "two frames of reference" argument was actually a very modest one. "My aim then was not to establish positively the possibility of incarnation, but only to rebut a long-standing argument about the doctrine being incoherent. The incarnation is a paradox (an apparent contradiction that on closer inspection proves not to be incoherent) but not a blatant, logical contradiction."[35]

When we inspect this paradox more closely, says O'Collins, we take our understanding of who God is and test it against the portrait of the Incarnate Word in the New Testament. As we enter more deeply into the paradox, we begin to notice the "two-directional nature of our thinking." We at first offer "some account of divine characteristics and then acknowledge that these characteristics are to be found in Christ. Yet, there is some feedback here. In light of Christ, we understand God afresh....What we make of Jesus and his Spirit ultimately shapes what we make of God."[36] The same "feedback" occurs when consider what it means to be human and then test those ideas against the portrayal of the Incarnate Word in the New Testament. To best appreciate this dynamic, O'Collins recommends that we turn our attention to poets, musicians, and artists, especially in works dealing with Christ's "humble birth and terrible death—episodes that stretch the tension between his divinity and humanity almost to the breaking point. The Christ Child's humanity is beyond question; he needs nurture, protection and affection to survive and grow. The crucified Jesus' humanity is also beyond question, as he dies in excruciating agony. Faith invites us to recognize also the true divinity of the One who is unquestionably human."[37]

The classic paintings of the Christ Child or the crucified Christ recall once again the Philippians hymn that proclaims that Christ, "though he was in the form of God, did not regard equality with God as something to be exploited, but emptied himself, taking the form of a slave, being born in human likeness. And being found in human form, he humbled himself and became obedient to the point of death—even death on a cross" (Phil 2:6–8). O'Collins poses the question: "Of what did the Son of

God 'empty' or divest himself in the incarnation?"[38] For O'Collins, the best answer may be found in a parable recounted by the nineteenth-century philosopher Søren Kierkegaard, a fairy tale that has become a familiar plot line in many children's movies. A king loves a poor maiden. "Would she be able to summon confidence enough never to remember what the king wished only to forget, that he was king and she had been a humble maiden?"[39] The king could certainly display his power in spectacular ways but "it could not satisfy the king, who desired not his own glorification but hers." This would also not result in a genuine mutual love, for "the unfathomable nature of love" is that it "desires equality with the beloved, not in jest merely, but in earnest and truth." Echoes of the Philippians hymn resound in Kierkegaard's reasoning: "In order that the union may be brought about, God must therefore become the equal of such a one, and so he will appear in the likeness of the humblest. But the humblest is one who must serve others, and God will therefore appear in the form of a *servant*."[40] In terms of the Incarnation, there must be a genuine union of the human and the divine in this servant. "But the servant-form was not mere outer garment, and therefore God must suffer all things, endure all things, make experience of things. He must suffer hunger in the desert, he must thirst in the time of his agony, he must be forsaken in death, absolutely like the humblest—behold the man!"[41] The Incarnation, concludes O'Collins, is a love story. "Paul's hymn and Kierkegaard's parable invite us to remember and cherish the love showed by the divine King in assuming the limited and painful operations and sufferings of our human condition."[42]

SEARCHING FOR GOD THROUGH CHALCEDON

Any search for God that proceeds along the line of Chalcedon would be centered on Christ ("christocentric"). The seventeenth-century mathematician and religious thinker Blaise Pascal reflected his own christocentric perspective when he wrote, "Jesus Christ is the object of all things, the centre towards which all things tend."[43] Pascal did important work in the area of geometric cones, so we will take the image of a cone to describe the two forms that a christocentric search for God could take. In the first form, we can picture beginning at the base of the cone and moving to the point. We might begin at the base with questions of importance to all humans (What is the meaning of life?), then perhaps narrow our focus to various religious responses to that question (e.g., the concept of enlightenment in Buddhism, the concept of living in harmony with the Tao in Taoism), and moving finally to Christ's teachings. The theologian Clyde Crews proceeds in this way in his work *Ultimate Questions*. Christianity claims that "in the life and death, actions and attitudes of the figure Jesus, there is to be found the key to human meaning and significance. And the claim is yet more: that he is the fullest revelation of God to humanity (true God) and the fullest manifestation of what humanity can be (true human)." While God's revelation extends far beyond the bounds of Christianity, "in the figure of Christ the revelation is fullest and normative."[44]

In the second form of this christocentric approach, we can imagine beginning with the point and moving toward the base. The point of the cone would serve as a lens on the world. In religious terms, we would see the world through the eyes of Christ. Offering his assessment of the present state of Catholic theology, the theologian Aidan Nichols believes that while excellent works in particular areas of Catholic doctrine continue to appear, there are not enough theological works that present the grand vision of Christianity. In his view, for works "to be termed a vision or system depends on their ability to present revelation in its entirety, albeit from a single, determinate starting point."[45] If we take the point of the cone to be this starting point, then a theological vision would move forward in all directions and we would survey all of life from the vantage point of the life, death, and resurrection of Christ.

In O'Collins's work, we detect both forms of the christocentric approach. We see the first (moving from the base to the point in the cone) in his incorporation of the early church thinking on the nature of the Logos into his own work. The term *Logos*, which is usually translated as "Word," also suggests a principle of rationality or order that underlies the entire universe. The second-century Christian apologist Justin Martyr spoke of the "seeds of the Word" present throughout creation. As O'Collins says regarding Justin and other like-minded theologians: "They understood the Logos to permeate the body of the world. No place or person lay or lies 'far from' God's creative Logos or Wisdom. The Logos was and is universally present to everyone and everything."[46] According to Justin, the wisdom that is present in fragmentary ways in the teachings of the great Greek philosophers finds the fullness of expression in Christ.[47] When thinking about the divine presence in the world, O'Collins, following Justin, suggests that we should, "be ready to acknowledge an endless variety in the qualitatively different possibilities of divine presence and activity" throughout human history.[48] For O'Collins, the human condition is "an incessant search for the absolute fullness of life, meaning, and love which is only to be found in God."[49] Countless poets, playwrights, and religious figures throughout history have offered valuable wisdom crafted in creative ways, but in Christ we have "the power of God and the wisdom of God" (1 Cor 1:24). In this first form, Christ is the goal, the summit, or perhaps the focal point, the point of greatest intensity of light as we find in the homey image offered by the twentieth-century Trappist monk Thomas Merton. "As a magnifying glass concentrates the rays of the sun into a little burning knot to heat that can set fire to a dry leaf or a piece of paper, so the mystery of Christ in the Gospel concentrates the rays of God's light and fire to a point that sets fire to the spirit of man."[50]

O'Collins also operates along the lines of the second form of the christocentric approach (moving from the point to the base in the cone) when he writes, "No human beings…can escape living in the presence of Christ. Whatever occurs, occurs in the presence of Christ. Whoever acts, acts in the presence of Christ, even if he or she does not discern and acknowledge his presence."[51] (We will consider the criticisms of this position in the chapter on the world's religions.) In the second form of a christocentric approach, Christ is the starting point, not the goal. Dorothy Day, co-founder of the Catholic Worker movement, sees all humans, but especially the hungry, homeless, and socially discarded persons, as Christ. In her 1945 Christmas Letter, Day offered a powerful reflection that recalls the statement by the Risen Christ, "Truly I tell you, just as you did it to one of the least of these who are members of my family, you did it to me" (Matt 25:40). We can imagine someone asking, "How can we who live so long after the time of Christ actually serve him?" Day begins, "It is no use saying that we are born two thousand years too late to give room to Christ. Nor will those who live at the end of the world have been born too late. Christ is always with us, asking for room in our hearts." She recounts the acts of kindness extended to Jesus: his mother was given shelter when she was to give birth; Peter's mother-in-law fed him; Martha, Mary, and Lazarus offered continual hospitality; and the women at the cross remained with him until his death. Day writes, "If that is the way they gave hospitality to Christ, it is certain that that is the way it should still be given. Not for the sake of humanity. Not because it might be Christ who stays with us, comes to see us, takes up our time. Not because these people remind us of Christ…, but because they *are* Christ, asking us to find room for Him, exactly as He did at the first Christmas."[52] Christ is present in everyone we meet, says Day, but we encounter his presence most forcefully when we serve the needs of those who lack food and water, clothing, or shelter.

If the Logos that took on flesh in Christ is indeed present in all places at all times, then the search for God knows no bounds. As O'Collins notes, "In 'the signs of the times' Christians note and seek to interpret current indications of Christ's personal presence and influence. That presence assumes a multiform diversity that allows us to acknowledge him as present everywhere and active in innumerable ways as the history of the world moves towards the end."[53] O'Collins concludes his investigation in *Incarnation* with the reminder that when we search for God we need to be ready for surprises. "The history of divine choices in the OT history repeatedly contains surprises. Over and over again God picks out less promising candidates, like younger sons and barren women, for special vocations....Whatever else we learn from the story of God's people, at least we should reach the conclusion: God's ways and choices are not our ways and choices."[54]

Discussion Questions

1. Is the Chalcedonian formula of Christ being "one person in two natures" intelligible to most Christians today? If not, is it possible to translate that formula into another language that is meaningful and intelligible to most Christians, and yet preserves the teaching of Chalcedon?

2. Is the relationship between Christ's human and divine natures, in your view, described better as a "unity" or an "association"?

3. Offer your own evaluation of Nestorius's position on the use of the title *Theotokos* for Mary. Is his argument better or worse than the one advanced by Cyril?

4. What did Cyril mean when he referred to God as "Life"?

5. Is O'Collins's argument for the centrality of the doctrine of the Incarnation for Christian belief a compelling one?

6. What is your favorite painting of Christ? What Christology is the artist conveying in the work?

7. Does Kierkegaard's parable of the king and the maiden shed any light on the Incarnation? If so, what should we take away from that parable?

Suggested Readings

For an overview of Cyril's thought, see the Introduction to Norman Russell, *Cyril of Alexandria* (New York: Routledge, 2000). Also helpful is John McGuckin's "Introduction" to Cyril of Alexandria, *On the Unity of Christ* (Crestwood, NY: St. Vladimir's Seminary Press, 1995); and Thomas G. Weinandy, "Cyril and the Mystery of the Incarnation," in *The Theology of St. Cyril of Alexandria*, ed. Thomas G. Weinandy and Daniel A. Keating (London: T & T Clark, 2003). For a detailed study of Cyril's Christology, see John McGuckin, *Saint Cyril of Alexandria and the Christological Controversy* (Crestwood, NY: St. Vladimir's Seminary Press, 2004).

For a collection of articles dealing with various aspects of O'Collins's thought, see Daniel Kendall and Stephen T. Davis, eds., *The Convergence of Theology* (Mahwah, NJ: Paulist Press, 2001), which also includes a bibliography of O'Collins's writing through the year 2000. O'Collins's "The Incarnation: The Critical Issues" in *The Incarnation*, ed. Stephen T. Davis, Daniel Kendall, and Gerald O'Collins (Oxford: Oxford University Press, 2002) provides a helpful summary of the issues involved in christological debates. See also O'Collins's earlier works *Interpreting Jesus* (London: Geoffrey Chapman, 1983) and *Focus on Jesus*, coauthored with Daniel Kendall (Leominster, England: Gracewing, 1996). For a discussion of O'Collins's method and Christology, see Craig A. Brown, "The Theology of Gerald O'Collins and Postmodernism," *American Theological Inquiry* 2, no. 1 (2009): 11–26.

PART THREE

The Search Intensifies

SACRAMENTS: ENCOUNTERING GOD

Ambrose of Milan and Louis-Marie Chauvet

While Christians hold that the Christ is the critical clue in the search for God, the mystery will not be solved until the last day. In the midst of this on-going inquiry, Christians are both investigators and collaborators. As investigators, the church assembles the witnesses ("a cloud of witnesses," Heb 12:1), records their testimony, and hands down their findings. As collaborators, the church harbors the one being sought. That is, the church believes that Christ will be present with us until the end of time (Matt 28:20). There is a tension, then, between our unity with Christ and our distance from the full realization of his will. The sacraments draw upon this tension between investigation and collaboration, presence and distance, promise and fulfillment. If the sacraments celebrate our unity with Christ, but fail to recognize the distance, the church could fall into shameful complacency. If the sacraments speak of the distance without celebrating the presence, the church could wither at the roots and not bear fruit. For help in understanding how the sacraments keep this creative tension alive in the Catholic tradition, we turn our attention to the early church thinker Ambrose of Milan and the contemporary theologian Louis-Marie Chauvet.

BACKGROUND TO AMBROSE OF MILAN

By virtue of his birth, Ambrose (339–97) enjoyed high social standing; by virtue of his upbringing, Ambrose possessed a deep piety. Both would serve him well during his episcopate in Milan. Ambrose's father (who was also named Ambrose) was the Roman governor of Gaul when the future bishop of Milan was born in Trier around 339.[1] Ambrose was the youngest of three children and he enjoyed a close relationship with his sister Marcellina and brother Satyrus. Ambrose's father died at a young age, and it was probably then that the family moved back to Rome. In Rome, Ambrose received the traditional education that prepared the son of a patrician to follow in his father's footsteps. After completing his studies, Ambrose served as a legal adviser to a powerful Roman official by the name of Probus, who was so impressed with Ambrose that he appointed him governor of a region in northern Italy that included the capital city of Milan. In the fall of 374, the bishop of Milan died, and the church was sharply divided over his successor. When Ambrose came to the cathedral in Milan to prevent the unrest from erupting into riots, the crowd unexpectedly acclaimed him bishop. Ambrose initially refused. Despite his pious upbringing, Ambrose was not baptized (his case does not seem unusual in the ancient world).[2] When the emperor Valentinian I offered his encouragement, Ambrose relented and was baptized, and eight days later was ordained bishop of Milan.

Ambrose dealt with six emperors over the course of his career as bishop, and as we might expect, he sometimes clashed with the imperial leader. Out of these conflicts, Ambrose crafted an understanding of church–state relations that would prove influential in the church's evolving thought in this area.[3] (The Edict of Milan that ended the Roman persecution of Christians had only been issued in 313.) To cite one example, in 385 the young emperor Valentinian II, spurred on by his mother Justina, requested that one of the churches outside the city walls of Milan, the Portian

Basilica, be put at his disposal so that the imperial court could worship there. The imperial court favored the teachings of Arius whose teachings had been condemned at the Council of Nicaea. Ambrose refused. Crowds filled the Portian Basilica; imperial forces were summoned and they surrounded the church. The situation grew increasingly tense. In a later letter to his sister, Ambrose describes his response to Valentinian.

> Do you think that you may seize the house of God? It is alleged that everything is permitted to the emperor and that all things are his. I reply: Do not so burden yourself, O Emperor, as to believe that you have any imperial right to those things that are divine. Do not so exalt yourself. Rather, if you wish to rule longer, be subject to God. It is written: "What is God's is for God, what is Caesar's is for Caesar" (Mark 12:17). The palaces belong to the emperor, the churches to the bishop.[4]

By week's end, the troops withdrew.

Ambrose's dramatic standoffs with the emperors should not overshadow the fact that his primary responsibility was for the pastoral care of his congregation in Milan. Ambrose was a renowned preacher and he introduced the Eastern practice of congregational hymn singing into Western liturgy.[5] One of his chief duties would have been the initiation of new members into the church. In the ancient church, new members were typically received into the church during Easter. Following from the theology of Paul (Rom 6:3–11), those who were baptized were baptized into his death and raised to new life in Christ. In the same Easter Vigil liturgy, the newly baptized were anointed (which becomes the separate sacrament of Confirmation in the West) and they then celebrated the Eucharist for the first time. It was Ambrose's custom to speak to the neophytes over the course of Easter Week and offer his reflections on the spiritual meaning of the various ritual actions that were included in the Easter Vigil liturgy.[6] These reflections come down to us in two works: *On the Sacraments*, which is believed to be a stenographic record of Ambrose's Easter Week reflections, and *On the Mysteries*, which is Ambrose's published revision of the same material.[7]

AMBROSE OF MILAN'S *ON THE MYSTERIES*

Drawing from both the Bible and Plato's philosophy, Ambrose distinguishes between the seen and the unseen, the physical reality and its spiritual meaning, when discussing the meaning of baptism, anointing, or Eucharist. Although Ambrose is not always consistent on this point, he uses the term *sacrament* to refer to the physical act (e.g., immersion in the water) and *mystery* to refer to the spiritual reality behind the action (rebirth).[8] In *On the Mysteries*, then, Ambrose concentrates on the spiritual significance of the sacramental acts. This sustained reflection on the meaning of the sacraments of initiation is called mystagogy. We encounter Ambrose's distinction between the seen and the unseen early in his mystagogical instruction. Referring to the water in the baptismal pool (the cathedral in Milan had an octagonal-shaped baptismal pool about twenty feet in diameter with three steps leading to the bottom), Ambrose says to new initiates:

> What did you see? Water, to be sure, but not only that. The levites [i.e., the deacons] who were ministering there, and the high priest [i.e., the bishop] questioning and consecrating. The first thing that the Apostle taught you was that we must not contemplate "what is visible but what is invisible, since what is visible is temporal, whereas what is invisible is eternal" (2 Cor 4:18). And elsewhere you read that, "since the creation of the world, the invisible things of God are understood by way of the things that have been made."[9]

Like any teacher, Ambrose needs to explain the meaning of the sacraments of initiation in terms that the hearers will understand. He could have related baptism to the beginning of the human life cycle, comparing physical birth and spiritual rebirth. He could have related baptism to the ministry of Jesus, paralleling Jesus' baptism in the Jordan with their own beginning of Christian discipleship. Instead, Ambrose chose to relate baptism to the entire biblical narrative, beginning with the opening scene at creation where the Spirit hovering over the waters is seen by Ambrose as a foreshadowing (what Ambrose calls among other things a "figure") of the reception of the Spirit at baptism.[10] Throughout the entire *On the Mysteries*, Ambrose continually extracts meanings from the biblical stories and overlays those meanings on the various moments in their sacramental initiation: baptism, a washing of the feet, the reception of white baptismal garments, an anointing, and the celebration of the Eucharist. Like a painter carefully layering colors on the canvas, Ambrose blends biblical stories and liturgical actions to draw out the shades of meaning in the sacraments of initiation.

The opening paragraph of *On the Mysteries* alludes to the preparation that the candidates for baptism underwent. In the ancient world, this period of instruction prior to baptism (known as the catechumenate) could last for years. In Milan, the custom seems to be that on Epiphany those who wished to be welcomed into the church submitted their names to Ambrose. As part of their Lenten formation, those who were to be received into the church (those Ambrose called the *competentes*) at Easter would gather twice daily Monday through Friday to hear Ambrose preach a sermon on the biblical patriarchs or the Book of Proverbs. These two sources provided the role models and the moral principles for living a sound moral Christian life. Now that their moral instruction is complete and they have been baptized, explains Ambrose, "the time has come to speak of the mysteries and to explain the structure of the sacraments. If we had thought mention should be made of this to you before your baptism, when you were not as yet initiated, we would have been considered betrayers rather than explainers."[11] With that, Ambrose begins to delve into the mysteries into which the newest members of his church have been initiated.

Ambrose reflects back on the first step of their initiation that took place on Holy Saturday, "the opening" or the "ephphatha." The background for this is the story of Jesus healing a deaf and mute man in Mark 7:31–37. In *On the Sacraments*, Ambrose explains that their ears were opened so that they could be attentive to the words spoken to them. He also states that the nostrils are touched.[12] In *On the Mysteries*, Ambrose emphasizes that the touching of the ears allows the candidates to hear (i.e., comprehend) what is being asked of them. Stating that it would be improper to touch a woman's lips, Ambrose does not touch the mouth. In the gospel story, Jesus uses spittle when he touches the lips of the mute man, but there is no mention of that in Ambrose's ritual.[13]

In his discussion of the baptism itself, we see Ambrose in full command of his technique of overlaying one biblical story over another. Before we turn to the specific stories he chooses and how he relates them to each other, it is important to recall the purpose behind it all. Ambrose is speaking to the newly baptized and reflecting on the spiritual significance of the events of the recent Easter Sunday. As the liturgist Mary Pierre Ellebracht explains, "Ambrose intertwines passages from Scripture with the step-by-step flow of sacramental actions in such a way that the two become the expression of a single reality." That single reality is the activity of God in history. Ellebracht concludes, "The economy [God's working through history] of salvation is still going on in our midst, and it is in our liturgical celebrations that we recognize in faith and celebrate God's saving activity which continues in our daily life."[14] While we stand centuries removed from the events in the Bible, the "mystery" is that what we are experiencing here and now is the saving activity of the same God who acted in the same way in the lives of our biblical forebears.

The activity of God present in baptism is prefigured, says Ambrose, by the movement of the Spirit over the waters of creation (Gen 1:2), the preservation of Noah (Gen 6:5—9:17), the exodus from Egypt (Exod 14), the miracle Moses performs at Marah (Exod 15:22–25), the cleansing of the leper Naaman (2 Kgs 5), and the healing of the paralytic in the waters of Bethesda (John 5). In the midst of his reflections on this series of biblical stories, Ambrose enunciates his central theme: "You ought not, then, to believe solely with the eyes of your body. What is invisible is more completely seen, because the other is temporal, whereas this is eternal. What is not grasped by the eyes but perceived by the spirit and the mind is more completely viewed."[15] The physical event of baptism is necessary, according to Ambrose, but the "mystery" (the spiritual knowledge or wisdom) it reveals about God is greater.

Ambrose draws his listeners into this mystery by describing their recent initiation into the church in terms of a spiritual reading of the various biblical stories. For example, the Noah story mentions the waters of the flood, the ark built of wood, and the dove that returns carrying an olive branch in its beak. "Water is where the flesh is dipped so that every earthly sin may be washed away; there is every misdeed buried. Wood is where the Lord Jesus Christ was fastened when he suffered for us. The dove it is in whose appearance the Holy Spirit descended, as you learned in the New Testament (cf. Matt 3:16); he breathes into you the peace of soul and tranquility of mind."[16] Likewise, Naaman was a Syrian commander who journeys to Israel to see the prophet Elisha in the hope that the prophet could cure him of his leprosy. When Elisha tells him to dip seven times in the Jordan River, Naaman is outraged. I traveled all this way to have this prophet tell me to dip myself in a river seven times? I could have done that in Damascus! Nevertheless, Naaman does as Elisha prescribes and he is cured. Ambrose then turns Naaman's response on his audience. They, too, have grown accustomed to seeing the water of the baptismal font. They might be tempted to think as Naaman did, "I see the water that I am accustomed to seeing every day. Is that water, which I have often gone into without ever being cleansed, to cleanse me now?"[17] Naaman dipped multiple times in the river and was healed physically; the initiates were submerged in the water of the baptismal font in the name of the Father, the Son, and the Holy Spirit and were healed spiritually. In the waters of baptism, they died to sin and were raised to eternal life. "And so you read that the three witnesses in baptism—namely, water, blood and the Spirit (cf. 1 John 5:6) are one because, if you remove one of them, the sacrament of baptism no longer exists."[18] The waters of baptism, the cross of Christ, and Spirit of God are, then, for Ambrose the rungs on the ladder taking us up into the mystery of God's salvation.[19]

The newly baptized now step out of the font and are anointed. The chrism (also called myron), which is a perfumed oil, is not applied to the forehead in the sign of a cross, but rather is poured over the head of the person. Ambrose again layers different scriptural passages on this step of the initiation. Kings (e.g., David) and priests (e.g., Aaron) in the Old Testament were anointed. As the Psalmist proclaims, "It is like the precious oil on the head, running down upon the beard, on the beard of Aaron, running down over the collar of his robe" (Ps 133:2). Ambrose joins this allusion to Aaron with a verse from the Song of Songs, the love song that Bernard of Clairvaux compared to the love between Christ and the individual soul, "your name is perfume poured out; therefore the maidens love you" (Song 1:3). They are anointed on the head because wisdom resides there (Eccl 2:14). In this assemblage of verses, the newly baptized are reminded of their elevated state before God, the desire they have to be with the resurrected Christ, and the wisdom they have been granted. In short, "you are a chosen race, a royal priesthood, a holy nation, God's own people, in order that you may proclaim the mighty acts of him who called you out of darkness into his marvelous light" (1 Pet 2:9).

Between the anointing and the celebration of the Eucharist, Ambrose mentions two components of the initiation process that will be important in subsequent theological debates. The first is the washing of the feet. In *On the Sacraments*, Ambrose explains to his audience that although the Roman churches do not include the washing of the feet in their initiation ritual, he sees great value in its practice. Not only does the act imitate Christ's own humble gesture (John 13:1–20) and highlight the place of service in the life that these newly baptized Christians have chosen, but it also removes sin. When Peter recoils at the thought of Jesus washing his feet, Jesus replies, "Unless I wash you, you have no share with me" (John 13:8). Ambrose comments, "Peter was clean, but he had to wash his foot, for he had in his turn the sin of the first man, when the serpent tripped him up and persuaded him to go astray (cf. Gen. 3:1–7). Therefore his foot is washed so that hereditary sins may be removed. Our own sins, on the other hand, are remitted by baptism."[20]

The explanation anticipates the concept of original sin that gained a wide audience through the writings of Augustine, who was baptized by Ambrose in 387. The second is "the spiritual seal" that follows the vesting of the newly baptized in white garments. "Recall, then, that you received a spiritual seal, 'the Spirit of wisdom and understanding, the Spirit of counsel and power, the Spirit of knowledge and piety, the Spirit of holy fear' (Isa. 11:2), and maintain what you have received."[21] The problem for contemporary scholars is that we do not possess sufficient evidence to know exactly what Ambrose meant by "the spiritual seal." It may have been an anointing or possibly a laying on of hands.[22] The theological importance of this surfaces in later debates over the number of true sacraments, and whether confirmation as it is currently practiced in the Roman Catholic Church is being described here by Ambrose.

Ambrose's commentary also anticipates future theological debates over the real presence of Christ in the Eucharist. After comparing the manna given to the Israelites to the Eucharist, Ambrose comments, "You have understood what is more excellent, for light is better than shadow, reality is better than symbol, the body of the Creator is better than the manna from heaven.

Perhaps you will say: 'I see something else. How can you assert to me that what I am receiving is the body of Christ?'"[23] In responding to his rhetorical question, Ambrose recounts some of the miraculous events in the Old Testament: Moses performing miracles before Pharaoh (e.g., Exod 4:1–5), the exodus (Exod 14), Joshua parting the Jordan River (Josh 3:7–17), water flowing from a rock (Exod 17:1–7), Moses purifying a spring with a piece of wood (Exod 15:22–25), and Elisha raising a sunken iron axe head (2 Kgs 6:5–7). "If a human blessing was so powerful that it could alter nature, what shall we say of that divine consecration in which the very words of the Lord, the Savior, are at work?" Ambrose adds, "The Lord himself declares: 'This is my body' (Matt. 26:26). Before the blessing with heavenly words occurs it is a different thing that is referred to, but after the consecration it called a body."[24] While the exact nature of the change to which Ambrose refers would be a source of great debate in subsequent centuries, Ambrose saw the eucharistic celebration of the fitting culmination of the initiation process. As the theologian Gary Macy writes, "For Ambrose, all things have been given a new identity in Christ. As the catechumens became new people through baptism, so in the celebration of the eucharist, the bread becomes the body of Christ."[25]

Ambrose's entire outlook on the sacraments is rooted in the conviction that God is mysteriously at work in them. As the theologian Craig Alan Satterlee writes, "For Ambrose, there is more going on in the rites of initiation than what is perceivable by human sight. Ambrose was convinced that the Triune God is present in the rites of initiation to both give the neophytes faith and to enable them to see the mysteries, themselves, and the world through the eyes of faith that they have received."[26] In *On the Sacraments*, Ambrose recalls the cure of the man born blind (John 9:1–12). Jesus applied mud to his eyes and told him to go wash in the pool of Siloam. When the man did so, he recovered his sight. For Ambrose, those who were washed in the pool of baptism had their eyes opened as well. "You went there, you washed, you came to the altar, you began to see what you had not seen before: that is to say, through the font of the Lord and the preaching of the Lord's passion, at that moment your eyes were opened. Before you seemed to be blind of heart; but now you began to perceive the light of the sacraments."[27] In *On the Mysteries*, Ambrose reaffirms his conviction that God is at work in the church through the sacraments. "I believe that the Lord Jesus is present when he is called upon in the prayers of the priests. . . . Where the church is, where the mysteries are, there he graciously grants his presence."[28] While Ambrose asserted that sacraments effect a change in those who participate in them and that God draws near to us through them, he did not offer a precise description of how exactly that occurred. Medieval scholastic theologians would be far more interested in the question of sacramental causality, and their way of thinking about the sacraments would shape the church's theology down to the present day. It is this heritage that provides the starting point for our discussion of the contemporary theologian Louis-Marie Chauvet.

Like houses, theological positions rest on unseen foundations. In the case of Ambrose, his preaching about the meaning of baptism or the Eucharist rested on a number of key assumptions drawn from the Platonic tradition regarding the relationship between the material, changing world that we perceive through our senses and the immaterial, unchanging world that we grasp through the use of our reason. If a building's foundation crumbles, the entire structure collapses. Later builders will salvage what they can or add new elements to the mix and construct what they believe to be a more durable structure. The same is true of Christian thought. As Platonic ideas were discarded, new foundations were sought for Christian theology and new theological systems were built. Some endured, but many fell. In our own day, postmodern thinkers believe that the foundational assumptions upon which much of modern philosophy has rested have crumbled. They even question whether the metaphor of a foundation is an accurate one when describing human knowledge. One such thinker is the postmodern theologian Louis-Marie Chauvet, and we will explore his proposals for understanding the sacraments as we make our way among the ruins of past theological fortresses.

CHAUVET'S THREE MODELS

Before Chauvet turns his attention to his own constructive proposals in his work *The Sacraments: The Word of God at the Mercy of the Body*, he situates his own approach in relation to three dominant models of sacramental theology. In the first, the objectivist model, we find a focus on the efficacy of the sacrament. Like a schematic diagram of a building's water system, this position speaks of the movement of grace from Christ to the church, and finally the grace is distributed through the sacraments. The sacraments channel the grace to those who are properly disposed to receiving it. In the second, the subjectivist model, God's spirit blows where it wills, and so the church plays a secondary role. Like a newspaper that reports what has happened elsewhere, the church is the gathering charged with proclaiming God's activity in our lives and in our world, but the church is not the primary locus of God's activity.[29] In the third, the Vatican II model, the church functions as the sacrament of salvation for the world. It is the means by which Christ's presence is mediated to the world, but the mediation is not understood in the mechanical manner that characterized the objectivist model. It shares with the subjectivist model the belief that the reign of God extends beyond the church, but it sees the church as playing an essential role in the mediation of God's grace.

Chauvet sees weaknesses in both the objectivist and subjectivist models, but because of the prominent role the objectivist model has played in history of Catholic sacramental theology, he concentrates on its drawbacks. His chief criticism is that this model reduces grace to an object, a thing that can be produced and transferred from one party to another. In this "productionist scheme," there is a great theological concern to show *how* grace is bestowed to the person through the sacrament. Consequently, the category of "causality" figures prominently in this model. In an earlier work, Chauvet points to Aquinas's treatment of the sacraments in the *Summa Theologiae* as a classic case in point. Chauvet argues that Aquinas's choice of terminology is significant: "sacraments *'cause* grace,' they *'work'* or *'produce'* it, they *'contain'* it, they *'add to'* grace considered in general a 'certain divine assistance.' They are 'necessary to produce certain special effects that the Christian life requires,' they *'confer* grace,' they derive their *'virtue of producing* [causativa] *grace'* from the Passion of Christ."[30] In this scheme, the priest is seen "less as a pastor and minister of the gospel than as a sacred intermediary" whose performance of the rite guarantees that the sacramental grace is actually bestowed on those who are properly disposed for receiving it.[31] Finally, as much as the sacraments are acts of the church, in the objectivist model "the whole perspective is rather individualistic: the church as a community of faith and mission is absent; when it is mentioned, it is essentially as an institution endowed by Christ with supernatural powers for the benefit of individuals."[32] The objectivist model, in Chauvet's view, is both theologically flawed and pastorally inadequate.

THE STRUCTURE OF CHRISTIAN EXISTENCE

Although Chauvet's theological training followed along fairly traditional scholastic lines in seminary, he became increasingly interested in postmodern thought, especially the philosophy of Martin Heidegger, through conversations with some of his fellow seminarians.[33] This postmodern turn in philosophy focused on questions regarding the role that language plays in shaping our view of reality. These philosophical discussions are often very abstract and couched in abstruse terms, but they do provide the necessary background for understanding Chauvet's sacramental theology. The traditional account of language assumes that language is a mirror that reflects the objective world to the mind of the human subject. In postmodern thought, our language plays a much more active role in shaping what we take to be reality. Reality is not simply something that is "there" waiting for a human subject to perceive it. Language does not merely *reflect* reality, but it actually *constructs* reality. Chauvet notes that "even though the physical composition of snow is the same every-where, it is not perceived in the same way by us Westerners and the Inuit who possess a score of words in their language to describe snow. For us, it goes without saying that work and play are separate, if not antagonistic, activities, but the same is not true of the Australian Aborgines, who have one word for both."[34]

A culture's "symbolic order" is the filter through which people understand both the world around them as well their own identity.

> In order for the [human] subject to reach and retain its status of subject, it must build reality into a "world," that is to say, a signifying whole in which every element, whether material (tree, wind, house) or social (relatives, clothing, cooking, work, leisure) is integrated into a sys-tem of *knowledge* (of the world and of society), *gratitude* (code of good manners, mythical and ritual code ruling relationships with deities and ancestors), and *ethical behavior* (values serving as norms of conduct).[35]

Acquiring a personal identity is, therefore, like learning a language.[36] It obviously requires mastering a body of knowledge, but true proficiency involves gaining fluency, appreciating nuance, and developing a rhetorical flair.[37] Language constructs a world, and the self inhabits it and makes it his or her own.

Chauvet's sacramental theology corresponds with his post-modern account of language. The categories of knowledge, grati-tude, and ethical behavior translate in theological terms into Scriptures, Sacraments, and Ethics. The Scriptures are the "foun-dational texts," and theology "is at the bottom nothing else than the orderly and critically organized elucidation of the difficulties present in our foundational texts."[38] The Sacraments are the celebrations of the mysteries contained within the foundational texts, and the Ethics are the actions that express individual and collective conformity to the way of life outlined in the foundational texts and celebrated in the sacraments. All three aspects are intertwined. This triad forms the basic symbolic order through which Christians view reality. Just as language mediates reality, the language of the church mediates our experience of the Risen Lord. Christian formation and discipleship consists, therefore, in gaining proficiency with the language of the church. "One becomes a Christian only by adopting the 'mother tongue' of the church."[39]

Chauvet illustrates this process of acquiring a Christian identity thorough his analysis of the Emmaus story (Luke 24:13–35). Following the crucifixion, two dejected disciples are traveling the seven-mile road from Jerusalem to Emmaus. They had received reports of the empty tomb, but they seem unsure what to believe. The Risen Lord draws near to them, but in a curious feature of this story, "their eyes were kept from recognizing him" (24:16). As they walk together along the way (an ancient expression referring to Christianity, see Acts 9:2), Jesus engages the two in conversation and explains the scriptures to them. As nightfall approaches, the two disciples ask Jesus to stay with them. "When he was at table with them, he took bread, blessed and broke it, and gave it to them. Then their eyes were opened and they recognized him; and he vanished from their sight" (24:30–31). The Risen Lord guides the disciples along "the way" by explaining the Scriptures to them. The disciples finally recognize Christ in the breaking of the bread (the verb sequence of Luke 24:30 recalls the Last Supper in Mark 14:22).[40] The Scriptures lead to the Sacrament. The Gospel of Luke and Acts emphasize how this community that breaks the bread together must share what they have with each other. In John's Gospel, the institution of the Eucharist is replaced with the washing of the feet. In both cases, the Sacrament leads to Ethics.[41]

CHAUVET'S SACRAMENTAL THEOLOGY

In his postmodern sacramental theology, Chauvet deliberately offers an account of the sacraments that contrasts with the one traditionally presented in Catholic theology in three important ways. First, he shifts attention away from the scholastic focus on "causality" to the postmodern emphasis on "mediation." This accounts for the prominence Chauvet assigns to "the body." As the theologian Luk De Volder explains, "In this new train of thought, L-M. Chauvet finds the words to describe the mediation structure or the symbolic order, i.e., the entirety of culture, language and symbols (signifiers) of which every human being is a part. He calls it the *'corporality'* (*'corporeite'*) of our existence.... Our body is more than mere flesh. Culture, history, space and time are also a part of it."[42] This shift leads to the second difference. Chauvet understands the traditional concept of "the efficacy of a sacrament" in a new way. Chauvet chooses "the path of the efficacy of the word, in human communication, and not the path of the efficacy of the 'instrument' as in classical theology" as the route for his discussion of the sacraments.[43] This path of "the efficacy of the word" carries Chauvet into a deep exploration of symbols and rituals in human communication. Lastly, Chauvet's rejection of the traditional objectivist model of the sacraments with its "productionist scheme" of grace requires that he offer a different account of the activity of God's grace in the sacraments.

Chauvet repeatedly insists that there is no unmediated reality. The spiritual is no exception to the rule. Chauvet claims that "faith cannot be lived in any other way, including what is most spiritual in it, than *in the mediation of the body*, the body of society, of a desire, of a tradition, of a history, of an institution, and so on. What is most spiritual always takes place in the most corporeal."[44] For Chauvet, "body" encompasses a wide array of realities that all play an essential role in mediating the spiritual to us through the sacraments.[45] Chauvet identifies three ways in which we can rightly say the body "plays its role in a ritual, therefore symbolic manner in the sacraments: (1) every individual body, through voice, gestures, postures, motions" (2) "the social body of the church," and (3) "the cosmic body, represented by a little water, bread and wine, oil, light or ashes, and received as God's 'creation.'"[46]

The issue of a sacrament's "efficacy" has been a long-standing topic in sacramental theology. The question takes on greater prominence in church history when controversies erupt over who has the authority to administer sacraments or what the number of true sacraments is. There was, however, always a crucial pastoral element involved in these debates because those who celebrated the sacraments wanted to be assured that the sacrament did, in fact, impart grace to those properly disposed to receive it. Chauvet prefers to speak of "symbolic efficacy." "Not only is language efficacious *but it is what is most efficacious.* However, let us hasten to specify that what is meant is a *symbolic* efficacy. By now it is clear: such an efficacy does not designate, as in science or technology, a transformation of the world but a transformation of subjects, a 'work' that is produced in them and allows them to accede to another way of being."[47] *Efficacy*, in Chauvet's use of the term, has little to do with the one who administers the sacrament and a great deal to do with those participating in the sacrament. For this reason, Chauvet insists that, "the efficacy of the sacraments has nothing of a guarantee....God gives freely through the power of the Spirit; but the fruitfulness of this gift in those who receive it, that is, the *reception* they give to this gift *as* grace, depends on their faith."[48]

Grace, then, for Chauvet is not a "reward" that is given by God and it certainly is not a "thing" that is produced through a sacrament. Chauvet insists, instead, that grace is both gratuitous (a pure gift from God) and gracious (that which is beautiful, possessing a value that cannot be calculated).[49] The symbol of the manna in the desert captures for Chauvet both elements of grace. It was a gift freely given by God for the well-being of the wayfarers in the desert, but it could not be stockpiled and commoditized. Those who stored some for the next day found in the morning that it had rotted and was worthless. The value of the gift is found only in sharing it with others. Chauvet draws upon the work of the cultural anthropologist Marcel Mauss to further illustrate his point. In his studies of Polynesian and Northwestern Native American cultures, Mauss reported the practice of gift-giving among members of the entire society. The curious feature of this practice for Westerners is that, in this elaborate system, the gifts that were exchanged were not of equal value. As the theologian Glenn Ambrose explains:

> The lavish gift-giving in these cultures defied the logic of the marketplace wherein one saved, invested and made only equal or advantageous trades....The extravagant symbolic exchanges...were basic acts of recognition that formed alliances and maintained order. For this reason, the gifts were not as free as they first appeared. Indeed, there was a system of "obligatory generosity" that demanded that there be a return gift. The return gift of the receiver was first and foremost the very recognition of the giver, expressed in terms of thankfulness, and secondly, there was an expectation that a return gift would be extended to a third party on an unspecified date. The [gift-giving] was then a social mechanism that not only forged social solidarity but also distributed the wealth of society.[50]

Grace, like manna, is a gift to be given, not a commodity to be stored.

How, then, does this focus on the body, symbolic efficacy, and the gift of grace translate into a theology of the Eucharist? The traditional Catholic eucharistic doctrine of Transubstantiation maintains that during Mass "the substance" (i.e., what something is in reality and not merely as it appears to the senses) of the physical bread and wine are changed into the Body and Blood of Christ.[51] In this view, the eucharistic "body" primarily refers to the consecrated host. Chauvet believes such an approach overlooks the role of the church as the Body of Christ. If we accept what the Catholic theologian Henri du Lubac called "the deadly dichotomy" between the eucharistic body and the ecclesial body, our eucharistic theology becomes distorted.[52] Chauvet is fond of quoting Augustine's eucharistic dictum, "Be what you see and receive what you are."[53] Augustine was imploring his congregation to see in the bread the Body of Christ so that they might better realize their own calling to be the Body of Christ (the church) in the world. Chauvet concentrates less on the issue of the bread being transformed into the Body of Christ (the consecrated host) and far more on the spiritual and ethical transformation of the Body of Christ (the church).[54] This is why Chauvet speaks of "symbolic efficacy." The efficacy of the sacraments, the assurance of grace, is demonstrated through our self-giving to others. The Liturgy of the Eucharist must flow seamlessly into "the liturgy of the neighbor."[55]

What insights into the search for God can be gleaned from Chauvet's postmodern sacramental theology? As Glenn Ambrose observes, "Rendering God 'present' as an object is the inherent danger Chauvet finds in [traditional theology]."[56] Chauvet speaks of the "necrotic temptation" to kill the Living God by locking God into our preconceived notions of who God is and where God is to be found. For example, Chauvet sees Christian identity as shaped by scripture, sacraments, and ethics. However, when we reduce God to an object "contained" in the Bible, in the sacraments, or in the service of others, we fall prey to the necrotic temptation.[57] Following upon the work of the philosopher and theologian Jean-Luc Marion, Chauvet sees all religious objects, activity, and deeds as having the possibility of being idols rather than icons. Idols present to our minds ways "for us to put our hands on the divine, to permanently place it at our disposal, to have it enslaved (and at the same time to be enslaved by it)." An icon, by contrast, accentuates "the non-visibility of precisely what it presents to the eye."[58] It is for this reason that Chauvet speaks of God as "different," "absent," and "silent." It is especially in the crucifixion that we realize, according to Chauvet, that we must leave behind a "simple notion" of God.[59]

Given Chauvet's emphasis on the role language plays in constructing "reality," his insistence on the impossibility of unmediated knowledge and his stress on the absence of God, we might conclude that Chauvet's approach leaves us with nothing more than agnosticism.[60] He, however, summons us during his analysis of the Emmaus story in Luke's Gospel to make the following theological leap of faith: "You too must convert your desire for immediacy and *assent to the mediation of the church.*"[61] We cannot have an unmediated experience of God. We can only know God through the life of the church in which we hear the Scriptures proclaimed, participate in the sacramental life, and go out into the world to serve in the name of the Lord. Drawing on the work of the theologian Stanislas Breton, Chauvet speaks of the written word being a "trace" of the actual event in history. The theologian David Power notes, "Breton likes to speak of 'trace' rather than representation and this carries over into Chauvet. God acts in human time, but what is left is the trace of the divine action. On the basis of the traces found in the Scriptures, the Church 'writes itself' through its preaching, its theology, its ritual, and its ethics."[62] As Chauvet puts it, "Through the Spirit, God becomes inscribed somewhere in humanity. But God is inscribed without being circumscribed, without being assigned to any one place."[63] Perhaps, then, Ambrose and Chauvet arrive at similar conclusions. When Satterlee describes Ambrose's basic conviction about the sacraments, it does not seem far removed from Chauvet's own postmodern position. "For Ambrose of Milan, through worship and preaching, God gives faith to perceive God's invisible activity in our lives and in the world. Ambrose declares, 'Through the font of the Lord and the preaching of the Lord's passion… your eyes were opened.' Seeing everything with eyes of faith, we pass into a new world of consciousness."[64] With the eyes of faith, Chauvet might say, we can detect the traces of God passing through time.

Discussion Questions

1. A traditional definition of a sacrament is "a visible sign of an invisible grace." What does that mean? What is meant by *sign* and *grace*? Do you accept that definition?

2. Ambrose wrote, "I believe that the Lord Jesus is present when he is called upon in the prayers of the priests....Where the church is, where the mysteries are, there he graciously grants his presence." Do you share Ambrose's belief? Why or why not?

3. Do the material elements included in the sacraments (water, bread, oil) represent spiritual realities? If so, offer a specific example.

4. What is the purpose of baptism?

5. Theologians traditionally have discussed the "efficacy" of the sacraments. Is that an important concern? Do you believe that the sacraments are "efficacious"?

6. In what ways do Ambrose and Chauvet agree and disagree about baptism?

7. In your view, do we encounter God through the sacraments?

Suggested Readings

For background on Ambrose, see the "Introduction" to Boniface Ramsey, *Ambrose* (New York: Routledge, 1997). For an examination of Ambrose's theology of baptism, see Craig Alan Satterlee, *Ambrose of Milan's Method of Mystagogical Preaching* (Collegeville, MN: The Liturgical Press, 2002); chapter 2 of Enrico Mazza, *Mystagogy* (New York: Pueblo Publishing Co., 1989); and chapter 4 of Everett Ferguson, *Baptism in the Early Church* (Grand

Rapids, MI: Eerdmans, 2009). See also chapter 3 of Maxwell E. Johnson, *The Rites of Initiation* (Collegeville, MN: The Liturgical Press, 1999).

For an introduction to Chuavet's theology, see Glenn P. Ambrose, *The Theology of Louis-Marie Chauvet* (Burlington, VT: Ashgate, 2012); and Timothy M. Brunk, *Liturgy and Life* (New York: Peter Lang, 2007). See also Vincent J. Miller, "An Abyss at the Heart of Mediation: Louis-Marie Chauvet's Fundamental Theology of Sacramentality," *Horizons* 24, no. 2 (1997): 230–47. For a collection of essays dealing with Chauvet's thought, see Philippe Bordeyne and Bruce T. Morrill, eds., *Sacraments: Revelation of the Humanity of God* (Collegeville, MN: The Liturgical Press, 2008). Joseph Christopher Mudd's dissertation dealing with Chauvet and Bernard Lonergan is available at: http://www.lonerganresource.com/pdf/dissertations/Eucharist %20and%20Critical%20Metaphysics_Joseph%20Mudd.pdf.

8

MORALITY:
RESPONDING TO GOD
Fritz Tillmann and
Servais Pinckaers

Thinking about the "search for God" often conjures up an image of a hermit sitting high atop a mountain absorbed in prayer. While the wisdom imparted by those who lived the life of solitude has been a constant source of spiritual nourishment for Christians, theirs is not the only way of finding God. For the vast majority of Christians, the search for God is intimately joined with the care of their family, support for their friends, and concern for the poor. As the First Letter of John reminds us, "Those who say, 'I love God,' and hate their brothers or sisters, are liars; for those who do not love a brother or a sister whom they have seen, cannot love God whom they have not seen. The commandment we have from him is this: those who love God must love their brothers and sisters also" (4:20–21). Moral theology is at its root the attempt to determine the way of life that most closely aligns with our deepest beliefs about God. In this chapter, we will follow the thinking of two influential moral theologians, Fritz Tillmann (1874–1953) and Servais Pinckaers (1925–2008), as they guide us to see and respond to both the presence of God and the needs of our neighbor.

CONSTRUCTING A MORAL THEOLOGY

Geologists tell us that the majestic Rocky Mountains formed when tectonic plates deep beneath the Earth's surface collided, heaving large sections of rock skyward. This process provides us with an image of how a moral theology takes shape. Our deepest convictions about the authority of the Bible, the nature of the human person, and the teaching of Christ are three of the "tectonic plates" that collide and give rise to our moral conduct.

While theologians agree that the moral life is grounded in Scripture, they frequently disagree about how the Bible is to be interpreted or how it should be applied to specific moral issues. As we saw in the earlier chapter on the Bible, some thinkers, such as Hugh of St. Victor, see the Bible as a source of divine revelation that contains several levels of meaning that can be brought to the surface through a spiritual reading of the text. Other thinkers, such as Sandra Schneiders, describe the Bible as a "revelatory text" that to some degree has been infected by the patriarchal attitudes of the biblical writers themselves.[1] These varying perspectives raise a host of questions about how to apply the biblical text to our own day and age. What weight should we give a set of biblical verses that advocates a certain practice (e.g., hierarchical household codes) or condemns a certain act (e.g., homosexual relations)? Instead of citing specific verses, should we be looking to extract general principles from the Bible (e.g., equality of all people)? Should Christians follow the lead of postmodern thinkers who insist that "meaning" is not a fixed idea located in a text, but rather is a fluid concept that emerges from a community's engagement with the text?

The second "tectonic plate" in the formation of a moral theology is our understanding of the human person. In terms of our search for God, it might turn out that the same innate capabilities that make it possible for us to make moral decisions (free will, conscience, etc.) might also help us find God. In our earlier discussion of Bernard of Clairvaux, we found that he believed

160

that all humans have a "natural kinship" with God based on the fact that we are created in the image of God. For Erasmus, our status as creatures created in the image of God means that we have free will; and for Copeland, it is the basis of our solidarity with the marginalized. If this is true, then the moral theologian's discussion of, among other things, conscience, free will, and the virtues might prove to be illuminating for our understanding of God's activity in our lives.

The third and most powerful force shaping our moral theology is our understanding of Christ and his mission. Just as Christ is the critical clue in our search for God, Christ's teachings are the signposts leading us along the moral path. In the discussion of Christ, we distinguished between the historical and dogmatic approaches to determining his identity. If we take the historical approach to his teachings, we might focus on Jesus' concern for the poor, his identification of the love of God and neighbor as the heart of the Law, and his disregard for social or religious strictures prohibiting contact with sinners. If we take the dogmatic approach, we might focus on his forgiveness of sins, his sacrificial death on the cross, or his role as judge at the end of time. In any event, both approaches converge on the same person who appears in a variety of ways throughout the gospels: the teacher in the Sermon on the Mount who challenges his hearers to turn the other cheek; the merciful and just Lord who pardons the woman caught in the act of adultery, but tells her to go and sin no more, and the fiery end-time prophet who warns us that we will be judged on how well we cared for the hungry, the homeless, and the imprisoned.

BACKGROUND TO FRITZ TILLMANN: THE MORAL MANUAL OF THOMAS SLATER

Given the high degree of diversity of biblical writings, understandings of the human person, and portraits of Jesus in the

Gospels, the number of combinations that could form a moral theology is exceedingly high. At the turn of the twentieth century, moral theology was most commonly presented in the form of a manual. As the name suggests, the moral manuals were systematic and orderly presentations of both the general and specific questions of moral theology. In his history of moral theology, the theologian John Gallagher observes, "General moral theology consistently dealt with the nature of the human act, conscience, law, and sin. Special moral theology considered the nature of sins. Some manuals defined sins as violations of the ten commandments, whereas others studied sins as acts contrary to the theological and cardinal virtues."[2] There were different points of emphasis in the works of the manualists (those who compose moral manuals) in the different religious orders (especially the Jesuits, the Dominicans, and the Redemptorists), but the similarity in their content far outweighed any structural variations.

The manuals served as the primary seminary texts for moral theology from the time of the Council of Trent (1545–63) to the Second Vatican Council (1963–67). Their origins can be traced back to the early Christian missionaries to Ireland who catalogued prescribed penances for various sins in texts known as "penitentials." With the later rise of canon law and the scholastic approach to theology in the universities, consideration was given to the nature of sin, the gravity of sin (e.g., mortal and venial sins), the issue of culpability (e.g., full consent of the will, sufficient reflection), and the role of conscience (correct conscience, certain conscience).[3] Further impetus for the manuals was given in 1215 when Pope Innocent III mandated that Catholics receive the Eucharist at least once a year during the Easter season. Catholics had to confess their sins to a priest so that they would be in a "state of grace" before receiving the Eucharist.[4] With the rise of the seminary system during the Counter Reformation of the sixteenth century, the manuals became a fixture in the seminary curriculum.

In the early twentieth century, the most popular moral manual in English was Thomas Slater's *A Manual of Moral Theology*.[5]

In this work, we can see how the three tectonic plates (Bible, human person, Christ) merge to form a moral theology that many found responsive to the needs of the church at that time. In terms of Slater's use of the Bible, the evaluation of the Protestant ethicist James Gustafson of the moral theology texts of that era seems applicable. "The Bible is used to substantiate the existence of a supernatural, ultimate end for man—namely, that he is to enjoy eternal beatitude in the vision of God. But the bulk of moral theology deals with the natural moral acts of man; here the Thomistic structure asserts itself vigorously as the dominant framework, and the Bible is quoted (so it appears to these Protestant eyes) to proof-text a point already established on principles independent of biblical discussion."[6] The understanding of the human person corresponds as well to the Thomistic definition of a human act. "The actions over which a man has control are in a special sense called human acts, because they are due to his free choice." In addition to free will, humans possess a rational nature that allows them to deliberate among possible choices. "For among the various objects offered to the will's acceptance, the reason can propose motives for the selection of one object rather than of another, and…until the deliberation is finished, the will need not decide between them."[7] In terms of Christ, there is a deep and abiding continuity between the Ten Commandments and the teachings of Christ. "If Our Lord called his precept of love new, He did not mean that the great commandment did not bind under the Old Law, but only that urged it anew, gave us new motives to practise it, and especially His own divine example and wish."[8]

Slater devotes a great deal of attention to the category of law in his moral theology. The natural law inscribed in our hearts by God, the Ten Commandments given to Moses, the teachings of Christ, and the laws promulgated by the Catholic Church form an unbroken chain in Slater's moral theology. "The great precepts of the natural law which binds all men are summed up in the Ten Commandments given by God to the Israelites, and which Our

Lord declared that he came not to destroy but to fulfil." Sin is likewise "defined as a free transgression of the law of God."[9] Given the prominent role that law plays in his exposition, we can conclude, then, that Slater understands holiness to be characterized by obedience.

THE MORAL THEOLOGY OF
FRITZ TILLMANN

Tillmann began his career as a scripture scholar, not as a moral theologian. He had written several works of his own when, in 1912, he edited a volume of scholarly articles devoted to the New Testament. In one of the articles written by Tillmann's friend Friedrich Wilhelm Maier, the author advocated the "two-source theory" that maintains that Matthew and Luke used both Mark and a collection of sayings of Jesus (known as Q) as sources when composing their own Gospels. Though widely accepted today, the two-source theory caught the eye of Vatican officials in 1912, and Tillmann was ordered to leave the field of New Testament study.[10] He became a moral theologian, and in 1937, published his popular overview of moral theology entitled *The Master Calls*. Tillmann brought his sensibilities as a biblical scholar to bear on the work, and in doing so, forged a new path in Catholic moral theology. The contemporary moral theologian James Keenan, who has almost single-handedly prevented Tillmann's work from slipping into the dustbin of history, speaks of it in glowing terms, "Demonstrating in 1937 a biblically based moral theology was, in my estimation, nothing short of miraculous."[11] The title, *The Master Calls*, is itself biblically based. It comes from a story dealing with Mary and Martha, the two sisters of Lazarus whom Jesus raises from the death. Martha calls to Mary, in the words of the old Douay version of the Bible, "The master is come, and calleth for thee" (John 11:28). Mary's response was immediate: "And when she heard it, she got up quickly and went to him" (11:29). Mary, then, represents the model of discipleship that we are all called to emulate; she is the one who responds when the Master calls.

Tillmann's overall approach differs noticeably from that found in Slater's text. As Keenan explains, "Tillmann's work is a thoroughgoing departure from the neo-Scholasticism of the moral manuals. By turning to the person of Jesus Christ, and by outlining the way of salvation according to the threefold Love Command, Tillmann gives us an integrated moral theology, rooted in the Sacred Scriptures, moving away from sin and toward union with God, neighbour, and self, deeply affected by Christian piety, and founded on love and the person of Jesus Christ."[12]

Tillmann did not eliminate all scholastic language or remove any mention of sin, but these elements are subsumed under the overarching theme of discipleship and the great command to love God "with all your heart, and with all your soul, and with all your mind" and to "love your neighbor as yourself" (Matt 23:37–38).

Tillmann's description of Christ as the Master might lead us to expect a strong emphasis on obedience, but Tillmann instead highlights the "irresistible attraction he exerts" and describes his disciples as those "captivated by love of him."[13] Those who take up the task of imitating the master are called to be nothing less than children of God. The loving master also makes demands of his followers. "When imitation and divine sonship are in question, Jesus allows no bargaining or bickering, no compromising. A man must be convinced that in order to lay hold of God and to become His child, no price can be too great, no burden too heavy." By submitting to the will of the Master, the Christian finds inner freedom. "Hence the Lord seeks to produce children of God who rest in God with every fiber of their beings and in all their activity, who find in devotion to Him the strength for the full development of their personalities, for interior freedom and complete detachment from the world."[14]

Detachment from the values and priorities of the world should not be confused with indifference toward our neighbors.

> He would certainly err who thought that the meaning of the following of Christ exhausted itself in God-soul and soul-God relationships and who perceived therein the sum-total of the Good News….However great stress [Christ] may have laid on the care of the soul as the one thing necessary—this soul which outweighs the whole world in value—still, in the field of man's endeavor, there are not two but three things that call for the same degree of attention: God, the soul, the neighbor.[15]

Indeed, Tillmann's text is divided into five parts: the first surveys the elements that comprise a life of "following Christ" and the fifth is a short section dealing with Christian marriage and church-state relations, but the three central parts that comprise the bulk of the work are devoted to the love of God, the love of self, and the love of neighbor, respectively. The range of topics included under this three-fold command of love varies from vegetarianism to capitalism.

GOD IN TILLMANN'S MORAL THEOLOGY

Tillmann's work, while addressing the question of how to best understand the moral life, also provides some helpful insights into the search for God. First of all, Tillmann emphasizes the connection between the moral life and the spiritual life (or "interior life"). Reflecting his training as a biblical scholar, he follows the lead of the prophets and of Christ himself as he traces all human moral activity back to the heart of the individual. "Thus [Christ] pointed out the birthplace of moral actions, both good and bad, as man's interior disposition. In this connection Jesus used the word 'heart' in the sense established in the language of the Old Testament and familiar to his hearers, to indicate the core of the religious and moral man as opposed to purely external behavior." Tillmann continues, "In other words, every act of man receives its moral imprint not from without, but from within, from his personal and interior life, from his good or bad disposition, which in the last analysis consists in his conformity to, or rebellion against the will of God."[16]

Determining the action that conforms to the will of God, of course, takes place in the conscience. While the word *conscience* itself does not appear in either the Old Testament or the Gospels (the preferred term being *heart*), the term does appear in Romans 2:15: "They show that what the law requires is written on their hearts, to which their own conscience also bears witness; and their conflicting thoughts will accuse or perhaps excuse them." Tillmann then concludes:

> For Paul, as previously for Jesus, the heart or the con-science is the guiding star of all religious and moral activity: "All that is not from faith is sin" (Rom. 14:23). Both share the conviction that the entire conduct of the Christian depends totally and decisively on the will of God and must be formed by that will. Only if man's conviction and God's will agree does the interior judgment, the dictate of conscience, assume unconditional validity and absolute binding force. Thus the voice of conscience in the disciples of the Lord is drawn into his new life in Christ, preserved against error and uncertainty, and becomes in the full sense *the voice of God in the soul* (emphasis added)."[17]

On this point, Tillmann is in agreement with the thinking of the great nineteenth-century Catholic intellectual and cardinal, John Henry Newman. In Newman's historical novel *Callista*, the main character gives voice to his own position:

> I feel that [one] God within my heart. I feel myself in His presence. He says to me, "Do this: don't do that." You may tell me that this dictate is a mere law of my nature, as is to joy or to grieve. I cannot understand this. No, it is

the echo of a person speaking to me. Nothing shall persuade me that it does not ultimately proceed from a person external to me. It carries with it its proof of its divine origin.[18]

If this is right, then our wrestling with our conscience may be spiritually akin to Jacob wrestling with the angel of God (Gen 32). Our moral struggles may be both a determined, honest effort to determine the proper course of action, and a source of contact with the One who speaks to us through our consciences.

The second feature of Tillmann's moral theology that sheds valuable light on our search for God is his spirituality of work for disciples.

Precisely because God is the very life of the soul, the disciple needs no special means to make Him present.... Where reverence for God nourishes and maintains the fire of devotion, the sense of His presence arises spontaneously and naturally, and expresses itself in the conduct of the disciple. There is no need for complicated system of rules and practices for which the hours of the day do not suffice. These things crush out the joyful and spontaneous and tend to disturb the principal thing: the daily duties of one's calling. This is shown by the example of the Lord; the Father was never so close to Him as when He was carrying out His messianic work. In his vocation and life's work, the disciple also must be conscious of God's presence. And so his love of God should develop and grow more profound, as he understands his vocation as a constant call of God and daily obeys that call.[19]

Just as Tillmann earlier described the conscience as the place where we hear the voice of God, it is in living our daily vocation that we respond to the "constant call of God." The active life, rather than being a distraction from God's call, is, in fact, the very place where that call is heard most clearly and lived most fully. In this way, the "will of God is like the disciple's daily bread."[20] It is the spiritual nourishment that sustains us on our journey.

The third feature of Tillmann's moral theology that sheds light on our search for God follows from his repeated insistence on the inseparable unity of the love of God, neighbor, and self. "The Christian loves himself truly only when his love includes his neighbor, who, like him, is an image of God and called to be a disciple of Christ. Thus the love of God, the love of self, and the love of neighbor can be visualized as three circles whose common center is God."[21] We tend to place on the circle devoted to the love of neighbor those whom we hold in high esteem, those who embody a set of values that we admire, but Jesus expanded the notion of who is our neighbor. Christ's litmus test for how well we love our neighbor is not how well we love those who embody noble virtues, but rather how well we love our enemies. Tillmann, in keeping with the message of Jesus, reminds us of the unsettling element of Christ's teachings: "the concept of 'neighbor' is extended to all men without distinction, even to enemies" and "a man has no true love at all unless he also loves his enemies."[22] Here, we confront the seemingly impossible demand that Christ placed on his disciples: "You have heard that it was said, 'You shall love your neighbor and hate your enemy.' But I say to you, Love your enemies and pray for those that persecute you, so that you may be children of your Father in heaven; for he makes his sun rise on the evil and the good, and sends rain on the righteous and on the unrighteousness" (Matt 5:43–45). When we can love our self, our friends, and our enemies with the same degree of love, then we have learned through God's grace, how to love as God loves. Those disciples who have been able to respond to this demanding call from the Master undoubtedly understand the nature of God in ways most of us can't begin to imagine.

Like Tillmann, Servais Pinckaers found the manualists' juridical account of the Christian moral life lacked the theological richness and spiritual vitality found in the classic Christian writings of

Paul, Augustine, and Aquinas.[23] In the same year that Pinckaers published his dissertation, Angelo Roncalli was elected pope and took the name John XXIII. Sensing a need for an updating of the church, John XXIII called the Second Vatican Council. Pinckaers shared the new pope's belief that a renewal of Catholic moral theology was needed. He writes:

> The perspective of the manuals reduces moral theology to the domain of legal obligations, an impoverishment arising from the separation of moral theology from asceticism and mysticism, both of which were now viewed as annexed disciplines. The theology of St. Thomas and that of the manuals constitute two different moral systems, both of which have their own inner logic. Consequently, the way to renew moral theology is by returning to St. Thomas, as the one who represents the best of the tradition nourished by the scriptures and the fathers of the Church.[24]

By returning to the ancient sources, Pinckaers insisted, we would restore the classic themes of happiness, friendship with God, and the gifts of the Spirit to their rightful place in a Christian account of morality.

Pinckaers presented his vision for moral theology in his *magnum opus, The Sources of Christian Ethics*, which appeared in English translation in 1995. The work falls into three parts. In the first part, Pinckaers paints in broad strokes the accounts of the Christian moral life found in classic Christian sources such as Paul's Letters, Augustine's *Commentary on the Sermon on the Mount*, and Aquinas's *Summa Theologiae*. In the second part, Pinckaers offers a short history of Christian ethics in which he narrates the story of how the common set of beliefs about the Christian moral life held by the luminaries such as Augustine and Aquinas begins to fragment under the influence of the philosophical movement of nominalism in the late Middle Ages (the chief representative of the movement is William of Ockham,

1288–1348). In the third part, Pinckaers focuses specifically on the issue of human freedom and suggests that Aquinas was right in situating freedom in the context of the virtues and the natural ends that we strive to achieve. With the recovery of this more holistic approach to morality, Pinckaers argues, moral theologians can draw upon the riches of the Christian tradition to craft a compelling account of the moral life that resonates with our natural desire to see God.

COMPETING ACCOUNTS OF THE CHRISTIAN MORAL LIFE

In Pinckaers's reading of Christian history, there are two dominant models of Christian ethics: one that focuses on the demands of moral obligation and another that situates morality within the broader question of human happiness. In the former, divine commands figure prominently, while in the latter, the virtues are central. While the former model won favor with the manualists, Pinckaers's own work is an extended argument for the superiority of the latter, as we can see in his own proposed definition of Christian ethics: "Christian ethics is the branch of theology that studies human acts so as to direct them to a loving vision of God seen as our true, complete happiness and our final end. This vision is attained by means of grace, the virtues, and the gifts, in light of revelation and reason."[25]

Pinckaers believes that a recovery of the virtues and a moral vision centered on genuine human happiness or fulfillment offers a number of advantages over the morality of obligation. First, it allows for a fuller appreciation of the range of writings found in the Bible. When reading the Bible through the lens of moral obligation, we focus on the legal writings, but gloss over the wisdom of Proverbs, the poetry of the Psalms, and the moral exhortation that Paul offers the earliest Christian communities. Second, an ethic of moral obligation leaves little room for the discussion of our friendship with God. As Pinckaers points out, friendship creates obligations, but obligations do not necessarily create friendship. In a similar vein, Pinckaers argues, obligations cannot produce true love, but true love can give rise to obligations. Third, an ethic of obligation assumes that morality has chiefly to do with rationality, and that passions and emotions are impediments to clear thinking. Pinckaers believes that such an approach "misunderstands the existence of what might be termed spiritual sensibility."[26] The medievals called the wisdom derived from this spiritual sensibility "connatural" knowledge. If connatural knowledge is, indeed, valid, then this suggests that humans possess a way of knowing truth that does not conflict with our rationality, but extends beyond it.

THE PATH OF HAPPINESS

The Sources of Christian Ethics can be seen as Pinckaers's account of the rise, fall, and possible recovery of the path of happiness in Catholic moral theology. Pinckaers traces the rise of this tradition, beginning with Paul's description of the way of life generated by faith in Christ. Faith, writes Paul, penetrates to the core of our being, which he describes as our "inner selves" (Eph 3:16; Rom 7:22), and stirs within us a deep desire to live according to Spirit and not the flesh (Gal 5:16). In Pinckaers's view, Paul "expresses in a single sentence the essence of Christian morality" in his Letter to the Galatians: "And the life I now live in the flesh I live by faith in the Son of God, who loved me and gave himself for me" (Gal 2:20).[27] In faith we are united with Christ (Rom 6:5); we are new creations in Christ (2 Cor 5:17) who died to our old selves and have been raised to new life in Christ through baptism (Rom 6:4). We are in a moral and spiritual sense "imitators of Christ," leading lives marked by humility, service, and above all, love. Paul does not develop a systematic moral theory as much as offer an account of the Christian life as grounded in faith, characterized by love, and sustained by hope. He then responds to the various moral questions presented to him by the churches based on their shared belief that they have been called to follow the example of Christ who handed himself over for us (Eph 5:2) so that we might be slave to sin no more (Rom 6:6), but capable of discerning "what is the will of God, what is good and acceptable and perfect" (Rom 12:2).

Deeply steeped in Paul's theology, Augustine echoed many of Paul's themes in the *Commentary on the Sermon on the Mount*, especially in his treatment of the Beatitudes (Matt 5). Augustine maintains that in the Sermon we find "the perfect pattern of the Christian life."[28] In keeping with ancient numerology, Augustine identifies seven (the number of perfection) beatitudes, designating the eighth as a summary of those that preceded it. Augustine's spiritual interpretation of the Beatitudes (which appear in a slightly different order than the one found in our present translations) sees each of them corresponding to a virtue on the ascent to spiritual wisdom. Augustine believes our spiritual and moral journey begins with a sense of humility possessed by those who are "poor in spirit." They have a clear-eyed assessment of our human condition and our complete dependence upon God. The meek are those who resist evil. Those who mourn have lost their former love for the things of this world, but are comforted by the Holy Spirit as they develop a new love for eternity. As they begin to hunger and thirst for righteousness, they are filled with mercy as they come to the aid of the poor. Those on this spiritual ascent become the clean of heart who yearn to see God. At the seventh and final stage on this ascent, the Christian reaches the summit of peacefulness. "Perfection lies in peace, where nothing is at war; and the children of God are peaceful for the reason that no resistance to God is present."[29]

Aquinas's *Summa Theologiae*, with its precise definitions and highly defined structure, seems at first glance to be far removed from Augustine's *Commentary on the Sermon on the Mount*. Pinckaers, however, contends that this initial impression is misleading, for while the writing style of the two authors differs significantly, the account of the Christian life contained in each is remarkably similar. In a section of the *Summa* (Ia–IIae, qq. 106–8) that Pinckaers labels "a small masterpiece," Aquinas discusses "the New Law" of Christ.[30] While many of Aquinas's interpreters would see in this expression an endorsement of an ethic of obligation, Pinckaers argues for its deep affinity with the thought of Paul and Augustine.[31] The New Law is not a list of precepts to be followed, but is rather the working of the Holy Spirit that has been "infused" or "instilled in our hearts."[32] It is a fulfillment of the promise of Jeremiah of the time in which God will make a new covenant with the people. "But this is the covenant that I will make with the house of Israel after those days, says the Lord: I will put my law within them, and I will write it on their hearts; and I will be their God, and they shall be my people" (Jer 31:33). As the influence of New Law increases within us, we develop the virtues of faith, hope, and love, and interestingly, according to Aquinas, we gain increased freedom. Pinckaers notes that it strikes modern readers as paradoxical to say that the increase of the New Law promotes greater freedom, but for Aquinas, freedom is always connected with the goal of human happiness or fulfillment in God. "This is precisely why the New Law is called 'the law of freedom': the action of the Spirit through the virtues creates within us a spontaneous, personal movement toward good acts."[33]

It is nominalism that shatters the Augustinian-Thomistic synthesis in which freedom and law play complementary roles, and in which the virtues are the primary concern of moralists who see the Christian life in terms of the human heart's pursuit of happiness. Nominalism dealt with the abstract philosophical question of whether "universals" exist. For example, we call various things in this world "beautiful." How do we explain this philosophically? Is there a pure eternal essence of beauty that all beautiful things in this world reflect in the some way (as Plato held), or do we name (nominalism) various things in this world "beautiful" and then create a theory of what constitutes beauty based on our various usages of the term? If the nominalists were wrong, then we can rightly speak of "the good" toward which all human beings are naturally drawn. If the nominalists were correct, then "the good" is determined by whatever God wills, and freedom—both human and divine—is the ability to do what one wills apart from any external influence. The formation of character through the practice of the virtues was now seen as an impediment to human freedom. God's absolute freedom could not be constrained in any way. God could therefore theoretically command a person to hate rather than to love God.

As Pinckaers sees it, the task before contemporary moral theologians is to regain the ancient understanding of freedom as a "freedom for excellence" as opposed to the "freedom of indifference" that grew out of the nominalist movement. A "freedom of indifference" is simply the "power to choose between contraries."[34] A person is free when he/she is able to sin or not sin. A "freedom for excellence," by contrast, consists of the progressive mastery of skills that allows us to move toward our desired goal of human fulfillment. Pinckaers applies the two understandings of freedom to learning to play the piano. A student is certainly free to hit the keys in a haphazard manner, but "the person who really possesses the art of playing the piano has acquired a new freedom. He can play whatever he chooses, and also compose new pieces. His musical freedom could be described as the gradually acquired ability to execute works of his choice with perfection."[35] Rather than seeing human choice as either an act of human freedom *or* of God's activity, Pinckaers believes that a freedom for excellence provides the framework for seeing the two working in unison. "The nearer man approaches to God through the moral progress that weakens his inclination to sin, the more he grows in full freedom, sharing in the divine freedom itself."[36]

GOD IN PINCKAERS'S MORAL THEOLOGY

In terms of how we think about the Christian moral life, Pinckaers sees two options before us: the path of obligation and

the path of happiness. Not only do the two paths offer competing views of law, freedom, and sin, each presents a different
understanding of God. "A moral theory of obligation," writes
Pinckaers, "depicts God as an all-powerful legislator issuing his
law in the midst of thunder and lightning. This is a God to inspire
fear and trembling, a sovereign Judge. The contemporary reaction
to such a picture has the advantage of highlighting the goodness
of God." He does not, at this point, explicitly state the understanding of God underlying the path of happiness, but instead
offers a cautionary note. "Yet there is a risk of devaluation. In
removing from God all power of judgment and punishment, and
in focusing exclusively on his universal pardon, we are left with a
soft and spineless God. Here we encounter one of the major
problems of Christian ethics today: how to reconcile God's love
and justice. Both stand at the very heart of morality."[37]

The challenge, then, for readers of Pinckaers is to extract from
his work a portrait of God that contrasts with the one found
along the path of obligation, without underwriting a "soft and
spineless view of God." Following Pinckaers's lead, we will see if
elements drawn from the Beatitudes as well as from Augustine's
and Aquinas's theology can be melded into a coherent whole.
The portrayal of God that emerges from this process would be
clearest alternative to the understanding of God found in the
moral theories of those who understand the Christian life in
terms of obligation.

In order to assemble the basic model, we need to retrace our
steps and return to the main sources of Pinckaers's own thought:
Paul's Letters, Augustine's theology, and the moral theology of
Aquinas as expressed in the *Summa Theologiae*. According to
Pinckaers, the cornerstone of Paul's theology is the transformative power of faith in Christ. By reading Paul's Letter to the
Romans, Pinckaers insists, "we see clearly that faith in Christ
influences all aspects of the Christian personality, from its inmost
depths to external actions."[38] Through faith, we experience a
reorientation of our whole being, a turn, as Paul describes it, from

the things of the flesh to the things of the Spirit. "For those who live according to the flesh set their minds on the things of the flesh, but those who live according to the Spirit set their minds on the things of the Spirit. To set the mind on the flesh is death, but to set the mind on Spirit is life and peace" (Rom 8:5–6). Later, Paul adds, "For all who are led by the Spirit of God are children of God" (Rom 8:14). One of the leading themes in Augustine's theology is the restlessness of the human heart. In the opening paragraph of his *Confessions*, Augustine pens one of his most famous lines, "The thought of you [God] stirs him so deeply that he cannot be content unless he praises you, because you made us for yourself and our hearts find no peace until they rest in you."[39] The Augustine scholar Maria Boulding translates the middle portion of the quote as "you have made us and drawn us to yourself."[40] Not only does Boulding's expression "drawn us" recall Christ's own words in John's Gospel ("No one can come to me unless drawn by the Father who sent me," John 6:44), but it also dovetails nicely with a point that Pinckaers emphasizes; namely, that one of Aquinas's favorite expressions when describing the gifts of the Holy Spirit is "instinct."[41] Our natural instinct for truth and goodness "is at bottom an instinct for God."[42] The same can be said of our natural instinct for family and friends. "Our relationship to God is not something external, but operates within family and social relationships and is fulfilled through them."[43]

We now have the basic components of our concept of God, but we need to find an image that will unite them. From Paul, we have a reorientation of our inmost being, a turning to the things of the Spirit that makes us children of God. From Augustine, we have the restlessness of the human heart and our desire to return to the Father who draws us home. Lastly, from Aquinas, we have a positive assessment of the instincts at the core of our being, including the love of a parent for a child. All of these elements are present in the parable of the prodigal son (Luke 15:11–32). The son has abandoned his home to pursue happiness, but his search is misguided. In a decisive moment of clarity, he turns back to his father and begins the long journey home. Unlike the older brother who protests in the name of justice, the merciful father runs to meet him, embraces his son, and calls for a celebration. In his own reflection on Rembrandt's painting *The Return of the Prodigal Son*, the spiritual writer Henri Nouwen writes, "Here is the God I want to believe in: a Father, who from the beginning of creation, has stretched out his arms in merciful blessing, never forcing himself on anyone, but always waiting; never letting his arms drop down in despair, but always hoping that his children will return so that he can speak words of love to them and let his tired arms rest on their shoulders."[44] The image of God that emerges from the pages of *The Sources of Christian Ethics* leaves us with the strong impression that Pinckaers shared Nouwen's belief.

Discussion Questions

1. Are there moral teachings found in the Bible that are no longer binding on Christians today? What implications follow from your answer?

2. What are the advantages and disadvantages of having a manual textbook for moral theology?

3. What is the moral vision offered by Christ in his teachings? Was Christ speaking literally when he commanded us to love our enemies and turn the other cheek?

4. Does God speak to us through our consciences? What implications follow from your answer?

5. What does Pinckaers mean by "an ethic of obligation" and "an ethic of happiness"? What is a specific example of each? Which is the more accurate account of the Christian moral life?

6. What are the skills that we need to cultivate to live moral Christian lives?

7. What view of God is implied in the moral theology you hold to be true?

Suggested Readings

For background on Tillmann, see chapter 4 of James F. Keenan, *A History of Catholic Moral Theology in the Twentieth Century* (New York: Continuum, 2010); and chapter 8 of John A. Gallagher, *Time Past, Time Future* (Mahwah, NJ: Paulist Press, 1990).

For an anthology of writings by Pinckaers, see John Berkman and Craig Steven Titus, eds., *The Pinckaers Reader* (Washington, DC: The Catholic University of America Press, 2005). Titus also has written a helpful article, "Servais Pinckaers and the Renewal of Catholic Moral Theology," *Journal of Moral Theology* 1, no. 1 (2012): 43–68. Both the Summer/Fall issue of *Josephinum* 17, no. 2 (2010); and the January issue of *The Thomist* 73, no. 1 (2009) are dedicated to Pinckaers's moral theology.

9

RELIGIONS OF THE WORLD: LISTENING FOR GOD

Jean Daniélou and Raimon Panikkar

Should Christians believe that God speaks only through Christ, or if we listen carefully, can we hear the voice of God in other religions? This question has occupied Christian thought from its outset as the earliest Jewish-Christians sought to integrate their newfound faith in Jesus with their ardent desire to remain faithful to Israel's covenants with God. Early Christian missionaries likewise faced a unique challenge when they had to determine which religious requirements should be placed on pagan converts to Christianity. In this chapter, we will examine the theology of Jean Daniélou (1905–74) as expressed in his 1946 work *The Salvation of the Nations*, and Raimon Panikkar (1918–2010) as found in his 2006 work *The Experience of God*. Daniélou played a pivotal role in shifting Catholic attitudes toward a more positive assessment of the world's religions in the years leading up to Vatican II (1962–65), and Panikkar was one of the most influential and creative Catholic theologians involved in interreligious dialogue in the past several decades.

THE FULFILLMENT THEORY
OF JEAN DANIÉLOU

As a student at the Sorbonne, Jean Daniélou began a lifelong study of ancient pagan and Christian writings that would profoundly shape his theological views toward the world's religions.[1] A member of the Society of Jesus, Daniélou began his roughly twenty-five-year tenure at the Institut Catholique in Paris at the age of thirty-seven. Along with his fellow Jesuit theologian Henri de Lubac, Daniélou spearheaded a movement in Catholic theology (*"nouvelle theologie"*) that sought to recover the theological and spiritual wisdom of the early church and reclaim its deep appreciation for biblical symbolism and liturgical expression. The approach and insights of Daniélou and his colleagues gained official recognition at the Second Vatican Council at which Daniélou served as a *peritus* (expert). His influence is evident in the documents of the Council dealing with the role of the church in the modern world (*Gaudium et spes*), the church's missionary activity (*Ad gentes*), and the relationship between the Catholic Church and the various religions (*Nostra Aetate*). Pope Paul VI appointed him a cardinal in 1969. His death in 1974 on the stairs of a brothel in Paris generated a great deal of whispering in church circles, though the reasons for his visit were far more likely pastoral than salacious.

Daniélou's own position regarding the relationship between Christianity and the other world religions is often labeled as a "fulfillment theory." In one of his earlier works, Daniélou explained, "I do not say [the other religions] are completely false: Judaism, Buddhism, the fetishist civilizations are not so much false as *old*: that is to say, they belong to the time before Christianity, and are, in some way, survivals; Christianity which perfects them has come and henceforth all that was good in them is fulfilled in it."[2] In a paper delivered at a symposium almost twenty years later, his position remained unchanged: "We are to avoid the extremes both of syncretism, which classifies Christianity as simply part of the general phenomenon of religion, while granting its preeminence, and sectarianism, which fails to recognize positive content in non-Christian religions."[3]

For Daniélou, Christianity fulfills both the "pagan" (or "cosmic") religions and Judaism. As scholars in the nineteenth and twentieth centuries investigated the beliefs and practices of the world's religions, both ancient and modern, they were struck by the similarities between the pagan practices and many traditional Christian acts of faith. This commonality was interpreted in one of two ways. Using terms employed by Daniélou at the symposium, the syncretists viewed the pagan and Christian practices as equally valid expressions of the same human experience, and the sectarians viewed these pagan practices as nothing more than idolatry. Daniélou, by contrast, argued, "The pagan religions are like rays of cosmic revelation, refracted through a humanity spoiled by sin and not yet enlightened by positive revelation." For example, various pagan religions had a myth that attributed the change of seasons to a deity's primal death and rebirth, practiced a ritual of initiation that included immersion in water, or included sacred stories involving the gods visiting a sacred mountain. For Daniélou, such similarities are shadowy reflections of the time when the fullness of truth would be revealed by Christ. "By revealing the new birth of faith, biblical religion does not destroy the riches of the religious soul, but rather takes them over. Whereas pagan prayer often goes astray in its reach for an object, and incarnates it in an illusory god, Christian piety is directed to the Father of Jesus Christ, to God, the Three in One. But it is the full range of the religious instinct that, once directed towards its true goal, finds there its fulfillment."[4]

Judaism, Daniélou insists, involves the one true God, but here, too, Judaism plays a preparatory role in terms of its relationship to Christianity. "Before He came in the flesh and accomplished fully the mystery of the salvation of the world, and the mystery of the salvation of the nations, the Word of God Himself began by preparing His ways in history. As a first step toward this, God chose Abraham and his race to tell them something of the mystery of Christ, in a way obscure and hidden, but none the less quite real." Daniélou employs the typological method of biblical interpretation that we discussed earlier in the chapter devoted to Hugh of St. Victor. In this method of biblical interpretation, persons and events in the Old Testament prefigure persons and events in the New Testament: The manna provided to the Israelites in the desert is a "type" of the Eucharist; the bronze serpent raised on a pole by Moses is a foreshadowing of the crucifixion (John 3:14), and Jonah's three days in the belly of the whale is a prefigurement of Christ's three days in the tomb (Matt 12:40). "Indeed, the whole of the Old Testament is a prefiguration of the New, inasmuch as through the events it relates we see dimly those same ways of God which the New Testament manifests so much more clearly."[5]

The influence of Daniélou's theology—both his positive assessment of the world's religions (against the sectarians) as well as his insistence that all religions find their ultimate fulfillment in Christ (against the syncretists)—can be detected in an important passage in the Vatican II document, *Lumen gentium.*

> For those also can attain eternal salvation who without fault on their part do not know the Gospel of Christ and His Church, but seek God with a sincere heart, and under the influence of grace endeavor to do His will as recognised through the promptings of their conscience. Nor does divine providence deny the help necessary for salvation to those who, without fault on their part, have not yet reached an explicit knowledge of God, and yet endeavor, not without divine grace, to live a good life, for whatever goodness or truth is found among them is considered by the Church as a preparation for the Gospel, a gift from Him who enlightens every man that he may finally have life.[6]

The historical importance of the passage lies in its rejection of the ancient idea, "Outside the church, there is no salvation," but it also echoes Daniélou's belief that God's revelation extends beyond the boundaries of Christianity. Like the bishops, Daniélou also regarded "whatever goodness or truth" he discovered as a "preparation for the Gospel," a gift from the Word who enlightens everyone that all may have life. It should also be noted that while the bishops made repeated calls throughout the conciliar documents for respect and cooperation among all religions, in *Nostra Aetate*, they made special note of the unique relationship between Christians and Jews. Citing the "common spiritual heritage" shared by Christians and Jews, the bishops denounced "all hatreds, persecutions, displays of antisemitism leveled at any time or from any source against the Jews."[7]

SETTING THE FRAMEWORK: SALVATION HISTORY

In *The Salvation of the Nations*, Daniélou provides a succinct account of his views toward the world's religions. In broad terms, this account consists of three major parts. Daniélou first presents the framework for a Christian understanding of the religions; second, he presents his method of engaging the religions of the world from a Christian perspective; and lastly, he envisions the desired outcome of this type of engagement for Christians.

The concept that underlies Daniélou's theological view of the world's religions is "salvation history"—a Christian view of history in which "the Word is made progressively manifest through the course of human history." He describes the history prior to the time of Christ as "divine pedagogy" (see Gal 3:24) preparing humanity for the fullness of revelation in Christ.[8] Daniélou sees this "divine pedagogy" unfolding in three stages, beginning with the moment of creation. The word of God was present at creation—it is for this reason that the natural world can reveal God in a way that those who have no contact with the historical revelation of the word can detect and admire. The second mission is found in the covenants with Israel. The covenants, the patriarchs and matriarchs, the various Old Testament priests, prophets, and kings as well the key events in the Old Testament prepare the way for the Messiah. The third mission, "the decisive stage in the manifestation of the Word in the world," is the Incarnation in which "the Word became flesh and lived among us" (John 1:14).[9]

ENGAGING THE RELIGIONS: MISSIONARY ACTIVITY

For Daniélou, Christians engage other religions through missionary activity. In order for the Gospel message to be well received and eventually flourish, Christian missionaries need to be attentive to the dual nature of their task: enculturation and transformation. If other cultures are going to embrace Christianity, Christian missionaries must adopt the way of life of the people whom they serve. Cultures have deeply rooted beliefs and traditions; therefore, those who bring the Gospel message to a new land must respect the cultural landscape and be sensitive to the local customs. Christians shouldn't presume that Gothic cathedrals are appropriate for China. Nor should they expect everyone to think in the categories provided by Aristotle. "People must be taken as they are, and diverse types of mental structure must be allowed for. It is good, it is normal, that Christianity should become incarnate in these structures." The Gospel call to conversion, however, cannot be blunted. "At the same time, we must not forget that this is merely the first step, that we must turn towards the world only in order to turn the world towards Christ." Just as each person must be transformed by the Spirit to become more Christ-like, the culture that is touched by the Gospel must be transformed by the Spirit in order for it to become more Christ-like. The Christian's engagement with the world involves this constant give and take. "Missionary activity consists in discerning all that is good in civilizations and cultures, so as to permeate them with Christianity and offer them up to Christ; meanwhile discerning all that is false, so that it may be eliminated and rejected."[10]

Daniélou insists that this dynamic process of enculturation and transformation has been at work in Christianity since its earliest days. Early Christian liturgy, for example, borrowed heavily from the synagogue service. Furthermore, the early Christians retained the dates in the pagan calendar, but had them serve a Christian purpose. "Christianity itself did not scruple to celebrate on the day of the winter solstice, when the *Natale Solis invicti* [Birthday of the Unconquered Sun] was celebrated, the birth of Christ, demonstrating by this means that He was indeed the eternally risen sun of the new Creation."[11] The challenge for the missionary is to determine which customs or traditions can be adapted and which beliefs or practices are non-negotiable.

THE DESIRED OUTCOME: UNITY IN CHRIST

What is the long-term goal of the church's engagement with the religions of the world? For Daniélou, it is nothing less than unity in Christ. The descent of the Holy Spirit at Pentecost signaled a new era in history. "Pentecost restored what had been broken; once again men of all nations communicated in the unity of the Spirit, by virtue of which a common language has been restored. Thus, the mystery of Pentecost inaugurated the economy [God's plan of salvation] in which we now live." The church's task in this final stage of salvation history is to grow into greater sacramental unity with Christ and preach the Gospel to all the nations. At the close of history, all will be united in Christ. "Not only shall we enjoy a vast blossoming of charity when all nations are gathered together in Christ, but also an increase in light in the measure that revelation becomes more luminous to us by having been expressed through all the nations of the earth."[12]

SEARCHING FOR GOD IN DANIÉLOU'S THEOLOGY

Salvation history provides the context in which Daniélou views the religions of the world. Not only does any mention of a "plan of God in history" raise the question of how human free will fits into such a scheme (as we discussed earlier with Erasmus), but it also assumes that God unilaterally intervenes in dramatic ways at various points in human history. These events, which Daniélou labels "divine irruptions," "wonders of God," and miracles of God (*mirabilia Dei*), include the key moments in salvation history, such as the creation of the world, the call of Abraham, the covenant with Moses, the Incarnation, and the Second Coming. "Faith does not consist in the belief that God exists, but that God intervenes in history. This is what seems unreasonable to humans: that at the heart of the framework of ordinary events, in the midst of the determinism of physics and the chain of sociological facts, there are irruptions of God—a properly divine activity—in which God creates, visits, and saves."[13] The search for God, therefore, focuses on the decisive moments in the plan of God that began with creation, found ultimate expression in Christ, and continues until the Last Day.

When we contemplate God's greatness manifested in these "divine irruptions," insists Daniélou, our hearts and minds fill with adoration for God. "To pray is first to discover what God is in himself and to wonder at it. Adoration means to awaken ourselves to the wonders of God, the *mirabilia Dei*, and let them astonish and delight us."[14] Adoration springs from our recognition of God's majesty and grandeur: "God's attraction is so compelling that the moment we glimpse it, it draws from our souls the cry of that admiration by which the soul knows that it adores. Adoration is that highest form of admiration addressed only to God because He absolutely surpasses all limitations that creatures bring to their admiration. And this is the noblest sentiment a man can experience."[15] Adoration is each person's own surrender to the God who disrupts plans, who called Abraham to leave his home and travel to a distant unknown land, who sent Moses who was slow of speech to the mighty Pharaoh, and who entrusted the birth of the Messiah to a young unmarried woman.

While the history of salvation is punctuated by a series of dramatic divine interventions, it is sustained by the constant presence of the God who dwells among us.

> The mystery of this "dwelling" is one of the great mysteries of the Old Testament. God dwells in the midst of his people. Dwelling means a *continual presence* as a principle of intimacy and a whole dynamic of relationships. This mystery is fully expressed in Christ in whom God dwells: "The Word was made flesh and dwelt among us" (John 1:14). He continues this dwelling in us, who are the "temples of the Spirit." That God dwells in the accessible depths of our soul is an incredible reality.

Salvation history, then, is as much about the God who appears on Mt. Sinai as it is about the God who whispers to us in the depths of our souls. We often find God by moving away from the noise of our lives, but we can also find God in the midst of the commotion of our lives. "There is certainly a way of finding God in his creative and effective activity in the world. We participate in it to the extent that we do our best to conform our lives, in their professional, familial, or intellectual dimensions, to the accomplishment of God's plan." For Christians, the plan of God is nothing less than becoming Christ to others. "The Christian life consists in allowing the Holy Spirit to transform us gradually into Christ. The unique end of every person is to become another Christ."[16]

CONCLUDING THOUGHTS ON DANIÉLOU

Daniélou's theology played a major role in changing Catholic attitudes toward the religions of the world. While maintaining the centrality of Christ, Daniélou provided a very positive assessment of the riches found in the world's religions. The influence of his work is clearly seen in the documents of Vatican II, especially *Nostra Aetate*. In the years following Vatican II, however, many scholars have questioned whether Daniélou's position fully appreciates the intrinsic value of the world's religions. Does the category of salvation history reduce all other religions to mere "preparations" for the Gospel? Shouldn't thinking about the other religions in terms of missionary activity be replaced with genuine interreligious dialogue? Does the goal of unity in Christ negate the salvific value of the other religions? It is with these questions in mind that we turn our attention to the pioneering work of Raimon Panikkar.

In Raimon Panikkar, we find not only a scholar specializing in the field of comparative religion, but a Catholic priest on a personal spiritual quest to craft a theological vision that is faithful to the deepest insights of Hinduism, Buddhism, and Christianity.[17] Born in 1918 in Barcelona to an Indian Hindu father and a Catalan Catholic mother, Panikkar earned doctorates in philosophy, chemistry, and theology. In 1940, he joined the newly formed Opus Dei movement and remained associated with it until the early 1960s. Ordained in 1946, Panikkar traveled in 1954 for the first time to India, where he studied Hinduism and Buddhism. This experience set him on a course of discovery that would continue until his death in 2010. Beginning in 1966, Panikkar moved between the United States, teaching both at Harvard and the University of California at Santa Barbara, and India. In 1987, he retired from teaching and returned to Spain, where he continued to publish up to the time of his death.[18] His approach provides an interesting contrast to the one taken by Daniélou. We will examine Panikkar's writings, especially his 2006 work *The Experience of God*, in terms of same three areas that we explored in Daniélou's thought: the framework for a Christian understanding of the religions, his method of engaging the religions of the world from a

Christian perspective, and the desired outcome of this type of engagement for Christians.[19]

THE FRAMEWORK: PLURALISM

Panikkar explicitly rejects the fulfillment theory that Daniélou proposed as the framework for viewing the religions of the world. Panikkar believes "that we are now at a turning point in history and that the encounter of present-day Christian consciousness and other cultures and religions can no longer follow the homogeneous and evolutionary pattern of what is sometimes termed fulfillment-theology."[20] Whereas the fulfillment theory sees all history heading toward one point in time (i.e., the Incarnation), Panikkar's theory of pluralism believes that there are several legitimate vantage points ("centers of intelligibility") from which we can survey the world's religions.[21] Furthermore, while the fulfillment theory argues that all differences in religious belief will be ultimately reconciled in Christ, Panikkar highlights the irreconcilable nature of human beliefs while at the same time not arguing that these differences will, or even should be, resolved. Panikkar holds out no hope for an eventual grand unified theory (or "supersystem") in which all religions will be brought into perfect harmony.

The starting point for Panikkar's theory of pluralism can be found in his belief that human experience, knowledge, and, especially, meaning are shaped by the "myth" through which we interpret reality. A cultural, religious, or scientific myth is the sum total of the conditions that allows us to make sense of human experience. Like Chauvet, Panikkar holds that our language in a certain sense "creates" reality.[22] All human knowledge is situated in a particular myth with its specific rules for what constitutes an "intelligible" statement and is, therefore, limited. We don't have the ability to step outside our own limited perspective and survey all the perspectives and determine which one is the truest. When we try to do this, asserts Panikkar, we are overreaching and mistakenly thinking that "the part is like the whole." For this reason, Panikaar rejects any universal theory or universal standards by which all religions are to be measured. As Panikkar explains:

> We all see through our respective windows. The more perfect the window the less conspicuous it is; we may easily forget that we are looking through a window, so transparent has it become for us. We do not see our windows, our myths. But there is still more. We realize that there are other people looking through different windows. We may even contest the alleged correctness of the visions through other windows, but we hear others describing to us their respective sceneries. Let me insist. Pluralism does not claim to see through all the windows or to control all (or some) of them. Pluralism simply acknowledges the existence of other windows.[23]

Panikkar's image of looking out windows suggests that reality is an independent entity that various groups perceive from different perspectives, but Panikkar goes one step further and argues that "reality itself is pluralistic."[24] Pluralism is not simply a matter of perspective for Panikkar, but runs down to the very fabric of reality. This complex notion carries us into the very heart of Panikkar's "cosmotheandric" vision of the world.

Panikkar rejects two understandings of reality that are commonly found among the cultures of the world: The first holds that matter and spirit are ultimately one reality; the second holds that matter and spirit are two independent realities. Panikkar steers a middle way between the two: Reality is both spirit and matter at the same moment. This type of thinking is more at home with the Hindu sense of *advaita* or non-duality than Western thought. "Man and God are neither two nor one."[25] Since religious experience includes the human element, Panikkar describes it as "cosmotheandric"—the "cosmos" (the world), "theos" (God or the Divine), and "aner" (the human). Here we may say that it is neither three nor one. As the theologian Paul Knitter explains:

So there are three components, as it were, to mystical experience and to what is revealed in such experience: the Divine, the human, and the world. All three are so interrelated that they have their being in each other; they can't exist without being related to each other. Certainly, the Divine is very different from the human, and the human from the material world; Panikkar is not talking about reducing one to the other. And yet they are as life-givingly related to each other as are fire and the oxygen that feeds it.[26]

In his study of Panikkar's work, the theologian Jyri Komulainen questions whether Panikkar is doing the very thing he says can't be done; that is, Panikkar insists that we can't step outside of history and compare competing claims about ultimate reality, yet he claims that all reality is cosmotheandric.[27] Komulainen asks, "Is not Panikkar himself adopting here a perspective from without? If so, is there not an evident contradiction with his denial of the existence of any bird's-eye perspective?"[28] In reply, Panikkar insists that pluralism is an attitude[29]—an awareness that all human knowledge is limited, and it is with this humility that Christians should approach the various religions' claims about the world, the divine, and the human.

ENGAGING THE RELIGIONS: DIALOGUE

The cosmotheandric view of reality serves as the framework in which Panikkar understands the meaning of Christ. This "experience of reality as trinitarian, though very differently understood, seems to be virtually universal."[30] This trinitarian process comes to fullest expression in the Christian tradition in Christ. In the revised edition (1981) of his influential early work *The Unknown Christ of Hinduism*, Panikkar writes, "Christ is still a living symbol for the totality of reality: human, divine, and cosmic....In this book Christ stands for that centre of reality, that crystallization-point around which the human, the divine, and the material can grow."[31] Christ is the symbol for that "crystallization-point" of the universal cosmotheandric process, and so while the name "Christ" belongs properly to Christianity, the reality to which the symbol "Christ" points belongs to other religious traditions. "Jesus is Christ, but Christ cannot be identified completely with Jesus of Nazareth."[32] In his later writings, Panikkar moves away from a Christology based on the historical existence of Jesus of Nazareth and speaks in more universal terms of "christophany" and "the christic principle." Panikkar adds, "If Christians are able to extricate from their own religion the christic principle, *this principle can be experienced as a dimension at least potentially present in any human being* [italics added], as long as no absolute interpretation is given."[33]

There are two poles in Panikkar's thought—his cosmotheandric view of all reality and his commitment to the pluralism of truth—and between them he clears the ground for dialogue among the religions. Because of the common cosmotheandric context, when we compare two different religions, we may find symbols or concepts that serve similar functions within their respective religions. Panikkar labels these "homeomorphic equivalents."[34] Because we are immersed in the reality we are describing, we all speak from a vantage point within the myth through which we see the world. For this reason, Panikkar insists that he is acknowledging the *relativity* of human knowledge, but is not endorsing moral *relativism*.[35] When we recognize both the cosmotheandric constitution of reality as well as the relativity of human knowledge, we can enter into genuine dialogue ("dialogical dialogue") with followers of other religions. In order for genuine dialogue to take place, both parties must be open to being transformed by the other. If one party presumes to be in possession of the fullness of truth, then true dialogue can't take place. In genuine dialogue, when both subjects willingly allow each other to shape their view of reality, "mutual fecundation" can take place.

Panikkar's openness to dialogue and his emphasis on the limited nature of human knowledge concerns even a sympathetic critic such as Paul Knitter, who questions whether Panikkar's position adequately addresses the problem of evil in the world, especially evil underwritten with religious ideology.

> In order to show how his position is one of "relativity" and not "relativism," he must make clearer how he can come to discern between what is "true and false," "good and evil." While he rightly insists that the diversity of religious experience is infinite, does that mean that *all* religious views can contribute to the dialogue? Are there ever situations where Panikkar would have to exclude someone from the table of dialogue? More specifically, it does not seem that Panikkar has sufficiently laid out the criteria—or the procedure—by which he can confront and oppose what seems to be the *intolerables* that are present within our contemporary world. I, and many others, find ourselves morally constrained to declare intolerable such realities as needless starvation, oppression of some human beings by others, torture, and economic injustice that destroys both human and planetary life.[36]

In his response to Knitter, Panikkar agrees that Christ is "the liberating symbol for the oppressed" and "another word for Justice."[37] This concern for the poor, of course, is not restricted to any one religious tradition and provides one of the common bonds that informs Panikkar's own hope for where genuine dialogue among the religions of the world may lead.

DESIRED OUTCOME: HARMONY

Of the three areas that we discussed, it is in this final one that we find the clearest difference between Daniélou and Panikkar. Daniélou once commented, "For me, the theology of history is the most important aspect of contemporary theology."[38]

As we discussed earlier, Daniélou frames the discussion of Christianity's relationship to the other religions in terms of salvation history. By contrast, "Panikkar has no linear view of history and, correspondingly, his thinking lacks an eschatological [end-time] dimension."[39] In Panikkar's own words, "history is the modern myth of the West."[40] Because Daniélou has a linear understanding of time, he interprets the Bible along typological lines (e.g., the Old Testament story of Isaac's near-sacrifice foreshadows Christ's death on the cross). The goal of history is the reunification of all creation in Christ. Because of Panikkar's commitment to pluralism and his deep affinity for Eastern thought, he does not identify one single, final goal to human existence.[41] So while the key idea that captures Daniélou's hopes for the future is unification, Panikkar emphasizes concord and harmony.

In Panikkar's vision of the future, the themes of pluralism, the relativity of knowledge, and the cosmotheandric nature of reality continue to play a decisive role. The goal of religious dialogue is not to convert the other party or to create one generic religion, but to preserve the diversity in a state of harmony.

> Concord is neither oneness nor plurality. It is the dynamism of the Many toward the One without ceasing to be different and without becoming one, and without reaching a higher synthesis. Music is here the paradigm. There is no harmonical accord if there is no plurality of sounds, or if those sounds coalesce in one single note. Neither many nor one, but concord, harmony.[42]

Harmony is neither a single voice nor a cacophony. The concord and harmony is that of a symphony. "Pluralism tells us here that one should not assume for oneself (person or culture) the role of the conductor of the human and much less of the cosmic orchestra. It is enough with the music (divine), the musicians (human), and their instruments (the cosmos). Let us play by ear!"[43]

SEARCHING FOR GOD IN
PANIKKAR'S THEOLOGY

In Panikkar's cosmotheandric vision of reality, the cosmic, the divine, and the human are neither completely separate nor completely identical. As Panikkar explains in his work *The Experience of God*, "God, the Human, and the World are not one, nor two, nor three. They are not three things, neither are they one."

In this trinitarian account of all that exists, God cannot be sifted out from the world. Rather, "the experience of God occurs in and with the totality of reality." God is not to be found, then, apart from the cosmic and the human, but rather through them, in them, and with them. "The experience of God cannot be separated from a stroll with a friend, a shared meal, the love that we feel, the idea that we defend, the conversation that unfolds, the pain that we endure—discovering in all of this…a dimension of depth, of love, of the infinite—and hence the ineffable."[44]

The question for Panikkar is not whether God is present in the world, but rather how well we perceive that presence. Here, Panikkar sees great wisdom in the idea of "the third eye" found in both the teachings of Tibetan monks and Hugh of St. Victor's student, Richard of St. Victor. Richard spoke of "three eyes"—the eye of the body, the eye of the mind, and the eye of faith. Each "eye" corresponds to a dimension of reality and our perception of it. The eye of the body perceives physical objects; the eye of reason grasps intellectual concepts, and the eye of faith understands the spiritual significance of all that the other two eyes see. This concept of the "third eye" recalls Bernard of Clairvaux's "spiritual senses" by which we "taste and see that the Lord is good" (Ps 34:8). Both "the third eye" and "the spiritual senses" refer to the religious capacity for discerning the deepest meaning of the moment in which we now stand. It is the awareness of Life. "This ideal is best summarized by commenting on a traditional experience, formulated by a number of sacred texts: God is Life. The experience of Life is equivalent to the experience of God."[45] Life is here not simply mere physical existence (what the Greeks called *bios*), but the fullness of life that we experience at peak moments in our lives (what the Greeks called *zoe*). In John's Gospel the word *zoe* appears in the passage in which Christ proclaims, "I came that they may have life, and have it abundantly" (John 10:10). It is this experience of Life that countless poets and mystics of all cultures have expressed in verse, wise sayings, and parables.

Because God is Life, "the experience of God is not the monopoly of any religious system, of whatever denomination, nor of any church, nor basically, of any culture." However, Panikkar insists that each of these experiences is a glimpse "of the cosmotheandric icon of reality at that moment of space and time, from the angle of our personal perspective and in light of our limited and concrete vision." This grounding in time and place is what gives each perspective its richness and uniqueness, yet it is also the basis for Panikkar's emphasis on pluralism and dialogue. "Pluralism is inherent to the human condition and prevents us from speaking of God by starting from a single perspective or a unique principle of intelligibility....The pretension of offering a unified scheme of intelligibility of the universal level is a remnant of cultural colonialism."[46] Once we dispense with this "cultural colonialism," we can enter into genuine dialogue with the other religious traditions of the world as equal partners and "mutual fecundation" can occur.

While the human experience of the cosmotheandric reality is pluralistic, as we move into the depths of our experience, we discover an ever-increasing sense of "universal solidarity" among people of all faiths. For Panikkar, the *interpretations* of the cosmotheandric reality vary immensely, but the *experience* of the cosmotheandric reality itself is universal.

> Those who consider that the label "Christian," for example, separates them from "nonbelievers" confuse their experience of God with their *interpretation* of the experience of God. The one who speaks as an "American," a

"scientist," a "male," except on predetermined scientific subjects, leaves aside or confuses the experience of God with *his* or *her* experience of God. Such an experience is not the oceanic, prelogical, or primitive feeling that has frequently been criticized. Rather, *it is the ultimate and universal experience incarnated in the concrete and the particular.*

God, says Panikkar, is an "infinite sea."[47] In this life we can only see to the horizon. When we have completed the voyage, we will learn how accurate our interpretations of the Divine were, but for now it would be a wise move on our part to listen to all those whose wisdom can help us navigate the often treacherous waters that we all must cross.

Discussion Questions

1. How should Christians view the beliefs and practices of other religions?

2. Should Christians see in the Old Testament foreshadowings of Christ's life, death, and resurrection?

3. Does the natural world reveal anything about God's nature?

4. Are all religions equally valid paths to salvation?

5. Do you agree with Daniélou that history is filled with the irruptions of God?

6. Panikkar once wrote of his journey to India, "I left Europe as a Christian, I discovered I was a Hindu and returned as a Buddhist without ever having ceased to be Christian." Is it possible to do this?

7. Panikkar states, "The experience of Life is equivalent to the experience of God." What does he mean by this? Do you agree with Panikkar's statement?

Suggested Readings

For a comprehensive overview of Catholic views toward other religions, see Karl Becker and Ilaria Morali, eds., *Catholic Engagement with World Religions* (Maryknoll, NY: Orbis Books, 2010). For background to *Nostra Aetate* and a review of its implementation, see Edward Idris Cardinal Cassidy, *Ecumenism and Interreligious Dialogue* (Mahwah, NJ: Paulist Press, 2005). See also Paul Knitter, *Theologies of Religion* (Maryknoll, NY: Orbis Books, 2002). For a recent study of Daniélou, see Marc C. Nicholas, *Jean Daniélou's Doxological Humanism* (Eugene, OR: Wipf and Stock, 2012). Nicholas's work also has a very helpful bibliography on pages 163–99. On Daniélou's view toward the world's religions, see Adam Sparks, "The Fulfillment Theology of Jean Daniélou, Karl Rahner and Jacques Dupuis," in *New Blackfriars* 89, no. 1024 (2008): 633–56. Dominic Veliath offers a comparison of Daniélou and Panikkar in his *Theological Approach and Understanding of Religion* (Bangalore, India: Kristu Jyoti College, 1988).

For studies of Panikkar's theology, see Jyri Komulainen, *An Emerging Cosmotheandric Religion?* (Boston: Brill, 2005); and John Francis Duggan, *Multireligious Experience and Pluralist Attitude: Raimon Panikkar and His Critics* (PhD diss., Toronto School of Theology, 2000). A helpful collection of articles devoted to Panikkar's theology can be found in Joseph Prabhu, ed., *The Intercultural Challenge of Raimon Panikkar* (Maryknoll, NY: Orbis Books, 1996).

10

ESCHATOLOGY: ANTICIPATING GOD

Johann S. Drey and Hans Urs von Balthasar

Like most investigations, the search for God involves gathering information, following leads, and refining positions over time. Whether it is a detective trying to solve a crime, a biomedical researcher working to find a cure, or an archaeologist hoping to locate an ancient tomb, the search does not end until the mystery has been solved. In theological terms, the search for God continues until the *eschaton*, the end of time when the mystery of God is fully revealed. Eschatology (the study of the end-time) covers a wide range of topics, but we can divide them into two general categories: those dealing with the end of human history (Judgment Day, Second Coming of Christ) and those dealing with the end of each individual's life (Heaven, Hell). In terms of the end of human history, no concept in the teaching of Christ receives greater attention than "the kingdom of God." For this reason we will examine the role the kingdom of God plays in the theology of Johann Sebastian Drey (1776–1853) as found in his 1819 work *A Brief Introduction to the Study of Theology*. Among the various eschatological issues relating to the life of each individual, one of the most frequently debated concerns the eternity of hell, especially as it relates to the love of God. Our springboard into this debate will be the 1986 work *Dare We Hope "That All Men Be Saved"?* by Hans Urs von Balthasar.

HISTORY AND ESCHATOLOGY

Eschatological passages in the Old Testament reflect the often painful awareness that the present state of the world bears little resemblance to how the world would operate if God's will were universally obeyed. Despite the fact that the righteous are persecuted for doing the will of God while the wicked prosper, the covenant community possesses an enduring hope that God has not abandoned them. In general, we can distinguish two patterns of thought in the Old Testament regarding the future. In the first, God will soon act dramatically to bring about a decisive overthrow of the present social order. In this apocalyptic eschatology (e.g., Dan 7), history has reached its final stage. The highly symbolic visions or oracles given long ago are being fulfilled in our midst and a catastrophic end to the present order is at hand. In the second, the prophetic literature, there is a correlation between the unfaithfulness of the community to the demands of the covenant and their impending fate, typically a massive defeat at the hands of their enemies. This defeat, however, will not result in absolute annihilation. Isaiah, for example, believed that "a remnant" (Isa 10:21) would remain and return to the Lord. They would once again be called to bring about a more just society, one in which justice will roll down like the waters and righteousness will be like an ever-flowing stream (Amos 5:24).

The relationship of history to the end-time is of particular concern to many of the New Testament writers. Some of the early Christian communities believed that Christ's death and resurrection signaled the decisive victory of God over the forces of evil, and therefore, expected his imminent return (the *parousia*). At that time, the living and the dead would be judged (1 Thess 4:13–18). While Paul discouraged his readers from trying to predict when this would occur, reminding them that "the Lord will come like a thief in the night" (1 Thess 5:2), he was convinced that "the present form of the world is passing away" (1 Cor 7:31). The most apocalyptically charged work in the New Testament is the Book of Revelation. The Four Horsemen (Rev 6), the fallen angels (Rev 12), the beast numbered 666 (13:18), the battle at Armageddon (16:16), and the thousand-year reign of Christ (Rev 20) are but a few of the images that have profoundly shaped Christian eschatological thought down through the centuries. By contrast, the author of Luke-Acts sees the missionary work of the church as playing an integral part in the plan of God (Luke 7:30). The end will come, but the gospel must first be preached to the ends of the earth (Acts 1:8). The idea that a certain body of believers or a specific nation has a special role and responsibility in the plan of God to instill Christian values at home and abroad has found expression in some of the most famous Christian sermons ever delivered. Even when there is not an imminent expectation of the end-time, a community's understanding of the relationship between history and eschatology directly informs its sense of identity and mission.

Modern theological reflection on history and its relation to eschatology focus on the meaning of "the kingdom of God" in Jesus' preaching. The theologian Michael Horton poses the question in the following way: "Does the kingdom of God grow within history, from an acorn to an oak tree? Or does it arrive like a violent wind, 'from above,' breaking up history and judging it?" In short, Horton asks, is the end of history a consummation or a catastrophe?[1] We can add yet another question into the mix. "What role do the members of the covenant community play in bringing about 'the kingdom of God'?" If the end-time is brought about by the activity of both God and humans, then one might speak of his/her work as a "building up" of the kingdom of God, or as something that hastens the arrival of the kingdom.[2] If the end-time is solely an act of God, then Christians are called to bear witness in their present way of life to the future peaceful kingdom that God will establish. The Mennonites, for example, ground their pacifism in this very conviction.[3]

The nineteenth century provides an interesting window on the shifting stance of the theological community toward the issue of history and eschatology in Jesus' proclamation regarding the kingdom of God. One of the leading theological voices in the early and mid-nineteenth century, Albecht Ritschl (1822–89), understood "the kingdom" as preached by Jesus to be a social order defined by the absolute love of God and neighbor. By creating a more just society, we play a role in the building up of the kingdom. In 1892, Ritschl's son-in-law, Johannes Weiss (1863–1914), published *Jesus' Proclamation of the Kingdom of God*, which the great twentieth-century New Testament scholar Rudolf Bultmann described as "epoch-making."[4] Weiss argued that the moral kingdom of God brought about through human effort is a modern construction draped on top of the preaching of the historical Jesus. When Christ's preaching is placed in its first-century Jewish context, Weiss argued, we discover that the coming of the kingdom of God refers to a future divine intervention into history. The modern idea that humans play some role in building the kingdom finds no support in the literature of the first century. Furthermore, Christ's preaching was not the peaceful beginning of a centuries-long process of creating a just and spiritual community. For Weiss, Christ spoke like a man who believed that the end of human history was imminent.[5] It is against this backdrop of nineteenth-century theology that we can both situate Drey's own understanding of the kingdom of God, which in many important ways resembles that of Ritschl, and anticipate the objections to his position by subsequent thinkers who adopted Weiss's view.

JOHANN SEBASTIAN DREY'S *A BRIEF INTRODUCTION TO THE STUDY OF THEOLOGY*

In 1817, Johann Sebastian Drey and two of his colleagues at the seminary in Ellwangen, Germany, traveled to the University of Tubingen to form the university's first Catholic theological faculty. Tubingen had a long and distinguished history as a center of Protestant theology, but the university was now to include both a Catholic and Protestant theological faculty. Drey could now realize many of the hopes that he expressed for Catholic theology in an article he published five years earlier, "Toward the Revision of the Present State of Theology." In that piece, Drey traces what he regards as the dissolution of the medieval synthesis of reason and revelation, prayer and study, and scripture and tradition. He chides Catholic theologians for a lack of creativity in their thinking and their insufficient awareness of intellectual movements that might help them shape the Gospel message in ways that would engage their contemporaries. "While one Catholic theologian copied another, and few looked further around at what might possibly be going on in the realm of the other sciences and in the altered manner of thinking of the time, they necessarily misunderstood the sciences and the time, and were in like manner misunderstood."[6] He was especially interested in recapturing a sense of the organic development of Christianity from Jesus to the church of the present day and the interrelation of the various components of the faith (e.g., biblical theology, morality, spirituality). Soon after his arrival at Tubingen, Drey composed his *A Brief Introduction to the Study of Theology*,[7] in which he sets out not only his proposal for a comprehensive theological curriculum, but also his own understanding of Christianity as formed by the one principal idea of the kingdom of God.

Drey places the blame for the aridity of the religious thought of his day on the modern tendency to completely separate matter and spirit, thought and emotion, and nature and grace. Drey, however, found in the work of two of his contemporaries philosophical and theological systems that offered a more satisfying account of human experience. Friedrich Schelling (1775–1854), associated with the movement known as German Idealism, saw matter and spirit as joined in a dialectical pattern of unification and differentiation. This process was not random, but rather guided by a supreme Mind. There was, therefore, a spiritual undercurrent to history. As the theologian Wayne Fehr explains, "There is a sense of the Infinite *in* the finite [in German Idealism], an awareness of the whole, a tendency to understand all particulars in their relation to the whole....For Schelling, as well as for Drey, the self cannot be thought of apart from the great whole, nor can the world be thought apart from God."[8] The theologian Frederich Schleiermacher (1768–1834) was deeply influenced by Romanticism, a philosophical and literary movement that celebrated our oneness with the natural world, and stressed the importance of feeling and intuition to the human personality. Deep within our consciousness—in a reality more profound than the language we have to describe it—we come into contact with a divine power upon whom we are absolutely dependent. Our religious doctrines and practices express the religious consciousness produced in this encounter with God in the very depths of our being.

In the opening section of his *Brief Introduction*, Drey speaks of religion in language drawn from Idealism and Romanticism. "All faith and all knowledge rests on the dimly felt or clearly perceived presupposition that every existing finite reality has not only emerged from an eternal and absolute ground (#1)," but that its life and vitality depends on its continued contact with this fertile ground. There is a "universal *connectedness* and true *dependence* of all things in and to this ultimate ground" (#3). Because consciousness and reality are not radically distinct, "man becomes conscious of God as he becomes conscious of himself" (#6). In the Romantic understanding, the child's experiences are the purest. Their consciousness is marked by wonder and awe. In the eyes of a child, a dandelion is a miniature sun glistening in a flowing field of green. For adults, a dandelion is a weed that has infested their finely manicured lawn. With age and social conditioning, we lose touch with this earlier state of innocence. In spiritual terms, in our innocence "religious affection responds gladly and willingly to the force of love for God," (#11) but as we develop a sense of self-identity apart from others, we exert "our self-will in opposition to the will of God" (#12). We grow estranged from the natural world and our fellow human beings. We recognize our need for healing. This is Drey's version, if you will, of the Fall.[9]

THE KINGDOM OF GOD IN DREY'S THEOLOGY

Now that Drey has set the stage, he leads the reader through "the drama of providence" (#114). In order to appreciate the harmonious relation of the various acts in this drama, we will pursue a very close reading of Drey's *Brief Introduction* and the various meanings he attaches to the concept of the kingdom of God. The dynamic that drives this drama is the dialectical relationship between "the idea" and the "the real." The idea is conceptual or the theoretical design. The real is the actual expression of that concept or theory in the existence of an actual entity (#71). In our state of innocence, before our state of "self-consciousness and freedom" (#18), we perceived the world as what it truly is: the kingdom of God. "The world was such a Kingdom of God from its beginnings; the most primitive original revelation announced this Kingdom to mankind. But as humanity, ignoring the Kingdom of God, exalted itself *above* this original revelation, the revelation too was raised above humanity and so the Kingdom of God was assigned to a higher order of reality as mystery.—This is the historical course of revelation up to Christ" (#27, emphasis his). This historical course of revelation was educative. As Drey once noted, "Revelation…is for the whole of mankind what education is for the individual."[10] The theologian Donald Dietrich notes the warmth that Drey conveys in his discussion of this process of revelation. "[God] established man's relation to him as that of a father to his children, formed and educated man in a similarly paternal way, taught him the difference between right and wrong, drew his attention to the dire results of his sinful acts to warn him against harm and misfortune, and finally revealed to man, who did not heed his warning, the ultimate consequences of his sin without, however, depriving him of his consolation and help."[11]

God is "*most perfectly* revealed" in the Incarnation and therefore Christ is "*the visible head of the Kingdom*" (#32, emphasis his). Through Christ, "the *idea of a Kingdom of God* is once again discovered…the idea which was expressed in the universe at its beginning, which grounded our first religious feelings, and which was forgotten during egoism's long dominance" (#32, emphasis his). Christ "refined the material idea of *an earthly Kingdom of God and worldly dominion* into the purity and universality of a *heavenly kingdom*, a moral kingdom within the universe" (#59, emphasis his). Christ "introduced the epoch when the mystery of the past would be uncovered and when from this brighter present a broader vision of the future could be seen" (#59).

Just as "the original revelation" of the kingdom at creation stands in continuity with Jesus' proclamation of the kingdom, the church is the embodiment of the kingdom of God in next act in the "drama of providence." The "visible expression and tangible realization" of the idea of the kingdom of God "is the *church*" (#32, emphasis his). In order for the kingdom of God to become real, Christians must cultivate a personal spiritual life, a public worship, and a moral code that creates "true citizens of that Kingdom" (#324). "The church is the temporal and sensible manifestation of the kingdom in which the key ideas of Christianity attain reality" (#275). It might be more accurate to amend Drey's statement to read, "the key ideas of Christianity *should* attain reality, but there is no guarantee that will happen." Drey used organic images, such as a seed developing into a fully grown plant, to describe the life of the church, but as the theologian Bradford Hinze reminds us, Drey was not unaware that disease can threaten the health of any living thing.[12] The church is an organic reality that grows and expands over time, and if it is healthy, it can expand the kingdom of God, but it also easily fall prey to those forces of disease that could stifle the kingdom's growth and possibly even seriously compromise the health of the ecclesial body.

The final act in the historical drama is judgment day and then the eternal kingdom is established.[13] As Frey notes, "The end-state of God's Kingdom will be the unity of all those who have been saved and sanctified in one perfect society with God and Christ. Only in this final, eternal condition of the world will the Idea of *Reich Gottes* [the kingdom of God] finally be actualized completely. Although this can only be an object of hope during the present age, it is nevertheless in continuity with what is already visible as Church."[14] As Drey described elsewhere, the fulfillment of the kingdom is "the perfect uniting of all things with God," a state in which everything "which is now opposed and hostile to God and the divine decrees will disappear utterly and be removed."[15] By attaching different meanings to the kingdom of God, Drey masterfully weaves a grand narrative, "a drama of providence," in which the idea of the kingdom links creation, the ministry of Christ, the life of the church, and the world to come. The result is a plot line uniting our faith in God, our love of neighbor, and our hope for the future.

CONCLUSION

Where Drey's theological vision and eschatological hope is marked by a deep sense of continuity running throughout the ministry of Christ, the present age, and the end-time, his critics see in Christ's life, death, and resurrection an in-breaking of a radically new aeon in history. In Paul's Letters, for example, we find a tension between the present age and the age to come (Gal 1:4). Christians, so to speak, live in two worlds. As disciples, they witness to the kingdom that they believe broke into history in Christ and that will one day, known only to God, be fully realized. The followers of Christ meanwhile live in a wider culture that often does not embrace their beliefs. Drey's critics charge that this eschatological tension of the kingdom as "already, but not yet" is lacking in his theology. The historian Grant Kaplan, for example, writes, "Drey does not see salvation history in such a way that human beings are in a new era after the Christ event and that they will remain in this stage until the eschaton. Instead Drey's conception of history is still too close to the framework of salvation history expressed in the German High Enlightenment. In this model, humanity enters various stages on the road from pupil to graduate."[16]

Drey's theology reminds us that any search for God necessarily entails speculation about the future. Questions concerning both our origin and destiny—be it the human race or our own individual lives—lead us to question about our life's purpose. The question of origin, "How did we get here?" leads to the question, "Why are we here?" In a similar way, the question of destiny, "Where are we headed?" raises the question "How should I live now?" Paul recognized that our knowledge about God in light of our ultimate destiny is dim, but he was confident in what it revealed about how we are to live in the present. "For now we see in a mirror, dimly, but then we will see face to face. Now I know only in part; then I will know fully, even as I have been fully known. And now faith, hope, and love abide, these three; and the greatest of these is love" (1 Cor 13:12–13).

In our discussion of Drey, we dealt with eschatological questions regarding the end of human history. We now turn our attention to eschatological questions regarding the end of each individual's lives. In the traditional categories of Catholic belief, this involves questions of heaven, hell, and purgatory as well as the communion of saints. Given our present focus on the nature of God, we will highlight the commonly asked question: Would an all-loving God condemn someone to eternal punishment in hell? In other words, how does God's mercy relate to God's justice? We will explore the issue of eternal damnation and whether there is any basis for the hope that all people might be saved by examining the argument advanced by the Swiss theologian Hans Urs von

Balthasar in his work *Dare We Hope "That All Men Be Saved"?* and its companion piece, published the following year, *Short Discourse on Hell.* In both of these works, von Balthasar offers his argument for why such a hope is, indeed, justified.

DARE WE HOPE "THAT ALL MEN BE SAVED"?

The public controversy involving von Balthasar over the question of universal salvation began in 1984 when Pope John Paul II presented him with the first Paul VI International Prize for Theology. At a news conference surrounding the event, von Balthasar was asked about his thoughts regarding the possibility that all humans might be saved—an issue that von Balthasar had raised in works throughout his career.[17] He replied that such was his hope. When the news reports appeared, they were, in the words of von Balthasar, filled with "gross distortions" of his position.[18] He, therefore, wrote a short piece on the matter that was reprinted in the German edition of the Vatican newspaper *L'Osservatore Romano.* A flurry of articles from his critics soon followed, and von Balthasar offered his response in *Dare We Hope "That All Men Be Saved?"* in 1986.

The constant refrain that runs throughout *Dare We Hope?* is von Balthasar's contention that we can *hope* that all persons are saved, not that we *know* for certain that all people will be. In fact, he charges, by insisting that some individuals are damned (e.g., Judas), his opponents are claiming to possess certain knowledge about the afterlife. Von Balthasar insists that his own position is more restrained and more modest in what it proposes than the certainty claimed by his opponents. He takes one of his critics, Gerhard Hermes, editor of the German publication *Der Fels,* to task for claiming that "we cannot hope that all men will enter heaven, because that is expressly excluded through revelation."[19] Von Balthasar continues:

Let us…attend solely to the end of the sentence, which at last reveals the source of the critic's 'certain knowledge.' It is of course, the texts in the New Testament, which in fact contain sufficiently abundant talk of hell fire (Mt. 5:22, 29 f.; 10:28; 23:33), of the 'outer darkness' (Mt. 8:12; 22:11 ff.; 25:30), or eternal punishment (Mt. 25:46), of the unquenchable fire (Mk. 9:43) and abundantly in Revelation, of the lake of fire (19:20; 20:10; 21:18).[20]

In addition to these verses, there are the warnings of Jesus in Matthew 7:20–13 ("I never knew you…") as well those against the unrepentant cities (Matt 11), the sin against the Holy Spirit (Matt 12), the unmerciful servant (Matt 18), the wicked tenants (Matt 21), and the worthless servant in the parable of the talents (Matt 25). Finally, and perhaps most famously, there is the parable of the Last Judgement (Matt 25) in which those who neglected "the least ones" are condemned to the "eternal fire prepared for the devil and his angels" (25:41).

Von Balthasar responds to this seemingly overwhelming amount of scriptural evidence in three ways. First, he insists that the New Testament record is not exclusively focused on the possibility of damnation. "It is generally known that in the New Testament, two series of statements run along side by side in such a way that a synthesis of both is neither permissible nor achievable: the first series speaks of being lost for all eternity; the second, of God's will, and ability, to save all men."[21] Von Balthasar especially highlights the passages that speak of Christ's death on behalf of all creation. "For in him all the fullness of God was pleased to dwell, and through him God was pleased to reconcile to himself all things, whether on earth or in heaven, by making peace through the blood of his cross" (Col 1:19–20). Second, the passages that do speak of an eternal hell are not to be taken as descriptions of a future that will definitely exist, but as warnings for those in the present that such a *possibility* exists. Because we possess genuine free will, we could close ourselves off to God. Third, the certainty of eternal damnation for even a few gives insufficient attention to both our solidarity with the entire human race and the love of neighbor that Christ commands.

Two Sets of Texts in the New Testament: Despite the number of passages referring to eternal damnation, "this does not hinder the fact that the universalist series of texts possesses an ineradicable gravity."[22] Chief among the texts cited as justification for the hope that all people will be saved is the declaration that God "desires everyone to be saved and to come to the knowledge of the truth" (1 Tim 2:4). Von Balthasar highlights two additional passages in particular. In the first (Rom 5:12–21), Paul offers an extended comparison of the disobedience of one man (Adam) that brought sin and death, and the obedience of one man (Christ) who overcame sin and death. "Therefore just as one man's trespass led to condemnation for all, so one man's act of righteousness leads to justification and life for *all*" (5:18, emphasis added). Von Balthasar comments, "The word 'all' is repeated nine times, and the predominance of grace is further emphasized by the fact that law led to an increase in trespass, while grace 'abounded all the more' through this added hindrance (Rom 5:12–21). The whole passage gradually intensifies into a true hymn of triumph."[23] The second passage that von Balthasar believes bolsters the hope of universal salvation appears in John's Gospel, "And I, when I am lifted up from the earth, will draw all people to myself" (12:32). While judgment is certainly a theme in John's Gospel, so, too, is the love of Christ, a love that extends "to the end" (13:1). Christ instructs his followers to live on in his love (15:10). Though they will face persecution from "the world," Christ love is greater than any power opposed to the love of God. As Christ proclaims, "In the world you face persecution. But take courage; I have conquered the world!" (16:33).

The mistake that theologians often make, according to von Balthasar, is trying to ignore either the universalist passages or the damnation passages, and thereby "know" that hell is empty or full. The early church thinker Origen believed that the "universal restoration" (Acts 3:21) that Peter mentions in his speech at the Temple in Jerusalem could, indeed, include the restoration of even the most vile sinner, including Satan himself, to God. Origen believed that "the end will be like the beginning." At the end of time, after countless episodes of punishment and rehabilitation, all souls (even Satan) will freely return to God, so that God will be all in all (1 Cor 15:28). On the other end of the theological spectrum, Augustine's predestination gave him great confidence that hell would not go unpopulated. In his *City of God*, he writes, "The fact is that there is no way of waiving or weakening the words which the Lord has told us that He will pronounce in the last judgment: 'Depart from me, accursed ones, into the everlasting fire which was prepared for the devil and his angels' [Matt 25:41]. In this way He showed plainly that it is an eternal fire in which the Devil and his angels are to burn."[24]

Critics of von Balthasar take him to task for dismissing a traditional solution to the problem of how to reconcile the two sets of passages in the New Testament regarding salvation. The theologian Thomas White comments:

> Balthasar is certainly correct, therefore, to insist on a contrasting emphasis on his "two sets" of texts in the New Testament. On the one hand, we are told that God desires the salvation of all, and that Christ has come to redeem the entire world. On the other hand, we are also warned that there will be those who refuse such initiatives, who come under the judgment of God. One evident solution to this "textual dualism" is offered by the distinction between the antecedent and consequent will of God, a solution that arises from within the classical theological tradition.[25]

God's "antecedent will" refers to God's desire that all will be saved, but not all persons freely accept that universal offer, and consequently (i.e., "the consequent will"), not all are saved. God does not *will* that some are damned, but God *allows* damnation to occur. In his critique of von Balthasar, the theologian Ralph Martin complains that this distinction is "dismissed by Balthasar without extensive argumentation."[26] Whether von Balthasar's argument is sufficiently developed is up to the reader, but there is certainly no doubt that the tone of his argument is biting.

> But what about Jesus' triumphant words when he looks forward to the effect of his Passion: "Now shall the ruler of this world be cast out; and I, when I am lifted up from the earth, will draw *all* men to myself" (Jn 12:31 f.)? Oh, he will perhaps attempt to draw them all but will not succeed in holding them all. "Be of good cheer, I have overcome *the world*" (Jn 16:33). Unfortunately, only half of it, despite your efforts, Lord. "The grace of God has appeared for the salvation of *all* men (Titus 2:11)—let us say, more precisely, to offer salvation, since how many will accept it is questionable. God does not wish "that any should perish, but that *all* should reach repentance" (2 Pet 3:9). He may well wish it, but unfortunately he will not achieve it.[27]

Von Balthasar seems to regard the distinction between God's antecedent and consequent will as a presumptuous move on the part of theologians that does not fully appreciate the power, majesty, and mercy of the Father "who did not withhold his own Son, but gave him up for all of us" (Rom 8:32).

Damnation Texts as Warnings: Von Balthasar follows the approach taken by the Jesuit theologian Karl Rahner when interpreting Christ's teachings on hell. Rahner argues "that what Scripture says about hell is to be interpreted in keeping with its literary character of 'threat-discourse' and hence, not to be read as a preview of something which will exist some day. Insofar as it is a report, it is rather a disclosure of the situation in which the persons addressed are actually to be found."[28] This "situation" is nothing else than the possibility of categorically rejecting God's offer of love, that is, hell. This for Rahner is the real meaning of the various biblical images of hell: "the possibility of man being finally lost and estranged from God in all the dimensions of his existence."[29] Following this line of reasoning, von Balthasar contends that hell was not created by God, but is, in fact, a state of self-condemnation. As the religious writer C. S. Lewis argues, "I willingly believe that the damned are, in one sense, successful, rebels to the end; that the doors of hell are locked on the *inside*."[30] The hope for the salvation of all, therefore, is rooted in the hope that even the most adamant refusal of God's love might in the end be surrendered. "The question, to which no final answer is given or can be given, is this: Will he who refuses [God's love] now refuse it to the last?"[31] Is it possible that each person will ultimately behave like the Ninevites who heeded Jonah's message of God's judgment and repented in dust and ashes? "When God saw what they did, how they turned from their evil ways, God changed his mind about the calamity that he said he would bring upon them; and he did not do it" (Jonah 3:10).

Critics have challenged von Balthasar's reading of the damnation teachings of the New Testament as warnings rather than descriptions of an actual state of affairs. The Franciscan Regis Scanlon contends that while von Balthasar is certainly correct when he states that the church has never definitively declared a specific person to be in hell, there are strong scriptural indications that hell will not go unpopulated. In John's Gospel, Jesus prays to the Father saying, "I guarded them, and not one of them was lost except the one destined to be lost, so that scripture might be fulfilled" (John 17:12). If the "one destined to be lost" refers to Judas, as many of the church's greatest theologians have held, then it is reasonable to assume that Judas is in hell. Scanlon sees further evidence in Christ's teaching on the narrow way. "Someone asked him, 'Lord, will only a few be saved?' He said to them, 'Strive to enter through the narrow door; for many, I tell you, will try to enter and will not be able'" (Luke 13:23–24). Scanlon concludes, "Thus, even though the Magisterium [the teaching office of the church] has not yet condemned Judas *by name* or the mere 'hope' for universal salvation, the Church is not in doubt about this matter. Scripture, Tradition, and the Magisterium certify that Judas and others have perished."[32]

The theologian James O'Connor makes a similar argument to that advanced by Scanlon, highlighting, in particular, the teachings found in the Vatican II document *Lumen gentium*, n. 48.

Since we know neither the day nor the hour, we should follow the advice of the Lord and watch constantly so that, when the single course of our earthly life is completed (cf. Heb. 9:27), we may merit to enter with him into the marriage feast and be numbered among the blessed (cf. Mt. 25:31–46) and not, like the wicked and slothful servants (cf. Mt. 25:26), be ordered to depart into the eternal fire (cf. Mt. 25:41), into the outer darkness where "men will weep and gnash their teeth" (Mt. 22:13 and 25:30).[33]

O'Connor reports that the Theological Commission responsible for drafting the document made a point of specifying that the reference to the damned is "grammatically future." O'Connor continues, "The significance of that remark is that when the Church speaks of damnation of humans she speaks, as Christ himself did, not in a form of a grammar which is *conditional* (i.e., speaking about something which *might* happen), but in the *grammatical future* (i.e., about something which *will* happen). And it was with this understanding that the bishops of Vatican II voted upon and accepted *Lumen Gentium*."[34]

Human Solidarity: Von Balthasar argues that a genuine love of neighbor necessitates our hope for their salvation. He offers the following thesis for our consideration: "Whoever reckons with the possibility of even one person's being lost besides himself is hardly able to love unreservedly....Just the slightest nagging thought of a final hell for others tempts us, in moments in which human togetherness becomes especially difficult, to leave the other to himself."[35] Genuine love does not turn its back on the neighbor or resign itself to the eternal torment of the other. It is on this point that the theologian Edward Oakes believes von Balthasar's thought is most compelling. "The great advantage of Balthasar's eschatology is that it puts us in touch once more with the essential solidarity of the human race, and schools us in compassion."[36]

Instead of delving into the great medieval engagements of Peter Lombard, Thomas Aquinas, or Bonaventure with the "shameful" problem of whether those in heaven might feel compassion or sorrow for their loved ones in hell, von Balthasar suggests, instead, that we consider the scenario from the perspective of God. "Does God no longer love the damned, for whom, after all, his Son has died? Or—if I may revert to the hypothesis that I developed earlier—do the absolute naysayers burn in the fire of absolute divine love that also embraces them, and what sort of effect does such a situation have on God?"[37] An all-loving God would, von Balthasar implies, be distressed by this prospect, and therefore, we should be as well.

CONCLUSION

Eschatology played a central role throughout the entire body of von Balthasar's work. As the theologian Geoffrey Wainwright observes, "The red thread of eschatology—thought and doctrine about ultimates—runs through Hans Urs von Balthasar's work from start to finish. He first took up this theme with his humanistic dissertation written at the University of Zurich on 'the history of the eschatological problem in modern German literature' (1930), a large work that was eventually incorporated into an even larger enterprise, a three-volume work on 'the apocalypse of the German soul' (1937–39)....The thesis of Balthasar's earliest work, both the dissertation and its later three-volume expansion, was that the ways in which a people envisions the End 'reveal' its 'soul.'" Wainwright then asks, "[If] the eschatological myths of a culture reveal something about a nation, does not the eschatological imagery, doctrine, and thought of the Christian religion reveal, in a focused way, the faith of the Church—and of the theologian?"[38] Nowhere does the church, the theologian, or the individual Christian more clearly display our understanding of God than in the eschatological vision we present. How do God's justice and mercy finally relate to each other? How does Christ's victory on the cross change the course of human salvation? How does God's grace operate in a way that does not violate human free will? In order to answer these questions, we might imagine that we had the talent of Michelangelo and could add a fresco to the Sistine Chapel.[39] How would we portray the afterlife of the entire human race? Would there be one, two, or three (or more) groups? Which colors would dominate the work? What impression would our fresco leave on those who gazed upon it? In this mental artistic creation, we might very well have the clearest picture of our most cherished beliefs about God as well as our deepest hopes for humanity.

Discussion Questions

1. What did Jesus mean when he spoke about "the kingdom of God"?

2. Do you agree with Drey when he writes, "Revelation… is for the whole of mankind what education is for the individual"?

3. Is the kingdom of God something that will be realized in the course of human history? If so, can humans work to bring about the kingdom of God?

4. Does hell exist? Is it likely that some persons will end up there?

5. Do you accept or reject von Balthasar's argument for the hope that all people might be saved? Why or why not?

6. Evaluate the following statement: "God wills that all people be saved. However, we can reject that invitation. Hell, therefore, is a self-condemnation, a definitive rejection of God's offer of salvation."

7. What does our vision regarding the afterlife for all humans suggest about our view of God?

Suggested Reading

For studies of Drey's theology, see Wayne L. Fehr, *The Birth of the Catholic Tubingen School: The Dogmatics of Johann Sebastian Drey*, American Academy of Religion Academy Studies 37 (Chico, CA: Scholars Press, 1981); and Bradford Hinze, *Narrating History, Developing Doctrine* (Atlanta: Scholars Press, 1993). For background on "the Catholic Tubingen school," see Donald J. Dietrich and Michael J. Himes, eds., *The Legacy of the Tubingen School* (New York: Crossroad Publishing Co., 1997); and Bradford Hinze, "Roman Catholic Theology: Tubingen," which appears as chapter 9 in David Fergusson, ed., *The Blackwell Companion to Nineteenth-Century Theology* (Malden, MA: Blackwell, 2010); and James Tunstead Burtchaell, "Drey, Mohler and the Catholic School of Tubingen," which appears as chapter 4 in Ninian Smart, John Clayton, Steven T. Katz, and Patrick Sherry, eds., *Nineteenth Century Religious Thought in the West*, vol. 2 (London: Cambridge University Press, 1985). See also chapter 5 of Bernard M. G. Reardon, *Religion in the Age of Romanticism* (New York: Cambridge University Press, 1985).

For background to von Balthasar, see Edward T. Oakes, *Pattern of Redemption* (New York: Continuum, 1994); David L. Schindler, ed., *Hans Urs Von Balthasar: His Life and Works* (San Francisco: Ignatius Press, 1992); and Edward T. Oakes and David Moss, eds., *The Cambridge Companion to Hans Urs Von Balthasar* (Cambridge, MA: Cambridge University Press, 2004). See also Karen Kilby, *Balthasar: A (Very) Critical Introduction* (Grand Rapids, MI: Eerdmans, 2012). In the "Disputed Questions" section of the journal *Logos* 1, no. 3 (1997), there are three articles dedicated to von Balthasar's *Dare We Hope "That All Men Be Saved"?*; and for a critique of von Balthasar's position, see chapter 6 of Ralph Martin's *Will Many Be Saved?* (Grand Rapids, MI: Eerdmans, 2012). John Sachs provides a helpful overview of Catholic thought on the question of universal salvation in his "Current Eschatology: Universal Salvation and the Problem of Hell," *Theological Studies* 52 (1991): 227–54.

NOTES

Introduction

1. Stanley Hauerwas, *Hannah's Child* (Grand Rapids, MI: Eerdmans, 2010), x.

2. Louis Dupre speaks of "ambiguous intimations of transcendence inherent in the very heart of [the believer's] worldly experience" in his "Experience and Interpretation: A Philosophical Reflection on Schillebeeckx's *Jesus and Christ*," *Theological Studies* 43 (1982): 31.

3. John S. Dunne and Rebecca Adams, "Myth and Culture in Theology and Literature: A Conversation with John S. Dunne, C.S.C.," *Religion and Literature* 25, no.2 (1993): 83.

4. John S. Dunne, *The Circle Dance of Time* (Notre Dame, IN: University of Notre Dame Press, 2010), 115.

5. John S. Dunne, *Time and Myth* (Garden City, NY: Doubleday, 1973), 37.

6. Charles Williams, ed., *The Letters of Evelyn Underhill* (London: Longmans, Green, and Co., 1944), 205–6. I discovered this quote in Joseph W. Goetz, *Mirrors of God* (Cincinnati, OH: St. Anthony's Messenger Press, 1984), 77.

7. John Baptist de La Salle, "Explanation of the Method of Interior Prayer" in *John Baptist de la Salle*, ed. Carl Koch, Jeffrey Calligan, and Jeffrey Gros, 218 (Mahwah, NJ: Paulist Press, 2004).

8. Luke Salm, "Jesus in Lasallian Hearts," at page 3 of http://churchresources.info/missionspirit/0511/8.pdf.

9. John S. Dunne, *Time and Myth* (New York: Doubleday, 1973), 37.

Chapter 1

1. The sign is partially visible in the photo at http://pho tos.nola.com/tpphotos/2010/11/new_orleans_school_desegre gati_5.html. The quote also appears in 1962 when Archbishop Rummel of New Orleans ordered the Catholic schools to be desegregated. See *Time*, April 13, 1962. The article is reprinted at http://romereturn.blogspot.com/2010/02/new-orleans-1962-archbishop-rummels.html.

2. The theologian John Dunne describes the quest for certainty as "self-defeating." See his *The Way of All the Earth* (Notre Dame, IN: University of Notre Dame Press, 1978), 42.

3. *The Cloud of Unknowing*, trans. Carmen Acevedo Butcher (Boston: Shambhala Publications, 2009), 21.

4. Thomas Aquinas, *Summa Contra Gentiles*, I, 4, trans. Anton C. Pegis (Notre Dame, IN: University of Notre Dame Press, 1975), 67.

5. Herbert McCabe, *God Still Matters* (New York: Continuum, 2002), 216.

6. Aquinas, *Summa Contra Gentiles*, I, 3, 63.

7. Ibid.

8. Thomas Aquinas, *Commentary on the Gospel of St. John*, 1:18 (n. 211), trans. James A. Weisheipl (Albany, NY: Magi Books, 1998). The text is available online at dhspriory.org/thomas /John1.htm.

9. Aquinas, *Summa Contra Gentiles*, I, 11, 82.

10. Ibid., I, 30, 140.

11. Jean-Pierre Torrell, *Saint Thomas Aquinas: The Person and His Work*, vol. 1 (Washington, DC: The Catholic University of America Press, 1996), 112–13.

12. Robert Barron, *The Priority of Christ* (Grand Rapids, MI: Brazos Press, 2007), 220. Emphasis his.

13. Augustine, *Confessions*, VII, 5.

14. Ibid., VII, 20.

15. Robert Barron, *Thomas Aquinas: Spiritual Master* (New York: Crossroad, 1996), 61.

16. Ibid., 99.

17. Aquinas, *Summa Contra Gentiles*, I, 43, 166.

18. Robert Masson, "Karl Rahner: A Brief Biography," www.krs.stjohnsem.edu/KarlRahner.htm.

19. Karl Rahner, *The Love of Jesus and the Love of Neighbor* (New York: Crossroad, 1983), 52.

20. Karl Rahner, *Encounters With Silence* (Westminster, MD: Newman Press, 1960), 7.

21. Aquinas, *Summa Contra Gentiles*, I, 30, 141.

22. Josef Pieper, *The Silence of St. Thomas* (New York: Pantheon, 1957), 69–70. Emphasis his.

23. Aquinas, *Summa Contra Gentiles*, I, 95, 290–91. Of course, when Aquinas says that God cannot will something, he does not mean that God is *unable* to do so.

24. Ibid., I, 96, 292–94.

25. Ibid., I, 91, 15 and 18, 281–82.

26. This issue of biblical interpretation has been a long-standing one in the Christian tradition. Augustine deals with this very issue in Book Three of *On Christian Teaching*, trans. R. P. H. Green (Oxford: Oxford University, 2008).

27. Aquinas, *Summa Contra Gentiles*, I, 91, 278.

28. Ibid., I, 91, 277.

29. Ibid.

30. Ibid., I, 91, 278.

31. Paul J. Wadell, *The Primacy of Love* (Mahwah, NJ: Paulist Press, 1992), 63.

32. See Rosemary Radford Ruether, *Sexism and God-Talk* (Boston: Beacon Press, 1993), 96–97.

33. See Catherine Mowry LaCugna, *God For Us* (San Francisco: HarperCollins, 1991).

34. Elizabeth A. Johnson, "Forging Theology: A Conversation with Colleagues" in Phyllis Zagano and Terrence W. Tilley, eds., *Things New and Old* (New York: Crossroad, 1999), 100.

35. Elizabeth A. Johnson, *She Who Is* (New York: Crossroad, 1992), 12.

36. Ibid., 9.

37. Ibid., 242–43.

38. Ibid., 33.

39. Ibid., 105.

40. Ibid., 114.

41. Ibid., 117, quoting Aquinas, *Summa Contra Gentiles*, I, 31, 4.
42. Johnson, *She Who Is*, 112.
43. Ibid., 117.
44. Ibid., 105. See also 7, 108.
45. Ibid., 108.
46. Ibid., 104.
47. Ibid., 39.
48. Ibid., 39–40.
49. Ibid., 38.
50. Robin Darling Young, "She Who Is: Who Is She?" *The Thomist* 58 (1994): 333.
51. Ibid., 325–26.
52. Johnson, *She Who Is*, 108.
53. Ibid., 142.
54. Ibid., 145.
55. Ibid., 36.

Chapter 2

1. Jerome Taylor, trans., *The Didascalicon of Hugh of Saint Victor* (New York: Columbia University Press, 1991), 137.
2. Hugh of St. Victor, *Didascalicon*, V, 3, 121.
3. Origen, *On First Principles*, I.9, trans. G. W. Butterworth (Gloucester, MA: Peter Smith, 1973), 14.
4. For background on the reform movements and the canons regular, see Margot Fassler, *Gothic Song* (Cambridge, MA: Cambridge University Press, 1993), 187–91.
5. Paul Rorem, *Hugh of St. Victor* (Oxford: Oxford University Press, 2009), 5.
6. For background information, see Margot Fassler, *Gothic Song* (Cambridge, MA: Cambridge University Press, 1993), 187–91.
7. Rorem, *Hugh of St. Victor*, 7.
8. Ibid., 11.
9. Hugh of St. Victor, *Didascalicon*, I, 11, 60.
10. Franklin Harkins, *Reading and the Work of Restoration* (Toronto: Pontifical Institute of Medieval Studies, 2009), 73.

11. Hugh of St Victor, *On the Sacraments of the Christian Faith*, trans. Roy J. Deferrari (Cambridge, MA: The Mediaeval Academy of America, 1951), 3.

12. Boyd Taylor Coolman, *"Pulchrum Esse*: The Beauty of Scripture, the Beauty of the Soul, and the Art of Exegesis in Hugh of St. Victor," *Traditio* 58 (2003): 178.

13. Hugh of St Victor, *On the Sacraments of the Christian Faith*, 6.

14. Ibid., 5.

15. Hugh of St. Victor, *Didascalicon*, III, 3, 138.

16. Boyd Taylor Coolman, *The Theology of Hugh of St. Victor* (New York: Cambridge University Press, 2010), 129.

17. These Christian interpretations of Old Testament passages as foreshadowings to persons or events in the New Testament are also called "typological."

18. Coolman, *"Pulchrum Esse*: The Beauty of Scripture, the Beauty of the Soul, and the Art of Exegesis in Hugh of St. Victor," 193–94.

19. Hugh of St. Victor, *Noah's Ark*. I, 10 in *Hugh of Saint-Victor: Selected Spiritual Writings*, trans. A Religious of the Community of St. Mary the Virgin (Eugene, OR: Wipf and Stock Publishers, 2009), 57.

20. Hugh of St. Victor, *Didascalicon*, VI, 2, 135.

21. Ibid., VI, 3, 138.

22. Ibid., V, 2, 121.

23. Grover A. Zinn, Jr., "Hugh of St. Victor's *De Scripturis et Scriptoribus Sacris* as an *Accessus* Treatise for the Study of the Bible," *Traditio* 52 (1997): 130.

24. Hugh of St. Victor, *Noah's Ark*. I, 1, 45.

25. Grover A. Zinn, Jr. *"De gradibus ascensionum*: The Stages of Contemplative Ascent in Two Treatises on *Noah's Ark* by Hugh of St. Victor," in *Studies in Medieval Culture* V, ed. John R. Sommerfeldt, Larry Syndergaard, and E. Rozanne Elders (Kalamazoo. MI: Western Michigan University, 1975), 65.

26. Hugh of St. Victor, *Noah's Ark*. I, 5, 51.

27. Ibid., I, 7, 52.

28. Grover Zinn, "Hugh of St. Victor and the Ark of Noah: A New Look," *Church History* 40 (1971): 263–64. I am relying on both

the Zinn article and John A. Lewis, "History and Everlastingness in Hugh of St. Victor's Figures of Noah's Ark," in *Time and Eternity: The Medieval Discourse*, ed. Gerhard Jaritz and Gerson Moreno-Riano (Turnhout, Belgium: Brepols, 2003).

29. Hugh of St. Victor, *Noah's Ark*. I, 14, 64.

30. Ibid.

31. Hugh later adds that the thirty cubits represent Christ, see II, 8 and III, 11.

32. Hugh of St. Victor, *Noah's Ark*. I, 14, 66.

33. Ibid., II, 3, 75.

34. Ibid., II, 1, 73.

35. Rorem, *Hugh of St. Victor*, 133.

36. Hugh of St. Victor, *Noah's Ark*. II, 8, 82.

37. Ibid., IV, 13, 140.

38. Ibid., IV, 9, 132.

39. Sandra M. Schneiders, *The Revelatory Text* (San Francisco: HarperSanFrancisco, 1991), 3. A second edition appeared in 1999. In the Preface to the second edition (Collegeville, MN: The Liturgical Press, 1999), Schneiders addresses some of the questions raised by readers of the first edition.

40. Sandra M. Schneiders, Preface to *The Revelatory Text*, 2nd ed. (Collegeville, MN: The Liturgical Press, 1999), xix.

41. Sandra Schneiders, *The Revelatory Text* (San Francisco: HarperSanFrancisco, 1991), 52.

42. Sandra Schneiders, "Scripture and Spirituality," in *Christian Spirituality: Origins to the Twelfth Century*, ed. Bernard McGinn and John Meyendorff (New York: Crossroad, 1985), 17.

43. Schneiders, *The Revelatory Text*, 142.

44. Elizabeth A. Johnson, *Consider Jesus* (New York: Crossroad, 1990), 97.

45. Schneiders, Preface to *The Revelatory Text*, xxxi.

46. Schneiders, *The Revelatory Text*, 54–55.

47. Schneiders, Preface to *The Revelatory Text*, xxxvii.

48. Schneiders does not deny that there is "a cognitive dimension of revelation," 45.

49. Schneiders, *The Revelatory Text*, 39.

50. Ibid., 45.

51. Ibid., 50.

52. Ibid., 59.
53. Ibid., 58.
54. Ibid., 165.
55. Ibid., 153. Emphasis hers.
56. Ibid., 143.
57. Ibid., 169.
58. Ibid., 181.
59. Sandra M. Schneiders, "The Gospels and the Reader," in *The Cambridge Companion to the Gospels*, ed. Stephen C. Barton (Cambridge, MA: Cambridge University Press, 2006), 116.
60. Schneiders, *The Revelatory Text*, 173 and 197.
61. The interpretation of John 4 also appears as chapter 8 of *Written That You May Believe* (New York: Crossroad, 1999).
62. See Schneiders, *Written That You May Believe*, chapter 6, for a fuller examination of this point.
63. Schneiders, *The Revelatory Text*, 187.
64. Ibid., 191.
65. Ibid., 196.

Chapter 3

1. A distinction is sometimes made between *philosophy of religion* and *philosophical theology*. The former is understood to be a philosophical analysis of beliefs common to most or all of the religions of the world (e.g., "Is there a Higher Power?") and the latter is an examination of the beliefs of a particular religious tradition (e.g., "How can God be triune in nature while still being one God?"). See the Preface of Michael J. Murray and Michael E. Rea, *An Introduction to the Philosophy of Religion* (Cambridge, MA: Cambridge University Press, 2008) and the Introduction to Charles Taliaferro and Chad Meister, eds., *The Cambridge Companion to Christian Philosophical Theology* (Cambridge, MA: Cambridge University Press, 2010).

2. For biographical information on Erasmus, I am relying on chapter one of Erika Rummel, *Erasmus* (New York: Continuum, 2004); James McConica's entry on Erasmus in Hans J. Hillerbrand, ed., *The Oxford Encyclopedia of the Reformation* (New York: Oxford University Press, 1996); J. Laurel Carrington, "Desiderius

Erasmus," in *The Reformation Theologians*, ed. Carter Lindberg (Malden, MA: Blackwell, 2002); and Sike Dorer-Gommermann's entry on Erasmus in Erwin Fahlbusch, ed., *The Encyclopedia of Christianity*, vol. 2 (Grand Rapids, MI: Eerdmans, 2001). There is scholarly debate on whether Erasmus's father was a priest at the time of his birth or would later become a priest, and also on the reason why Erasmus's parents never married.

3. Michael Woodward, "Brethren and Sisters of the Common Life," in *HarperCollins Encyclopedia of Catholicism*, ed. Richard P. McBrien (San Francisco: HarperCollins, 1995), 196. See also John H. Van Engen, *Sisters and Brothers of the Common Life* (Philadelphia: University of Pennsylvania Press, 2008).

4. Rummel, *Erasmus*, 2.

5. Erasmus, *A Handbook of the Militant Christian*, trans. John P. Dolan (Notre Dame, IN: Fides Publishers, 1962), 80.

6. Erasmas, "The Godly Feast," in *Ten Colloquies*, trans. Craig R. Thompson (Indianapolis, IN: Bobb-Merrill, 1957), 158.

7. Ibid., 155.

8. John C. Olin, *Christian Humanism and the Reformation: Selected Writings* (New York: Harper and Row, 1965), 92.

9. Erasmus, *Paraclesis*, in Olin, *Christian Humanism*, 94.

10. Ibid., 97.

11. Ibid., 100.

12. Erasmus, *The Education of a Christian Prince*, trans. Neil M. Cheshire and Michael J. Heath (Cambridge, MA: Cambridge University Press, 1997), 15.

13. Erasmus, *The Praise of Folly*, trans. Clarence H. Miller, 2nd ed. (New Haven, CT: Yale University Press), 87–88. Italics his.

14. Quoted in George Faludy, *Erasmus* (New York: Stein and Day, 1970), 195.

15. Brummer, *What Are We Doing When We Pray?* 65.

16. Austin Farrer, *Saving Belief* (New York: Morehouse-Barlow, 1965), 121. Quoted in Charles C. Hefling, Jr., *Jacob's Ladder* (Cambridge, MA: Cowley Publications, 1979), 37.

17. Austin Farrer, *The End of Man*, ed. Charles C. Conti (London: SPCK, 1973), 143. Quoted in Hefling, *Jacob's Ladder*, 37.

18. Erasmus, *On the Freedom of the Will*, trans. E. Gordon Rupp, in *Luther and Erasmus: Free Will and Salvation* (Philadelphia:

The Westminster Press, 1969), 47. For a critique of Erasmus's definition, see Harry J. McSorley, *Luther: Right or Wrong?* (New York: Newman Press, 1969), chap. 9. McSorley points out that Erasmus is attacking Luther's rejection of free will, but Luther's position deals more specifically with the question of whether the human will, without any assistance from God's grace, can do the right action.

19. The citation of the Book of Wisdom invites a further discussion of Luther's position on the biblical canon. Following the Greek translation of the Old Testament, known as the Septuagint, Catholics accept Wisdom as one of the forty-six canonical books. Protestants accept the shorter Hebrew canon of thirty-nine Old Testament books, which does not include Wisdom.

20. Erasmus, *On the Freedom of the Will*, 80.

21. Ibid., 79.

22. Ibid., 65.

23. Albert Rabil, Jr., *Erasmus and the New Testament: The Mind of a Christian Humanist* (San Antonio, TX: Trinity University Press, 1972), 142.

24. Erasmus, *On the Freedom of the Will*, 41.

25. Quoted in Roland Bainton, *Erasmus of Christendom* (New York: Charles Scribner's Sons, 1969), 146–47, translating the Latin in *Lugduni Batavorum*, VII, 407–8.

26. Bainton, *Erasmus of Christendom*, 147.

27. I am relying heavily on the discussion of Luther in Joseph M. Incandela, *Aquinas's Lost Legacy: God's Practical Knowledge and Situated Freedom* (PhD diss., Princeton University, 1986), 175–81.

28. Luther, *On the Bondage of the Will* in Rupp, 242.

29. Ibid., 243–44.

30. Gerhard O. Forde, *The Captivation of the Will: Luther vs. Erasmus on Freedom and Bondage*, ed. Steven Paulson (Grand Rapids, MI: Eerdmans, 2005), 38–39. Also in support of Luther on this point is Lee Gatiss, "The Manifesto of the Reformation—Luther vs. Erasmus on Free Will," *Churchman* 123, no. 2 (2009): 203–25.

31. Luther, *On the Bondage of the Will*, 122.

32. For an introduction to such problems, see George I. Mavrodes, "Prayer," in *Routledge Encyclopedia of Philosophy*, ed. Edward Craig (London: Routledge, 1998).

33. For a fuller treatment of this question, see Thomas P. Flint, "Praying for Things to Have Happened" in *Midwest Studies in Philosophy*, ed. Peter A. French, Theodore E. Uehling, Jr., and Howard K. Wettstein, XXI (Notre Dame, IN: University of Notre Dame Press, 1997). See also Peter Geach, *God and the Soul* (London: Routledge and Kegan Paul, 1969), chap. 7.

34. I am relying on the argument of Scott A. Davidson, "Petitionary Prayer," which appears as chapter 13 in Thomas P. Flint and Michael C. Rea, eds., *The Oxford Handbook of Philosophical Theology* (Oxford: Oxford University Press, 2009), 287–89.

35. Søren Kierkegaard, *Purity of Heart* (New York: Harper and Row, 1948), 15. Quoted in Vincent Brummer, *What Are We Doing When We Pray?* (London: SCM Press, 1984), 24.

36. Eleonore Stump, "Petitionary Prayer," *American Philosophical Quarterly* 16, no. 2 (1979): 81–91, at 85. This article has been reprinted in several works. See Stump's curriculum vitae at http://sites.google.com/site/stumpep/ for a listing of texts in which it may be found.

37. Stump, "Petitionary Prayer," 86.

38. Ibid., 87.

39. Ibid.

40. Ibid. Emphasis hers.

41. Ibid., 88.

42. Ibid., 90.

43. Erasmus, *On the Freedom of the Will*, 94.

44. Stump, "Petitionary Prayer," 90. Emphasis hers.

45. Vincent Brummer, *What Are We Doing When We Pray?* (London: SCM Press, 1984), 46. Emphasis his.

46. Ibid., 47. Emphasis his.

47. Michael J. Murray, "God Responds to Prayer," in *Contemporary Debates in Philosophy of Religion*, ed. Michael L. Peterson and Raymond J. VanArragon (Malden, MA: Blackwell, 2004), 253.

48. David Basinger, "Reply to Murray," in *Contemporary Debates in Philosophy of Religion*, ed. Peterson and VanArragon, 266.

49. Richard P. McBrien, *Catholicism*, new ed. (San Francisco: HarperSanFrancisco, 1994), 1197. Emphasis his.

50. This issue raises the question of whether there is such a thing as an unmediated or uninterpreted experience of any kind. See Edward Schillebeeckx, *Christ* (New York: Crossroad, 1981), 31–36.

51. Augustine, *Confessions*, III, 11, trans. R. S. Pine-Coffin (New York: Penguin Books, 1961), 69.

52. Stump, "Petitionary Prayer," 89.

53. Ibid., 90.

54. Boris Pasternak, *Doctor Zhivago* (New York: Pantheon, 1958), 68. I thank Kevin Coyne for directing me to this quote.

Chapter 4

1. Emero Stiegman, "Bernard of Clairvaux, William of St. Thierry, the Victorines," in *The Medieval Theologians*, ed. G. R. Evans (Malden, MA: Blackwell, 2001), 131.

2. The highly respected authority on Bernard of Clairvaux, Jean Leclercq dates his entrance into Citeaux at 1112 (Jean Leclercq, "Introduction" to G. R. Evans, trans., *Bernard of Clairvaux: Selected Works* (Mahwah, NJ: Paulist Press, 1987), 17.

3. Christopher M. Bellitto, *Renewing Christianity* (Mahwah, NJ: Paulist Press, 2001), 72.

4. Leclercq, "Introduction," 24.

5. Jean Leclercq, Françoise Vandenbroucke, and Louis Bouyer, *The Spirituality of the Middle Ages*, Volume Two of *A History of Christian Spirituality* (New York: Seabury, 1982), 151.

6. Ian Stuart Robinson, *The Papacy 1073–1198* (Cambridge, MA: Cambridge University Press, 1990), 67.

7. Bernard McGinn, *Three Treatises on Man* (Kalamazoo, MI: Cistercian Publications, 1977), 78; and John R. Sommerfeldt, *The Spiritual Teachings of Bernard of Clairvaux* (Kalamazoo, MI: Cistercian Publications, 1991), 3.

8. Though this distinction appears throughout Bernard's writings, the meaning he attached to each of the terms varied.

See Bernard McGinn, "Introduction" to Bernard of Clairvaux, *On Grace and Free Choice* (Kalamazoo, MI: Cistercian Publications, 1977), 31.

9. Michael Casey, *Athirst for God* (Kalamazoo, MI: Cistercian Publications, 1988), 136–37.

10. Bernard of Clairvaux, "Sermon Eighty" and "Sermon Eighty-Two" in *On the Song of Songs IV*, trans. Irene Edmonds (Kalamazoo, MI: Cistercian Publications, 1980), 146, 148, and 172–73.

11. Sommerfeldt, *Spiritual Teachings*, 22.

12. Casey, *Athirst for God*, 140–41.

13. Charles Dumont, *Pathway of Peace* (Kalamazoo, MI: Cistercian Publications, 1999), 34.

14. Bernard of Clairvaux, *On Loving God*, 25.

15. Ibid., 40.

16. Bernard of Clairvaux, "Sermon 20," vol. 2 of *On the Song of Songs I*, trans. Killian Walsh (Spencer, MA: Cistercian Publications, 1971), 152.

17. Ibid., 152–53.

18. Bernard includes an intermediate stage that he labels a "rational love."

19. Casey, *Athirst for God*, 203.

20. Bernard of Clairvaux, *On Loving God*, 27.

21. Louis Bouyer, *The Cistercian Heritage* (London: A. R. Mowbray, 1958), 51.

22. Bernard of Clairvaux, *On Loving God*, 26.

23. Ibid., 28.

24. Ibid., 41.

25. Vincent Brummer, "God and the Union of Love," *Bijdragen* 52 (1991): 265.

26. Bernard of Clairvaux, *On Loving God*, 30.

27. Bernard of Clairvaux, "Sermon 74" in Evans, *Bernard of Clairvaux*, 254–55.

28. Michael Casey, "In Pursuit of Ecstasy: Reflections on Bernard of Clairvaux's *De Diligendo Deo*," *Monastic Studies* 16 (1985): 148.

29. Bernard of Clairvaux, *On Consideration*, Book V, XIII, 27–31 in Jean Leclercq, *Bernard of Clairvaux and the Cistercian Spirit* (Kalamazoo, MI: Cistercian Publications, 176), 152–56.

30. Quoted in Casey, *Athirst for God*, 82.

31. See M. Shawn Copeland, "Freedom, Emancipation, and Deliverance: Toward a Theology of Freedom," in Magdala Thompson, *Full of Hope* (Mahwah, NJ: Paulist Press, 2003), 43–49.

32. M. Shawn Copeland, "A Theology of the Human Other: Interview with M. Shawn Copeland," interview by Margot Patterson, *National Catholic Reporter*, July 18, 2003, at www.nat cath.org/NCR_Online/archives2/2003c/071803/Copeland.htm.

33. Christopher Pramuk, "'Living in the Master's House': Race and Rhetoric in the Theology of M. Shawn Copeland," *Horizons* 32, no. 2 (2005): 296. Emphasis his.

34. M. Shawn Copeland, *Enfleshing Freedom* (Minneapolis, MN: Fortress Press, 2010), 8.

35. Ibid., 10 and 17.

36. Ibid.

37. Ibid., 21. Emphasis hers.

38. Ibid., 24, 23.

39. Ibid., 24.

40. Ibid., 29 and 48.

41. Ibid., 73.

42. Ibid., 86, 87, 94, and 100.

43. Ibid., 128.

44. M. Shawn Copeland, "Toward a Critical Christian Feminist Theology of Solidarity," in *Women and Theology*, ed. Mary Ann Hinsdale and Phyllis H. Kaminski (Maryknoll, NY: Orbis Books, 1995), 31.

45. Bernard of Clairvaux, *On Loving God*, 5. See also Mark S. Burrows, "Bernard of Clairvaux (1093–1153) *On Loving God*," in *Christian Spirituality*, ed. Arthur Holder, 89 (London: Routledge, 2010).

46. M. Shawn Copeland, *The Subversive Power of Love* (Mahwah, NJ: Paulist Press, 2009), 54. Quotation is Bernard Lonergan, *Method in Theology* (New York: Herder and Herder, 1972), 106, 111.

47. Bernard of Clairvaux, "Sermon 1," in Evans, *Bernard of Clairvaux: Selected Works*, 214–15. I discovered this quotation in Dumont, *Pathway of Peace*, 28.

48. Quoted in Copeland, *Enfleshing Freedom*, 39.

Chapter 5

1. Alfred Loisy, *My Duel with the Vatican*, trans. Richard Wilson Boynton (New York: Greenwood Press, 1968), 86–87.

2. Ibid., 87.

3. Valentine G. Moran, "Loisy's Theological Development," *Theological Studies* 40, no 3 (1979): 416.

4. Bernard B. Scott, "Introduction" to Alfred Loisy, *The Gospel and the Church* (Philadelphia: Fortress Press, 1976), xx.

5. James C. Livingston, *Modern Christian Thought*, vol. 1, 2nd ed. (Upper Saddle River, NJ: Prentice Hall, 1997), 366.

6. Leonard E. Boyle, "A Remembrance of Pope Leo XIII: The Encyclical *Aeterni Patris*," in *One Hundred Years of Thomism*, ed. Victor B. Brezik, 7–9 (Houston: Center for Thomistic Studies 1981).

7. For a discussion of Loisy's distinction between the two approaches, see Norman Provencher, "Loisy's Understanding of Theology and History," *Science et Espirit* 36, no. 1 (1984): 109–18.

8. Marvin R. O'Connell, *Critics on Trial* (Washington, DC: The Catholic University of America Press, 1994), 242.

9. Loisy, *My Duel with the Vatican*, 227–28.

10. Adolf von Harnack, *What is Christianity?* trans. Thomas Bailey Saunders (Gloucester, MA: Peter Smith, 1978), 6.

11. Ibid., 15, 19, and 55.

12. Ibid., 56. Emphasis his.

13. Loisy, *The Gospel and the Church*, 70, 66.

14. Harnack, *What is Christianity?*, 61.

15. Loisy, *The Gospel and the Church*, 72, 59.

16. Harnack, *What is Christianity?*, 144 (emphasis his), 63, 128, and 142 and 144 (emphasis his).

17. Loisy, *The Gospel and the Church*, 96, 121.

18. Ibid., 13, 16, 166.

19. Ibid., 210, 215.

20. Ibid., 11, 12.

21. Bernard M. G. Reardon, *Roman Catholic Modernism* (Stanford, CA: Stanford University Press, 1971), 17.

22. Raymond Brown, *The Virginal Conception and Bodily Resurrection of Jesus* (Mahwah, NJ: Paulist Press, 1973), 3.

23. Ibid., 4.

24. Raymond E. Brown and John P. Meier, *Antioch and Rome* (Mahwah, NJ: Paulist Press, 1983).

25. John P. Meier, *A Marginal Jew*, vol. 1 (New York: Doubleday, 1991), 168.

26. Ibid., 171.

27. Ibid., 175.

28. Ibid., 177.

29. Ibid., 180.

30. John P. Meier, *A Marginal Jew*, vol. 2 (New York: Doubleday, 1994), 411.

31. Ibid., 414.

32. Ibid., 415.

33. Ibid., 421.

34. Ibid., 905.

35. Ibid., 908.

36. The quotation of the Greek version of Job 38:16 is found in Meier, *A Marginal Jew*, vol. 2, 915. The NRSV translates the expression as "walked in the recesses of the deep."

37. Ibid., 917.

38. Ibid, 920, 921, 923.

39. Loisy, *The Gospel and the Church*, 268.

Chapter 6

1. Philip Jenkins, *Jesus Wars* (New York: HarperCollins, 2010), 54.

2. Susan Wessel, *Cyril of Alexandria and the Nestorian Controversy* (Oxford: Oxford University Press, 2004), 3.

3. Norman Russell, *Cyril of Alexandria* (New York: Routledge, 2000), 34.

4. "Nestorius's First Sermon Against the *Theotokos*" in Richard A. Norris, ed., *The Christological Controversy* (Philadelphia: Fortress, 1980), 124–25.

5. "Nestorius's First Sermon" in Norris, *The Christological Controversy*, 126. Emphasis his.

6. Ibid., 130.

7. Ibid., 131.

8. John McGuckin, *Saint Cyril of Alexandria and the Christological Controversy* (Crestwood, NY: St. Vladimir's Seminary Press, 2004), 131.

9. Jenkins, *Jesus Wars*, 56.

10. "The Third Letter of Cyril to Nestorius," in McGuckin, *Saint Cyril of Alexandria and the Christological Controversy*, 271.

11. Ibid., 273.

12. For the history of the Council of Ephesus, I am relying on Russell, *Cyril of Alexandria*, 46–51; Wessel, *Cyril of Alexandria and the Nestorian Controversy*, 4–5; Jenkins, *Jesus Wars*, chap. 5; and John Anthony McGuckin, "Introduction" to Cyril of Alexandria, *On the Unity of Christ* (Crestwood, NY: St. Vladimir's Seminary Press, 1995).

13. Cyril of Alexandria, *On the Unity of Christ*, 54.

14. Ibid., 55.

15. Ibid., 59.

16. Ibid., 64.

17. Cyril of Alexandria, *Commentary on the Gospel According to John*, vol. 2, trans. T. Randell (London: Walter Smith, 1885), 321. See Thomas G. Weinandy, "Cyril and the Mystery of the Incarnation," in *The Theology of St. Cyril of Alexandria*, ed. Thomas G. Weinandy and Daniel A. Keating (London: T & T Clark, 2003), 24–25.

18. Cyril of Alexandria, *On the Unity of Christ*, 69 and 131.

19. Russell, *Cyril of Alexandria*, 20.

20. Ibid.

21. Roger Haight, *Jesus: Symbol of God* (Maryknoll, NY: Orbis, 1999), 289.

22. For a bibliography of O'Collins's work up to 2000, see Daniel Kendall and Stephen T. Davis, *The Convergence of Theology* (Mahwah, NJ: Paulist Press, 2001), 370–98.

23. See Gerald O'Collins, *Christology*, 2nd ed. (Oxford: Oxford University Press, 2009), 245–47 for a discussion of Chalcedon's "ongoing validity." O'Collins believes that we are justified in retaining the "one person in two natures" formula, though he does say that we should do so "cautiously," given the difference between the ancient and modern understanding of *personhood*. For a similar assessment of Chalcedon in one of O'Collins's earlier works, see *What Are They Saying About Jesus?* (New York: Paulist Press, 1977), 8.

24. Gerald O'Collins, *Interpreting Jesus* (London: Geoffrey Chapman, 1983), 174. Emphasis his.

25. Gerald O'Collins, *Incarnation* (London: Continuum, 2002), 8.

26. Ibid., 12.

27. Ibid., 13.

28. Gerald O'Collins, "The Incarnation: The Critical Issues," in *The Incarnation*, ed. Stephen T. Davis, Daniel Kendall, and Gerald O'Collins (Oxford: Oxford University Press, 2002), 3.

29. O'Collins, *Incarnation*, 23. Emphasis his.

30. Ibid., 41.

31. Ibid., 43.

32. Gerald O'Collins, *Christology* (Oxford: Oxford University Press, 1995), 234. Emphasis his.

33. John McIntyre, *The Shape of Christology*, Second Edition (Edinburgh: T & T Clark, 1998), 291.

34. Ibid.

35. O'Collins, *Christology*, Second Edition, 240.

36. Ibid., 234.

37. O'Collins, *Incarnation*, 51. O'Collins suggests the work by the seventeenth-century Spanish painter Murillo, *The Heavenly and Earthly Trinities*. See also David Brown, "The Incarnation in Twentieth-Century Art," in *The Incarnation*, ed. Davis, Kendall, and O'Collins, 332–72. Brown includes pictures of eight works (six paintings and two sculptures) at the end of the piece.

38. O'Collins, *Incarnation*, 55.

39. Søren Kierkegaard, *Philosophical Fragments* in Robert Bretall, ed., *A Kierkegaard Anthology* (Princeton: Princeton University Press, 1946), 165–66.

40. Ibid., 167–68. Emphasis his.

41. Ibid., 169.
42. O'Collins, *Incarnation*, 63.
43. Blaise Pascal, *Pensées*, trans, A. J. Krailsheimer (New York: Penguin Books, 1966), 449, 169.
44. Clyde Crews, *Ultimate Questions* (Mahwah, NJ: Paulist Press, 1986), 109.
45. Aidan Nichols, *The Shape of Catholic Theology* (Collegeville, MN: The Liturgical Press, 1991), 345.
46. O'Collins, *Christology*, Second Edition, 344.
47. Ibid., 175.
48. Ibid., 342. See also 345.
49. Ibid., 235.
50. Thomas Merton, *New Seeds of Contemplation* (New York: New Directions, 1961), 150.
51. O'Collins, *Christology*, Second Edition, 345–46.
52. Dorothy Day, "Room for Christ" in Robert Ellsberg, ed., *Dorothy Day: Selected Writings* (Maryknoll, NY: Orbis Books, 1992), 94–97. Emphasis hers. The piece is also available at http://www.catholicworker.org/dorothyday/daytext.cfm?TextID=416.
53. O'Collins, *Christology*, Second Edition, 349.
54. O'Collins, *Incarnation*, 132.

Chapter 7

1. For biographical information on Ambrose, I am relying on Boniface Ramsey, "Introduction" to *Ambrose* (London: Routledge, 1997); and Ramsey's entry on Ambrose in G. R. Evans, ed., *The First Christian Theologians* (Malden, MA: Blackwell, 2004); as well as chap. 2 of Craig Alan Saterlee, *Ambrose of Milan's Method of Mystagogical Preaching* (Collegeville, MN: The Liturgical Press, 2002).
2. Saterlee, *Ambrose of Milan's Method of Mystagogical Preaching*, 48.
3. Ivor Davidson, "Ambrose" in Trevor A. Hart, ed., *The Dictionary of Historical Theology* (Grand Rapids, MI: Eerdmans, 2000), 10.
4. Ambrose, Letter 20.19 in Ramsey, *Ambrose*, 27.
5. Davidson, "Ambrose," 10.

6. Mary Pierre Ellebracht, "Today This Word Has Been Fulfilled in Your Midst," *Worship* 60, no. 4 (1986): 347.

7. Saterlee, *Ambrose of Milan's Method of Mystagogical Preaching*, 20; and Pamela Jackson, "Ambrose of Milan as Mystagogue," *Augustinian Studies* 20 (1989): 96.

8. For this distinction in Ambrose's thought, see Enrico Mazza, *Mystagogy* (New York: Pueblo Publishing Co., 1989), 23. Mazza concedes on page 29 that Ambrose does not always adhere to this distinction.

9. Ambrose, *On the Mysteries* 3.8 in Ramsey, *Ambrose*, 147. The text of *On the Mysteries* is found on 146–60. All quotations of *On the Mysteries* are from Ramsey, unless otherwise noted. For the shape and size of the baptismal pool in Milan, see Saterlee, *Ambrose of Milan's Method of Mystagogical Preaching*, 158–61.

10. For a discussion of the different terminology Ambrose uses in this regard, see Mazza, *Mystagogy*, chap. 2.

11. Ambrose, *On the Mysteries* 1.2, 146.

12. Ambrose, *On the Sacraments*, in Edward Yarnold, *The Awe-Inspiring Rites of Initiation*, Second Edition (Edinburgh: T & T Clark, 1994), 101. The touching of the nostrils is implied, but not explicitly stated in *On the Mysteries* 1.3.

13. On the possible use of spittle or oil, see Yarnold, *The Awe-Inspiring Rites of Initiation*, 18, including n. 80.

14. Ellebracht, "Today This Word Has Been Fulfilled in Your Midst," 348.

15. Ambrose, *On the Mysteries* 3.15, 149.

16. Ibid., 3.11, 148.

17. Ibid., 4.19, 149–50.

18. Ibid., 4.20, 150.

19. In *On the Sacraments*, Ambrose refers to baptism as the "sacrament of his cross" (2.23).

20. Ambrose, *On the Mysteries* 6.32, 153.

21. Ibid., 7.42, 155.

22. For a discussion of the possible meanings of "the spiritual seal," see Maxwell E. Johnson, *The Rites of Christian Initiation* (Collegeville, MN: The Liturgical Press, 1999), 137–40.

23. Ambrose, *On the Mysteries* 8.49—9.50, 157.

24. Ibid., 9.52, 54, 258–59.

25. Gary Macy, *The Banquet's Wisdom* (Mahwah, NJ: Paulist Press, 1992), 50.

26. Saterlee, *Ambrose of Milan's Method of Mystagogical Preaching*, 311.

27. Ambrose, *On the Sacraments, III, 15*, in Edward Yarnold, *The Awe-Inspiring Rites of Initiation*, 126–27.

28. Ambrose, *On the Mysteries*, 5.27. Here I am using the translation provided by Ellebracht in "Today This Word Has Been Fulfilled in Your Midst," 353.

29. Chauvet has in mind here the later work on the church by the Reformed theologian Karl Barth. In regard to Barth's later view of the church, Tom Trinidad notes, "The Church is not in possession of anything for which it is the distributive means" in *The Word of God in Ecclesial Rites and the Formation of Christian Identity: A Comparison of Karl Barth and Louis-Marie Chauvet* (PhD diss., University of Notre Dame, 2007), 203.

30. Louis-Marie Chauvet, *Symbol and Sacrament* (Collegeville, MN: The Liturgical Press, 1995), 21. For a criticism of Chauvet's assessment of Aquinas, see Bernard Blankenhorn, "The Instrumental Causality of the Sacraments: Thomas Aquinas and Louis-Marie Chauvet," *Nova et Vetera* (English Edition) 4, no. 2 (2006): 255–94.

31. Louis-Marie Chauvet, *The Sacraments: The Word of God at the Mercy of the Body* (Collegeville, MN: The Liturgical Press, 2001), xv.

32. Ibid.

33. Philippe Bordeyne, "Louis-Marie Chauvet: A Short Biography," in Philippe Bordyne and Bruce T. Morrill, eds., *Sacraments: Revelation of the Humanity of God* (Collegeville, MN: The Liturgical Press, 2008), x.

34. Chauvet, *The Sacraments*, 9–10.

35. Ibid., 13. Emphasis his.

36. The contemporary classic that develops this idea is George A. Lindbeck's *The Nature of Doctrine* (Philadelphia: Westminster Press, 1984).

37. Chauvet, *Symbol and Sacrament*, 171.

38. Chauvet, *The Sacraments*, 29.

39. Ibid., 17.

40. Ibid., 25n5.
41. Ibid., 26–27.
42. Luk De Volder, "Do We Still Need the Sacraments?" *Questions Liturgiques* 82, no. 1 (2001): 38. Emphasis his.
43. Chauvet, *The Sacraments*, 51.
44. Ibid., xii. Emphasis his.
45. See Chauvet, *Symbol and Sacrament*, 150. Chauvet speaks here of "the triple body—social, ancestral, and cosmic."
46. Chauvet, *The Sacraments*, 65.
47. Ibid., 91. Emphasis his.
48. Ibid., 94. Emphasis his.
49. Ibid., 88.
50. Glenn P. Ambrose, *The Theology of Louis-Marie Chauvet* (Burlington, VT: Ashgate, 2012), 89–90. For a discussion of this aspect of Chauvet's thought, see Darren M. Henson, "Symbolic Exchange: Chauvet's Approach to the Sacrament," *Assembly* 33 (6), 2007. My thanks to the Notre Dame Center for Liturgy for providing me with a copy of this back issue.
51. For a discussion of Chauvet's views on Transubstantiation, see Trinidad, *The Word of God in Ecclesial Rites and the Formation of Christian Identity: A Comparison of Karl Barth and Louis-Marie Chauvet*, 167–70.
52. Chauvet, *The Sacraments*, 139.
53. Ibid., 143.
54. See Chauvet, *Symbol and Sacrament*, 388.
55. Ibid., 265.
56. Ambrose, *The Theology of Louis-Marie Chauvet*, 4.
57. Chauvet, *Symbol and Sacrament*, 173–77.
58. Ibid., 217.
59. Chauvet, *The Sacraments*, 161.
60. I was first made aware of this by reading Theresa Sanders, "The Otherness of God and the Bodies of Others," *The Journal of Religion* 76, no. 4 (1996): 578. Glenn Ambrose makes a similar point when discussing the influence of Heidegger on Chauvet. "Heidegger was adamant that Being was not God and rejected any passage from Being to God" (*The Theology of Louis-Marie Chauvet*, 16).
61. Chauvet, *The Sacraments*, 28. Emphasis his.

62. David N. Power, "Postmodern Approaches" in "Sacramental Theology: A Review of the Literature: Postmodern Approaches; Feminist Theology; African Contributions," *Theological Studies* 55, no. 4 (1997): 688.

63. Chauvet, *The Sacraments*, 169.

64. Craig Alan Satterlee, "Patristic Principles for Post-Christendom Preaching," *Liturgy* 25, no. 4 (2010): 20. The quote from Ambrose is *On the Sacraments*, III, 15.

Chapter 8

1. Sandra Schneiders writes, "One cannot assume, in other words, in reading the biblical text that it gives us an accurate picture of women in the community of salvation. We get the picture of women that men created, which corresponds to the male understanding of women and their place in society at the time of the writing of these documents." *The Revelatory Text* (San Francisco: HarperSanFrancisco, 1991), 182.

2. John A. Gallagher, *Time Past, Time Future* (Mahwah, NJ: Paulist Press, 1990), 29–30.

3. The discussion of conscience produced a number of key distinctions in moral theology. The conscience involved an act of judgment on the part of the individual. If the person's information was correct and his/her reasoning was sound, then the person was acting on a "correct" conscience. If the information was incorrect or the person's reasoning was unsound, then the person was said to be acting on an "erroneous conscience." This was distinguished from the question of whether the person doing the action was "certain" or "doubtful" about its moral correctness. See Andrew C. Varga, *On Being Human* (Mahwah, NJ: Paulist Press, 1978), 125–32.

4. James F. Keenan, *A History of Catholic Moral Theology in the Twentieth Century* (New York: Continuum, 2010), 2.

5. Keenan writes that Slater's 1906 text "was for twenty years the most consulted manual in English, going through five editions, the last appearing in 1931." *A History of Catholic Moral Theology in the Twentieth Century*, 10.

6. James M. Gustafson, "Christian Ethics in America," in *Christian Ethics and the Community* (New York: Pilgrim Press, 1979), 54.

7. Thomas Slater, *A Manual of Moral Theology*, vol. 1, 3rd ed. (New York: Benzinger, 1909), 18–19.

8. Ibid., 119.

9. Ibid., 207, 133.

10. For an interesting reflection on this episode, see statement by then Cardinal Joseph Ratzinger (now Pope Emeritus Benedict XVI) on the one hundredth anniversary of the Pontifical Biblical Commission at http://www.vatican.va/roman_curia /congregations/cfaith/pcb_documents/rc_con_cfaith_doc_2003 0510_ratzinger-comm-bible_en.html.

11. Keenan, *A History of Catholic Moral Theology in the Twentieth Century*, 61. See also Keenan's lecture "Innovation: The Recovery of History and Scripture for Moral Theology" delivered on July 9, 2008, at the Lane Center for Catholic Studies and Catholic Social Thought at the University of San Francisco, available at: https://www.usfca.edu/uploadedFiles/Destinations /Institutes_and_Centers/Lane/Events/documents/KeenanLectu re7.9.08forhtml.pdf.

12. James F. Keenan, "John Mahoney's *The Making of Moral Theology*," in *The Oxford Handbook of Theological Ethics*, ed. Gilbert Meilander and William Werpehowski (Oxford: Oxford University Press, 2005), 505.

13. Fritz Tillmann, *The Master Calls* (Baltimore: Helicon Press, 1961), 3.

14. Ibid., 6, 8.

15. Ibid., 8–9.

16. Ibid., 36.

17. Ibid., 39. This raises the question of how we would know whether our "interior judgment" of conscience coincides with the will of God. The area of moral theology deals with the difference between a correct conscience and a certain conscience.

18. John Henry Cardinal Newman, *Callista: A Tale of the Third Century* (London: Longmans, Green, and Co., 1904), 236. I am using the e-book version at http://www.gutenberg.org/files /30664/30664-pdf.pdf.

19. Tillmann, *The Master Calls*, 94.

20. Ibid., 30.

21. Ibid., 184.

22. Ibid., 255, 265.

23. Servais Pinckaers, "Dominican Moral Theology in the 20th Century," in *The Pinckaers Reader*, ed. John Berkman and Craig Steven Titus (Washington, DC: The Catholic University of America Press, 2005), 86.

24. Servais Pinckaers, "My Sources," *Communio* 26 (Winter 1999): 914.

25. Servais Pinckaers, *The Sources of Christian Ethics* (Washington, DC: The Catholic University of America Press, 1995), 8.

26. Ibid., 19, 28, 26.

27. Ibid., 123. For a study of the role Paul's theology plays in Pinckaers's theology, see William F. Murphy, Jr., "Transformation in Christ: Pauline Foundation of Christian Moral Action," *Josephinum* 17, no. 2 (2010): 277–304.

28. Augustine, *The Lord's Sermon on the Mount*, trans. John J. Jepson (Westminster, MD: Newman Press, 1956), I, 1, 11.

29. Ibid., 15.

30. Pinckaers, *The Sources of Christian Ethics*, 174.

31. Aquinas cites Augustine's *Commentary on the Sermon on the Mount* in support of his position (*Summa Theologica* I–II, q. 108, art. 3).

32. Thomas Aquinas, *Summa Theologica*, I–II, q. 106, art. 1, trans., Fathers of the English Dominican Province (New York: Benzinger, 1947), 1104.

33. Pinckaers, *The Sources of Christian Ethics*, 185.

34. Ibid., 375.

35. Ibid., 355. For an excellent investigation of Aquinas's view of "situated freedom," see Joseph M. Incandela, *Aquinas's Lost Legacy: God's Practical Knowledge and Situated Human Freedom*, (PhD diss., Princeton University, 1986).

36. Pinckaers, *The Sources of Christian Ethics*, 376.

37. Ibid., 30.

38. Ibid., 117.

39. Augustine, *Confessions* 1.1, trans. R. S. Pine-Coffin (New York: Penguin Books, 1961), 21.
40. Augustine, *Confessions*, trans. Maria Boulding (Hyde Park, NY: New City Press, 1997), 14.
41. Pinckaers, *The Sources of Christian Ethics*, 186.
42. Ibid., 404.
43. Ibid., 444.
44. Henri Nouwen, *The Return of the Prodigal Son* (New York: Doubleday, 1992), 95–96.

Chapter 9

1. Aidan Nichols, "The Theology of Jean Daniélou: Epochs, Correspondences, and the Orders of the Real," *New Blackfriars* 91, no. 1031 (2010): 51.
2. Jean Daniélou, *The Advent of Salvation* (Glen Rock, NJ: Deus Books, 1962), 18. Emphasis his.
3. Jean Daniélou, "Christianity and Non-Christian Religions," in T. Patrick Burke, ed., *The Word in History* (New York: Sheed & Ward, 1966), 86.
4. Jean Daniélou, *God and the Ways of Knowing* (New York: Meridian Books, 1957), 21, 22, 37.
5. Daniélou, *The Advent of Salvation*, 25, 36.
6. *Lumen gentium* n. 16 in J. Neuner and J. Dupuis, eds., *The Christian Faith* (New York: Alba House, 1982), 287. See also James Fredericks, "The Catholic Church and the Other Religious Paths: Rejecting Nothing That is True and Holy," *Theological Studies* 24 (2003): 226–33.
7. *Nostra Aetate* n. 4 in Austin P. Flannery, ed., *Documents of Vatican II* (Grand Rapids: Eerdmans, 1975), 741.
8. Jean Daniélou, *The Salvation of the Nations* (Notre Dame, IN: University of Notre Dame Press, 1962), 28.
9. Ibid., 27.
10. Ibid., 58, 49–50, 65.
11. Daniélou, *God and the Ways of Knowing*, 26.
12. Daniélou, *The Salvation of the Nations*, 91, 108.
13. Jean Daniélou, *Prayer* (Grand Rapids, MI: Eerdmans, 1996), 38.

14. Ibid., 9.
15. Daniélou, *The Salvation of the Nations*, 113.
16. Daniélou, *Prayer*, 18–19 (emphasis his), 10, 73.
17. Panikkar is also known by the first names Raimundo and Raymond.
18. Panikkar also was married in a civil ceremony at the age of seventy. The details of this are not well known, see http://ncronline.org/blogs/ncr-today/panikkars-marriage for more information.
19. For biographical information, I am relying upon J. Abraham Velez de Cea, "Raimon Panikkar 1918–2010," *Buddhist-Christian Studies* 31 (2011): 215–19; and Ursula King, "Celebrating a Great Scholar," *Religions of South Asia* 6, no. 1 (2012): 7–11.
20. Raimundo Panikkar, "Chosenness and Universality: Can Christians Claim Both?" *Cross Currents* 38, no. 3 (1988): 320. See also Raimundo Panikkar, "The Jordan, the Tiber, and the Ganges: Three Kairological Moments of Christic Self-Consciousness," in *The Myth of Christian Uniqueness*, ed. John Hick and Paul Knitters (Maryknoll, NY: Orbis Books, 1987), 101.
21. Raimon Panikkar, "A Self-Critical Dialogue," in *The Intercultural Challenge of Raimon Panikkar*, ed. Joseph Prabhu (Maryknoll. NY: Orbis Books, 1996), 252.
22. Ibid., 239.
23. Ibid., 247.
24. Raimon Panikkar, "The Pluralism of Truth." This article originally appeared in *World Faiths Insight*, 1990: 7–16. I am using the on-line article available at http://www.dhdi.free.fr/recher ches/horizonsinterculturels/articles/panikkarpluralism.pdf. The quote appears on page 7 of the pdf.
25. Raimundo Panikkar, *The Trinity and the Religious Experience of Man* (New York: Orbis, 1973), 74.
26. Paul F. Knitter, *Introducing Theologies of Religion* (Maryknoll, NY: Orbis Books, 2002), 127.
27. "It is evident that the fact that Panikkar exercises metaphysics obliges him to articulate sentences describing reality *per se* even though he denies in his fundamental thinking any possibility of detaching of one's own limited perspective and speaking about things 'objectively.' Perhaps this kind of dilemma is

unavoidable in the context of metaphysics." (Jyri Komulainen, *An Emerging Cosomtheandric Religion?* [Boston: Brill, 2005], 76).

28. Ibid., 76.

29. Panikkar, "A Self-Critical Dialogue," 245–57.

30. Raimon Panikkar, *Christophany* (Maryknoll, NY: Orbis Books, 2004), 144–45.

31. Raimundo Panikkar, *The Unknown Christ of Hinduism*, New Edition (London: Darton, Longman, and Todd, 1981), 27.

32. Panikkar, *Christophany*, 150.

33. Panikkar, "The Jordan, the Tiber, and the Ganges," 112.

34. Panikkar, *Christophany*, 12.

35. Raimon Panikkar, "The Invisible Harmony," in *Invisible Harmony* (Minneapolis, MN: Fortress, 1995), 156.

36. Paul Knitter, "Cosmic Confidence or Preferential Option?," in *The Intercultural Challenge of Raimon Panikkar*, 184. Emphasis his.

37. Panikkar, "A Self-Critical Dialogue," 280.

38. Jean Daniélou, *Et qui est mon Prochain?: Memorias* (Paris, 1974), 91. Quoted in Nichols, "The Theology of Jean Daniélou: Epochs, Correspondences, and the Orders of the Real," 50.

39. Komulainen, *An Emerging Cosomtheandric Religion?* 62n69.

40. Panikkar, *Christophany*, 162.

41. According to the theologian Don Schweitzer, "In Panikkar's vision, salvation is experienced through detachment from history." *Contemporary Christologies* (Minneapolis, MN: Fortress, 2010), 106.

42. Panikkar, "The Invisible Harmony," 178.

43. Ibid., 180.

44. Panikkar, *The Experience of God* (Minneapolis, MN: Fortress Press, 2006), 66, 53, 138.

45. Ibid., 13, 135.

46. Ibid., 27, 140, 19.

47. Ibid., 108, 138 (emphasis his), 141.

Chapter 10

1. Michael Horton, "Eschatology," in *Mapping Modern Theology*, ed. Kelly M. Kapic and Bruce L. McCormack (Grand Rapids, MI: Baker Academic, 2012), 381.

2. For reflections on the idea of "building up the kingdom," see William A. Barry, "The Kingdom of God and Discernment," *America* (Sept. 26, 1987): 156–59 and his follow-up piece "The Kingdom of God: What Role Do We Play?" *America* (Sept. 23, 1989): 165–66.

3. See John H. Yoder, "If Christ is Truly Lord," which appears as chap. 3 in his *The Original Revolution* (Scottdale, PA: Herald Press, 1977).

4. Rudolf Bultmann, *Jesus Christ and Mythology* (New York: Charles Scribner's Sons, 1958), 12. See Richard H. Hiers, *Jesus and the Future* (Atlanta: John Knox Press, 1981), 2. For the influence of Weiss on German Protestant theology, see Walter E. Wyman, Jr., "The Kingdom of God in Germany: From Ritschl to Troeltsch," in *Revisioning the Past*, ed. Mary Potter Engel and Walter E. Wyman, Jr. (Minneapolis, MN: Fortress Press, 1992), 257–77.

5. Norman Perrin, *The Kingdom of God in the Teachings of Jesus* (Philadelphia: Westminster Press, 1963), 17.

6. Johann Sebastian Drey, "Toward the Revision of the Present State of Theology," in *Romance and the Rock*, ed. Jospeh Fitzer (Minneapolis, MN: Fortress Press, 1989), 71–72.

7. Johann Sebastian Drey, *A Brief Introduction to the Study of Theology*, trans. Michael Himes (Notre Dame, IN: University of Notre Dame Press, 1994). Drey's work is a "theological encyclopedia" and is comprised of 388 numbered paragraphs. Citations to the text are to the numbered paragraph.

8. Wayne L. Fehr, *The Birth of the Catholic Tubingen School: The Dogmatics of Johann Sebastian Drey*, American Academy of Religion Academy Studies 37 (Chico, CA: Scholars Press, 1981), 28. Emphasis his.

9. Fehr writes of Drey's view of the Fall, "Hence, what man falls away from is not an already established paradisaical state, but rather a divinely intended direction of development." *The Birth of the Catholic Tubingen School*, 214. He also notes that, "The origin and fact of evil is…difficult for Drey to integrate into his system," 220.

10. Drey, *Tubingen Theologische Quartalschrift* 8, 1826, 266, quoted in Fehr, *The Birth of the Catholic Tubingen School*, 58.

11. Donald J. Dietrich, *The Goethezeit and the Metamorphosis of Catholic Theology in the Age of Idealism* (Berne: Peter Lang, 1979), 79.

12. Bradford Hinze, *Narrating History, Developing Doctrine* (Atlanta: Scholars Press, 1993), 72–76. I would like to thank Professor Hinze for his kindness in answering some questions I had regarding Drey's theology.

13. Ibid., 284–85.

14. Fehr, *The Birth of the Catholic Tubingen School*, 206.

15. Drey "Praelectiones Dogmaticae," III, 69, quoted in Fehr, *The Birth of the Catholic Tubingen School*, 237.

16. Grant Kaplan, *Answering the Enlightenment* (New York: Crossroad Publishing Co., 2006), 110.

17. Jan Ambaum, "An Empty Hell: The Restoration of All Things?: Balthasar's Concept of Hope for Salvation," *Communio* 18 (1991), 45–46n30. See also Nicholas J. Healy, "On Hope, Heaven, and Hell," *Logos* 1, no. 3 (1997): 81.

18. Hans Urs von Balthasar, *Dare We Hope "That All Men Be Saved"?* (San Francisco: Ignatius Press, 1988), 17.

19. Gerhard Hermes, "Hoffnung auf das Heil aller? Bei H. U. von Balthasar nichts Neues" [Hope for the salvation of all? From H. U. von Balthasar nothing new], *Der Fels* 15 (November, 1984), 318. Quoted in von Balthasar, *Dare We Hope?* 20.

20. Von Balthasar, *Dare We Hope "That All Men Be Saved"?* 20.

21. Ibid., 29.

22. Ibid., 35.

23. Ibid., 40. For background on the translation of *all and the many*, see Joseph A. Fitzmyer, SJ, *Romans*, vol. 33 of *The Anchor Bible* (New York: Doubleday, 1993), 419.24. Augustine, *City of God*, XXI, 23 (Garden City, NY: Image Books, 1958), 504–5.

25. Thomas Joseph White, "Von Balthasar and Journet on the Universal Possibility of Salvation and the Twofold Will of God," *Nova et Vetera*, English Edition 4, no. 3 (2006): 643.

26. Ralph Martin, *Will Many Be Saved?* (Grand Rapids, MI: Eerdmans, 2012), 161.

27. Von Balthasar, *Dare We Hope "That All Men Be Saved"?* 184–85.

28. Karl Rahner, "Hell," in Karl Rahner, ed., *Encyclopedia of Theology: The Concise Sacramentum Mundi* (New York: Crossroad, 1982), 603.

29. Ibid.

30. C. S. Lewis, *The Problem of Pain* (London: The Centenary Press, 1941), 115. Emphasis his.

31. Von Balthasar, "A Short Discourse on Hell" in *Dare We Hope "That All Men Be Saved"?* 178.

32. Regis Scanlon, "The Inflated Reputation of Hans Urs von Balthasar," *New Oxford Review*, LXVII, no. 3 (2000): 20. Emphasis his.

33. *Lumen gentium* in Austin P. Flannery, ed., *Documents of Vatican II* (Grand Rapids, MI: Eerdmans, 1975), 408–9.

34. James T. O'Connor, "Von Balthasar and Salvation," *Homiletic and Pastoral Review*, LXXXIX, no. 10 (1989): 17–18. Emphasis his.

35. Von Balthasar, "A Short Discourse on Hell" in *Dare We Hope "That All Men Be Saved"?* 211.

36. Edward T. Oakes, *Pattern of Redemption* (New York: Continuum, 1994), 319.

37. Von Balthasar, "A Short Discourse on Hell" in *Dare We Hope "That All Men Be Saved"?* 202.

38. Geoffrey Wainwright, "Eschatology," in Edward T. Oakes and David Moss, eds., *The Cambridge Companion to Hans Urs Von Balthasar* (Cambridge, MA: Cambridge University Press, 2004), 113, 114.

39. See Christine M. Panyard, *The Sistine Chapel: A Biblical Tour* (Mahwah, NJ: Paulist Press, 2013); and John E. Thiel, *Icons of Hope* (Notre Dame, IN: University of Notre Dame Press, 2013).

Twelve

Christology: What did Jesus know, and when?

The Bible: Is everything written in scripture really true?

God's Presence: How does God speak to us?

Salvation: Do we need Christ, or can we save ourselves?

Theological

Evil: Why does God let innocent people suffer?

World Religions: Is Christianity the only true religion?

Dissent: Can we disagree and still be faithful?

The Secular World: Is it a place of grace or temptation?

Dilemmas

Ethics: How do we decide what's right and wrong?

Commitment: Do promises always mean forever?

Faith and Reason: Should we just believe and not think?

Continuity: Should religion change with the times?

Gregory C. Higgins

Twelve Theological Dilemmas
Gregory C. Higgins

A fresh, impartial presentation of timeless theological questions that Christians have found puzzling, accompanied by equally differing and valid explanations for them.

0-8091-3232-X   Paperback

Where Do You Stand?
Eight Moral Issues Confronting Today's Christians
Gregory C. Higgins

Examines the particulars behind eight crucial moral issues of the day and challenges the reader to take a personal stand on them.

0-8091-3608-2 Paperback

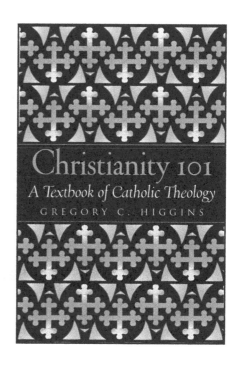

Christianity 101
A Textbook of Catholic Theology
Gregory C. Higgins

Christianity 101 is an introductory text for college-level courses in Christian theology. The text provides a history of Christian thought in each of the key areas of Christian theology and discusses the major debates and thinkers in the tradition.

0-8091-4208-2 Paperback

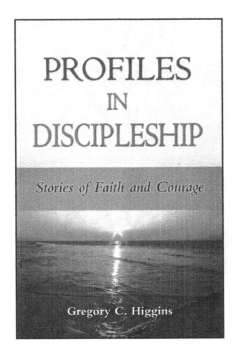

Profiles in Discipleship
Stories of Faith and Courage
Gregory C. Higgins

Profiles in Discipleship explores twelve images of Christian discipleship that have guided the thought and action of two dozen influential figures in the Christian tradition.

978-0-8091-4745-8   Paperback